Fit For Life 3

Harvey Diamond

The New Path to Vibrant Health

Prentice Hall Canada
Scarborough, Ontario

Canadian Cataloguing in Publication Data

Diamond, Harvey, 1945–
    Fit for life : the new path to vibrant health

Includes bibliographical references.
ISBN 0-13-918160-1 (trade)
ISBN 0-13-975376-1 (special)

1. Breast – Cancer – Prevention. 2. Breast – Cancer – Diet therapy.
I. Title. II. Title: The new path to vibrant health.

RC280.B8D52 1998   616.99′449052   C97-932788-1

© 1998 Harvey Diamond

Prentice-Hall Canada Inc., Scarborough, Ontario
A Division of Simon & Schuster/A Viacom Company

Prentice-Hall, Inc., Upper Saddle River, New Jersey
Prentice-Hall International (UK) Limited, London
Prentice-Hall of Australia, Pty. Limited, Sydney
Prentice-Hall Hispanoamericana, S.A., Mexico City
Prentice-Hall of India Private Limited, New Delhi
Prentice-Hall of Japan, Inc., Tokyo
Simon & Schuster Southeast Asia Private Limited, Singapore
Editora Prentice-Hall do Brasil, Ltda., Rio de Janeiro

ISBN 0-13-918160-1 (trade)
ISBN 0-13-975376-1 (special)

Director, Trade Group: Robert Harris
Acquisitions Editor: Dean Hannaford
Editorial Assistant: Joan Whitman
Editor: Liba Berry
Production Editor: Avivah Wargon
Production Coordinator: Julie Preston
Cover Photo: Ray Boudreau
Page Layout: B.J. Weckerle

1 2 3 4 5   RRD   02 01 00 99 98

Printed and bound in the U.S.A.

Visit the Prentice Hall Canada Web site! Send us your comments, browse our catalogues,
and more at **www.phcanada.com**.

"Greens+® is a registered trademark of Orange Peel Enterprises, Inc., a Florida
corporation, Vero Beach, Florida, U.S.A."

Bravo! Harvey Diamond has done it again. He clearly reveals how we can take charge of our own health and prevent disease.

Dr. Wayne Dyer
Author of **Manifest Your Destiny:
The Nine Spiritual Principles for
Getting Everything You Want**
and **Your Erroneous Zones**

Harvey Diamond gives everyone a powerful tool for the restoration of health. He speaks from a point of view so many of us now want: with an awareness of nature, consciousness and their role in healing. I deeply welcome this book into my own life.

Marianne Williamson
Author of **A Return to Love;
A Woman's Worth; Illuminata**

A magnificent job of ordering and documenting the vast body of information into a cogent, irrefutably sensible and wise program.

Jesse Lynn Hanley, M.D.
Director, Malibu Health and Rehabilitation

This is the health book we've been looking for. Harvey demystifies modern medicine's incurable disease, and puts you in charge.

Dr. Marcus Laux, N.D.
Editor, **Naturally Well**

This book represents the first ray of hope in conquering cancer. It could very well save your life or the life of someone you love.

Dr. Gayle Black, Clinical Nutritionist
President, Eating Smart Company

In my practice specializing in women's health, I have often wished for a book that would dispel the current hysteria and melodrama around disease. A book that would clearly and succinctly describe the changes necessary to prevent heart disease and cancer. A book that was engaging and easy to understand. A book that was free of preaching and dogmatic statements. A book that proposed simple changes that anyone could make no matter what the size of their pocketbook, or how difficult their circumstances. You hold such a book in your hands.

Carolyn DeMarco, M.D.
Author of **Take Charge of Your Body**

This book will empower as no medical encounter can with the knowledge and confidence to prevent disease naturally.

Zoltan P. Rona, M.D.
Columnist, **The Toronto Star**

This extremely well-researched book sends a welcome message of hope to millions of potential victims.

Edward A. Taub, M.D.
Author of **The Wellness Rx**

Harvey Diamond's belief that cancer is preventable goes along with my own experience, beliefs and research.

Barbara L. Joseph, M.D.
Author of **My Healing of Breast Cancer**

Mr. Diamond provides candid insight and powerful, beneficial advice for women in the challenge of the prevention of breast cancer.

J. William La Valley, M.D.
Founder, Complementary Medicine Section,
Canadian Medical Association

An empowering resource for anyone interested in improving the quality of their life, FIT FOR LIFE 3 delivers not only hope, but also the information you need to free yourself from fear.

Anthony Robbins
Author of **Awaken the Giant Within; Unlimited Power**

Contents

Foreword

Fit For Life 3 is no ordinary book.

More than a review of cancer or its management, this important book makes the strategic transition from treatment to prevention. Harvey Diamond makes a strong case for the fact that people are increasingly taking responsibility for decisions concerning their health. Indeed, *Fit For Life 3* empowers the individual to make health care decisions that are based on personal research; indeed, it accelerates this process.

The traditional view of the doctor as all-knowing is undergoing dramatic change as people use their knowledge to demystify such diseases as cancer. So what do physicians actually know about the cause of cancer? Precious little. In fact, no one knows for sure what causes most cancer. And while heart disease is still the country's number-one killer, cancer is our greatest fear. Unfortunately, some cancers—breast cancer, for example—have been on the rise for decades. We still don't know why. Despite 26 years of the U.S. government's War on Cancer, a program launched by then-President Richard Nixon, and an expenditure of some $30 billion, cancer deaths have not been significantly reduced. In a 1997 article on cancer research expenditures versus cancer mortality rates, published in the *New England Journal of Medicine*, Dr. John Bailor and Dr. Heather Gernick, from the University of Chicago, conclude that new treatments for cancer have been "largely disappointing" and that "the most promising approach of the control for cancer is a national commitment to *prevention.*"

And so, back to Harvey Diamond and *Fit For Life 3*. The book was not meant to be a medical textbook on cancer. Medical texts deal exclusively with diagnosis and treatment, while *Fit For Life 3* covers a much broader landscape. While Harvey does discuss diagnosis and treatment, his real message is that *you can prevent cancer*. Moreover, where medical books are objective, analytical, and usually completely unexciting to read, this book is alive with real people, stimulating ideas, and common-sense approaches to how you can take control of your health. It beats with a heart of its own as it covers a number of areas: Natural Hygiene, inspiring cancer recoveries, radical surgery, nutrition, the mind-body connection, vegetarianism, chemotherapy, exercise, radiation and the lymphatic system, and most important—the three principles of CAREing.

Fit For Life 3 is an exciting examination of a complex subject. Harvey Diamond penetrates much of its mystery with a prevention program couched in the life-sustaining principles of Natural Hygiene and an approach that challenges conventional thinking. The author takes doctors to task for stubbornly clinging to the past for cancer diagnosis, management, and treatment. He points out that researchers really do not know what causes most cancer, that there is a worrisome increase in the frequency of some cancers, and that cancer remains society's greatest fear. Harvey discusses what, in his view, causes cancer, and proposes a simple, effective program to address these causes. But this isn't just somebody's theory or wild guess. Harvey Diamond's program is based on a growing body of sound scientific evidence from the world's most respected researchers. Harvey translates this information so that it is accessible to everyone, as only the author of the best-selling diet-health book of all time, *Fit For Life* (approximately 11 million copies in 29 languages), could do.

Fit For Life 3 is enjoyable, inspiring, and will change how you live, eat, play, and think about cancer. I know of no popular or scientific book on cancer that brings together the wealth of wisdom contained in these pages. Everyone should read it and reread it. It is a book with *answers*, a book of *real hope*. It will help end your fears about cancer.

Harvey addresses the subject of women and breast cancer not only with passion, but with carefully compiled and analyzed facts and studies accrued from a number of reliable sources. He has also drawn from 28 years of his own study of diet and health, disease prevention, Natural Hygiene, yoga, and Eastern medicine. *Fit For Life 3* is a treasure trove of exciting health information to prevent breast cancer, and most other cancers as well. Harvey's program to promote and restore vibrant health allows you to enjoy that all-important sense of security you feel when you take responsibility for your own health. Once again you can feel renewed joy and hope knowing that a life free of the fear of cancer is an attainable goal.

I've treated thousands of cancer patients. During my general surgery training, I participated in many radical cancer surgeries. These experiences were unpleasant, and the patients who endured these operations lost more than a breast, or stomach, or prostate. All too often the cancer would recur and the hopelessness of a broken spirit would be added to their physical plight. I felt each patient's despair, and I knew I had nothing more to offer medically, except morphine-type drugs when the pain became intolerable. Occasionally I visited these patients in their homes. The fortunate ones had loving families and supportive religious beliefs that saw them through. I felt strongly that we in medicine had to find a way to stop this awful disease that destroyed so many lives. I knew, however, that there was very little we could do. Until now. Until *Fit For*

Life 3. What makes me excited about Harvey Diamond's program is that I believe it works, and that *prevention* is where the real hope is in the struggle against cancer.

So, is there absolute scientific proof that the program in this book will positively prevent cancer? No, of course not. Life is seldom that simple. My guess is it would take $50 million, and studying 20,000 cancer patients for 20 years to "prove" such a thing. I recall the 40-year controversy on whether cigarette smoking caused lung cancer! Even today, the struggle continues to keep smoking out of public places, even though, in those 40 years of debate, 14 million Americans died from smoking-related diseases. Harvey Diamond's plea is that we not wait for the millions of new cases of cancer to occur in the next 20 years, but to do something to prevent them *now*. When new scientific evidence and epidemiological studies start to point strongly to major lifestyle changes that *do* prevent cancer, which the author outlines extensively in this book, one must conclude that Harvey's program will work. At the very least, people who follow it will have more energy, stay slimmer, and feel healthier. At the most, it will prevent a wide variety of cancers and degenerative diseases from occurring.

While physicians are still focused on treating cancer already present, Harvey Diamond moves the focus to taking charge of your life so you can prevent cancer. I am convinced that *Fit For Life 3* will become a modern health classic. The book should be read by everyone. It will transform cancer worry and fear into real hope.

Kenneth M. Kroll, M.D.
Fellow, International College of Surgeons
*(Dr. Kroll received his medical degree from Harvard Medical School
and surgical training at Stanford Medical Center.)*

An Important Message
From the Author

If you could be granted *one* gift, what would it be? Imagine being given the opportunity to have *one* wish fulfilled, no matter what it was. What would you request? Perhaps your immediate reaction might be to wish for some mind-boggling amount of money, more than could be spent in a lifetime. But upon reflection, most people invariably say that they would wish for uninterrupted, vibrant health. Think about it; to not only be free of any illness whatsoever, but also free of the fear of developing an illness. After all, what good is a lot of money if you're too sick to enjoy it? If money could buy health, there would be no sick rich people.

This book is my attempt to grant you that wish. Having studied in this area for nearly 30 years, I am convinced that vibrant health is not only a real and reasonable goal, but also that it is our natural state of being. It *can* be achieved. We have been told that some form of ill health is inevitable, and only the fortunate few manage to actually experience long-term good health, but that is not true. Vibrant health is part of the gift of life. We were not put here to suffer from an endless array of painful maladies, starting at infancy and ending in a hospital bed with tubes poked into us to keep us alive. Our creator is kinder and more loving than that.

The reality is that our actions determine whether or not we will live in pain and disease or vibrancy and health. In every area of our lives, be it health, relationships, profession—everything—we are constantly making choices. The sum total of all of these choices determines what our lives will be like. I can tell you with a good degree of certainty that when it comes to your desire to experience the highest level of health available to you, there are choices that can help you live a long, healthy life, free of disease. You are going to learn what some of these choices are, so that you can have a greater sense of control in that ever-so-important area of your life: your health.

I wrote this book in order to give you a brand-new way of viewing good health and a brand-new way of viewing ill health. Thus, the subtitle, The "New" Path to Vibrant Health. The focus of *Fit For Life 3* is prevention, not treatment. I don't want to show people what to do after they're sick, I want to show them what to do so they don't *become* sick. Mark Twain said, "Everyone complains about the weather but nobody does anything about it." That's how I feel about the prevention of disease. Everyone talks about prevention, but that's all it is—talk. The goal of this book is to end all that by giving you something definite, specific, and real that you can immediately start using to ensure that you experience what our Grand Creator had in store for us all along: a healthy, pain-free, and disease-free existence. In other words—vibrant health! Be assured: that exalted state of being to which we all aspire is far easier to attain than you may think.

I have a specific strategy to bring this awareness to you. It requires looking at both sides of the issue. Have you ever heard the statement, "Every stick has two ends"? It means the same thing as, "Every coin has two sides." In order to understand one side of an issue, the other side also has to be examined. And that is most certainly the case here. I recall hearing the following statement many times: "Knowing what you *don't* want is every bit as important as knowing what you *do* want." How about you? For example, someone trying to figure out what profession to go into might be told by a trusted adviser, "Figuring out what you don't want to do for a living will help you figure out what you do want to do."

In order to ascertain what vibrant health is and how to attain it, we must simultaneously examine what is at the very opposite end of the spectrum. In this case, "the other end of the stick" is *the* most classic lifestyle disease there is: cancer. The vast majority of people, I have found, don't have the vaguest idea what factors lead to cancer. When you *do* know what those factors are, it is then an easy matter to avoid them. This may turn out to be one of the most controversial statements I have ever put in print, but preventing cancer is a remarkably easy thing to do. By learning how to adopt a lifestyle that results in vibrant health, which is exactly what you will learn from this book, you automatically make cancer an impossibility. Obviously, the two cannot co-exist.

Cancer is North America's number-two killer (heart disease is number one), and takes more than half a million lives every year. The world over, cancer is considered to be a major problem. In fact, it is a problem that has become progressively more troublesome every year for about the last half century. A predominant reason for this is that the nature of cancer is invariably misinterpreted and misunderstood. You see, *cancer is not the problem, it is the end result of the problem.* And because this simple truth has been so universally misunderstood, billions upon billions of dollars have been squandered in a futile attempt to treat and/or cure people *after* it's too late and they are in jeopardy of losing their lives. Worse yet is that so many millions of people have already suffered immeasurably before ultimately dying *unnecessarily* from something that could have been prevented in the first place.

If someone is in a devastating auto accident, it's done. That's it. There's no curing it, the damage is already done. Had that person been better instructed on how to drive defensively, be ever alert to expect the unexpected and take no unnecessary risks, there's a good chance that the accident could have been avoided before it happened. I'm going to show you how to prevent becoming sick before it happens. You see, being sick, experiencing pain, represents the preamble to cancer. The information contained in this book will help you fully appreciate and understand that pain, discomfort, and ill health are totally unnatural and abnormal states of being and are the first, faint warning signs that something is not right and must be changed or the situation will worsen. At that point in time the appropriate measures must be taken to remove the *cause* of the pain and discomfort. If, instead, you ignore the cause or take drugs to silence these warnings, then you are taking those first fateful steps onto a path that, with continued neglect, can lead to that most dreaded of diseases—cancer.

By the time you finish reading this book you will not only know how to prevent cancer, but also how to prevent becoming sick at all, which, as mentioned above, is the precursor to cancer. A recent poll revealed that people's number one health complaint is pain. You will learn exactly what pain is, the extremely important role it plays, how to remove it and how to prevent it from ever recurring. The means by which this is accomplished is so obvious and so simple it absolutely astonishes me that it has been missed for so long.

The way this is all achieved is not by studying cancer—the effect—but by studying the factors that bring on cancer—the cause. The universe operates under the law of cause and effect. Things don't just happen, they happen for a definite reason. There is an action and then a reaction. In this instance, the things we do, knowingly or unknowingly, that jeopardize our health are the actions and cancer is the reaction. Studying cancer, which is the end result of prolonged abuse and neglect, would be like rushing out to lock your garage door after someone has already driven off in your car.

The approach I have taken in this book is to use breast cancer as the example for all the other kinds of cancer. In fact, it doesn't matter which kind of cancer I use as an example because *the only thing that differentiates one type of cancer from another is its appearance, not its nature.* Now, some of you might ask: "Breast cancer? That only affects women, for the most part. Why not focus on something like stomach or colon cancer, which affects both men and women?" Or, "What's a man doing writing about breast cancer, why not prostate cancer?" If you are asking these questions, you are missing an important point: you're focusing on the result, which is the reaction, instead of the cause, which is the action. As you will learn, the factors involved in turning a healthy cell cancerous, are the same, regardless of where in the body the cancer occurs. The only difference between breast cancer, prostate cancer, colon cancer, or any other cancer is that they appear at different sites in the body.

In order to obtain the maximum benefit from this book it is crucial that you understand that when you focus on the reaction instead of the action that caused it—when you focus on the effect instead of the cause that brought it about—then you are forced into that unenviable position of having to focus on treatment instead of prevention, because it means you're already sick and it's too late for prevention.

It's what I was referring to above when I said I wanted to give you a brand-new way of thinking about health and disease. The old way of thinking is to wait until you're sick and then battle your illness with the latest weapon—in other words, treat disease. The new way of thinking is to learn what factors cause you to become sick, and then avoid them—in other words, prevent disease. And that is why it makes no difference which type of cancer (the reaction, the effect) is used as an example to reveal the causes of illness so that you can successfully avoid them. I'll give you a quick example to illustrate my point. Both breast cancer and prostate cancer have the same approximate number of deaths per year. And with both we are told that early detection is the key factor. In fact, early detection is said to be the key factor in cancer regardless of the type. Indeed, whether we're talking about breast cancer, prostate cancer, colon cancer, stomach cancer or any other type of cancer, common or obscure, we are told that early detection is the key. And *early detection means you have something to detect.* The only thing I want you to be able to detect after reading this book is pain-free, disease-free, vibrant health! And you are going to learn how to achieve that goal by studying and learning about causes, not effects.

So what else inspired me to focus on breast cancer? First, something happened to me in 1979 (Chapter 1) that so affected me, I knew from that day on that I would someday write about breast cancer. Second, since the lymph system is most important in keeping you consistently healthy, and since nearly every discussion of breast cancer invariably refers to the body's lymph system, a focus on breast cancer seemed the perfect approach to take. By the time you finish reading the chapter titled "Your Very Best Friend," you will never look at the workings of your body in the same way again. It will change you and it will put you in charge and control of your health.

Chapters 1 and 2 use a discussion of breast cancer to lay the conceptual groundwork for the rest of the book, but as stated above, this discussion will serve as the basis for explaining all cancers, and disease in general. Chapters 3 to 13 will show you not only how to prevent all cancers, but also how to obtain that most prized and praised gift of gifts: a long, pain-free, disease-free life.

I ask only one thing of you, dear reader—to do the best you can to read this book with an open mind and a minimum of preconceived ideas about health and disease. It is likely that some of your beliefs will be challenged by what you read here. All I am asking for is a fair hearing. Read the book in its entirety and I promise, you will not be disappointed.

Our life on this glorious planet is an ongoing journey of discovery of ourselves and our surroundings. When you proceed on this magnificent journey in a healthy body that is operating at optimum efficiency, the road before you is made smooth and your life becomes a joyous song of gladness. That is the glory of vibrant health.

All God's Blessings,

Harvey Diamond

Part One

HEALTH IS YOUR BIRTHRIGHT

1

Encounters with Breast Cancer

Encounter #1

In the midst of a conversation with a casual acquaintance, the woman I was talking to asked me if I was working on another book. Since I was deep into the research for this book, I said, "You bet," and proceeded to give her an enthusiastic overview, starting with the fact that I would be focusing on a discussion of breast cancer. At that time, whenever I had occasion to describe the book to a woman, I jumped at the opportunity. After all, I'm a man writing a book that discusses breast cancer, a subject of tremendous concern to women. I welcomed and greatly appreciated every woman's feedback.

I told my acquaintance that this would be like no other book that addresses breast cancer. It wasn't going to be one more recap of a bad situation getting progressively worse that posed lots of questions and no answers, one more treatise that left women feeling like helpless victims waiting for the axe to fall, with no hope beyond that of "early detection." I told her I was convinced that women were being made to unnecessarily worry, anguish, live in fear and suffer immeasurable pain. It simply did not have to be the case. The only reason it was, I went on to tell her, was that the true nature of lumps in the breast was not understood. The measures women could take to prevent them, or quickly remove them if they developed, were unknown to them. Women had been whipped into such a frenzy of fear that the mere mention of the diagnosis "breast cancer" filled them with horror and dread, and invariably resulted in them prematurely and unnecessarily "going under the knife." This fear was so intense that women were increasingly having both of their breasts removed before there was any sign whatsoever of cancer or *before* there was even a lump![1]

I told the woman that this book would liberate all women from this cycle of fear and pain and put them in complete control of their bodies and lives so that they could live with the confidence that they would not become one of the ever-growing statistics. I wanted her to know that women had a choice in the matter, that they were not hapless victims with no control over whether they developed breast cancer or not.

On the contrary, there were absolute, concrete actions they could take to *dramatically* reduce their chances of ever developing breast cancer and, equally important, steps they could take to remove lumps from the breast without ever undergoing surgery— steps that prove themselves relatively quickly, so that any and all other forms of treatment would still be available to them if need be. But they should know that their first line of defence could eliminate the problem before it became a problem, with no surgery, radiation or chemotherapy.

Whenever I gave this quick description of the book to women, I always looked forward to their initial reaction and feedback so as to confirm to myself the level of interest women had on this subject. Invariably, I received comments like, "Wow! Tell me more!" or "What a timely subject," or "Hurry up and write it, I can't wait to read it." Comments from women who had already had some experience with breast cancer were different: "Too bad you didn't write it three years ago," or "I wish I could have heard that I had choices before my surgery, I thought it was a mastectomy or death."

But when I looked at the woman I'd been talking to, I realized I would get no such comment. In fact, as I spoke, her face became flushed and her eyes filled with tears. It didn't take a psychic to see that either someone very close to her or she, herself, had been to the mat with breast cancer.

I have wanted to write a book on this subject for more than 15 years. In all of that time, as I gathered information and experience on the subject, I knew deep in my heart of hearts I could never rest or feel fulfilled until I wrote it. If there was ever even the slightest, most infinitesimal doubt in my mind that I should write about this subject, for whatever the reason may be, those doubts were forever obliterated as I listened to the story this woman told me about her personal experience with breast cancer.

There are no words to describe what this woman had lived through for six years and was still dealing with. I have seen plenty and I have heard plenty, but looking into her face as I listened to her describe her ordeal was almost more than I could handle. Here was a very pretty, vivacious woman in her late thirties telling me what would have sounded like science fiction to most people. By the time she'd finished her story, I was beside myself. I felt infuriated, angry, outraged. I thought I would explode. I wanted to scream or smash something, just somehow vent the unbridled rage I felt for the injustice of what this woman had been put through. I couldn't possibly give you the detailed, long version of her story because, number one, it would take too long and, number two, I don't want to repel you to the point that you put down the book. Even the short version, which I must share with you, will "strain the friendship."

Starting in 1987, this woman has had no less than seven surgical procedures. The first was a double mastectomy (one of which was a radical) and removal of lymph nodes from both sides including from under her arms. The second operation was to insert expanders under the skin of her chest to sufficiently stretch the skin so as to accommodate implants which were to be put in. Every ten days or so, for months, she would have a saline solution injected into the expanders to keep them full, as the solution would constantly seep out of the expanders into her system. Operation number three was to have silicone implants put in. Operation number four was to replace one of the implants because it punctured. Operation number five was to replace the other implant because it, too, punctured. Operation number six was to replace both silicone implants with saline implants because the first one that was replaced punctured again! Operation number seven was to make and attach nipples to her chest out of flesh from her buttocks.

She insisted on having numerous photos taken of her body at every stage of her treatment, from the very beginning when she had her breasts intact, to the end when she had nothing but scars and implants. As I looked at these photos and the large, brutal scars that are a permanent part of her body, I became physically ill. If you could see these pictures, you would think this woman a saint that she can still smile so readily.

Although she was heavily pressured to submit to chemotherapy and radiation, she refused because she was already in so much pain that she couldn't imagine surviving any more—especially the degree and intensity of pain that accompanies chemotherapy. For years she'd had so many shots in her thighs for pain that both legs were constantly black and blue and ached all the time.

She had no health insurance and had to pay for everything herself. She owned her own business which she lost, along with her house and her car. She could not get credit, and for seven years, through all the pain and operations, she still had to work in order to pay for her medical expenses. For seven years all the money she earned went toward paying for her next operation. By merely reading the words on these pages, you could never fully grasp the unrelenting physical and emotional pain and suffering this woman has had to overcome. Not only has her body been ripped apart and torn away, but everything she had worked so hard for has also been destroyed. And she had to pay for the entire ordeal out of her own pocket. It was more money than she had and she is still paying, still in pain and working on herself every day to get beyond the anger, put the entire ordeal behind her and move on. This woman's story so disturbed me and is the basis for the beginning of this book because the torment she experienced all happened as a result of one tiny lump in one breast that was no larger than the size of a single pea!

Now, right now, you may be thinking something like, "Hey, cancer is cancer. No matter what size it was, it had to be dealt with." Dealt with, yes. But in a far more sane and sensible way. Not the go-for-broke, all-out assault that is overkill in the extreme and which, unfortunately, has become standard medical treatment. By the end of this book you will see that the appearance of a lump in your breast, whether the size of a pea or a walnut, is no reason to run out like a scalded cat to have your body mutilated and disfigured and then bombarded with the most deadly and harmful treatments known: radiation and chemotherapy. This is especially so considering that members of the medical profession, the experts in the field, admit that they don't even know what breast cancer is. They don't know what causes it, they don't know how to cure it and they don't know how to prevent it. So, to compensate for this total lack of knowledge, the cancer is attacked with a vengeance, in the hope that an assault on the body will somehow exorcise the cancer without killing the patient. This overly aggressive treatment is like demolishing an entire city because there is a criminal hiding in it somewhere.

This is precisely what happened to the woman whose story I have related here. After discovering the lump, which was not painful, not even tender, she had a biopsy. She was told that cancer cells were found and that she should immediately have her breast removed and all the surrounding tissues and muscle as well. Everything, right down to the bone. "Just to be sure." That is a radical mastectomy.

She was still trying to deal with the shock of learning that she had cancer when her physician recommended that while she was having her right breast removed, she should just go ahead and have her left breast removed too. The reasoning was, if cancer appears in one breast, there is a certain likelihood that it could appear in the other breast as well. "Why take a chance of going through this again? Let's just get rid of both of them in one fell swoop and then you'll never have to worry about breast cancer again. And, oh yes, while we're at it, we'll remove all your lymph nodes from your chest and both your arms as a *precautionary* measure."

She was devastated. She went from feeling fine one day, no pain, no discomfort, to finding out the next day that the whole upper part of her body was going to be torn asunder, leaving her with no breasts and the prospect of considerable further surgery to reconstruct what was taken away. "Are you sure that's the best course of action?" she asked. "Can I get a second opinion?" Three other doctors from the *same hospital* gave their concurring opinions, and between the four physicians, she was, according to her, "frightened to death of what *might* happen to her and made to feel like a fool if she did not submit to the surgery." This all happened so fast that she was hardly given time to even think her decision over. At this most vulnerable time in her life, she was being literally bullied into this radical course of action. With no one to turn to, and no one to give her another point of view, she gave in and allowed this ultra-extensive, disfiguring surgery to take place.

After telling the woman about my experiences of helping women with breast cancer and about others who successfully overcame their breast cancer without surgery, she said, "My God, why couldn't I have known you then?" I told her that, for whatever the reason—and we may never know what those reasons are—she had to go through this in her life. This woman' story changed me. I decided that, although it may be of very little consolation to her now, I was going to see to it that millions of women would have the opportunity to avoid a fate similar to hers.

Women have choices outside of surgery, chemotherapy, and radiation and they are not being told about them. This book is going to change all that. If a woman learns about her options and still chooses to go the traditional medical route, so be it. At least she had the chance to consider other options. But to not even be given the opportunity to *hear* about her choices while being pressured, bulldozed, and terrorized into surgery, as though it was the only viable course of action, is outrageous and entirely unacceptable. It would be one thing if the incidence of, and death rate from, breast cancer were steadily decreasing, but the exact opposite is true. It has been getting worse and worse for more than *one hundred years!* In light of both this and the fact that those in charge don't know what causes breast cancer, let alone what to do about it, I would think that another course of action, other than the one that has failed so miserably to date, would be welcomed with open arms—*and minds!*

I told you that I have wanted to write this book for more than 15 years. There are three reasons why I did not do so until now. First, I wanted to have more experience with cancer in general and breast cancer specifically. I have that experience now. Second, I wanted a major success in some area of health that would validate me as a credible proponent of the relationship between diet and health. *Fit For Life* has succeeded in doing that. And third, I wanted to be 50 years old. Silly, perhaps, but I've always felt that by virtue of living for half a century one automatically earns the right to at least be listened to. I turned fifty in February 1995.

Encounter #2

In 1979 I had my second encounter with breast cancer. Because of that experience, I knew that I would someday write a book about the subject. I had been studying the field of Natural Hygiene for nine years and the publication of *Fit For Life* was still six years off. I was as convinced then as I am today that people who understood and practised the principles of Natural Hygiene, even moderately, could ensure for themselves long, pain-free, disease-free lives.

In 1971 I was particularly gung-ho because I had recaptured my own health, and had seen, firsthand, hundreds of people do the same by following the simple principles of Natural Hygiene I outlined for them in one-on-one counselling sessions. At that time, I loved talking about health to anyone who would listen and my enthusiasm for the subject was boundless. I welcomed any challenge from people to show them how they could heal even the most seemingly catastrophic problems. I had seen so many examples of individuals overcoming serious health problems that my excitement for the subject was often catalyst enough for people to start making the simple changes I suggested. I had, and still have, the utmost confidence that because the human body is self-repairing and self-healing, it can, given the right environment for healing, overcome any ailment so long as it has not suffered irreparable damage.

This was precisely my frame of mind when I received a phone call that day in 1979 from a woman friend to whom I had spoken on several occasions about the beautiful and remarkable healing capabilities of the human body. Our conversations must have made an impression on her because she was calling me from the hospital where she had just been given the results of a mammogram she had taken. It was obvious from her voice that she was highly agitated. Her voice was so shaky and she was so upset I could hardly understand her. The mammogram had detected a rather large lump in her breast. Compared to the pea-sized lump that was the rationale for the carnage performed on the woman described earlier, this one was huge, about the size of a walnut.

Part of the problem was that her physician was *there* at the phone with her berating her for being so foolish as to call "some nutritional friend" for advice when he had just finished telling her that she must make arrangements *at that moment* for the removal of her breast or she would die!

Now, try to picture this. She goes to her doctor to find out what, if anything, was found on her mammogram and he shows her a huge lump and then proceeds to scare the juices out of her by telling her that without an *immediate* mastectomy she would die. No biopsy, no tests, no anything. He doesn't even know if cancer was present or not. It was "let's cut now and talk later." He didn't say that she *might* die or that with a lump that size the chances are that there's cancer and she *could* die. No. He says to her, no mastectomy and you're dead!

So she tells him she knows someone who knows a lot about nutrition and she wants to call him first and he erupts at her. "How could you do something so stupid when your life is at stake? This is not time for nutrition, this is time for surgery. You had better do what I say and stop messing around." He was standing next to her at the phone harassing her while she was trying to tell me what was going on. It was a real scene, believe me.

Finally, I said to her that if she had a lump in her breast as big as she described, it had been growing for some 10 to 15 years at least. No matter what she decided to do, she certainly could take 24 to 48 hours to go home, reflect, talk to friends and make a rational decision without her doctor yelling in her face that either she listens to him or *dies!* I suggested that she hang up the phone, tell her doctor that she would call him in a day or two, and come directly to my office so that I could tell her about an option she will never hear from her doctor.

Within an hour, we were sitting and talking. When she walked into my office she looked horrible. Her face was ashen and there was fear in her eyes that was so obvious you could have sliced it up and served it on a platter. Her voice was still shaky, and as soon as she started to talk, she began to cry uncontrollably. I assumed she was crying because she had found out she possibly had cancer, and might have to undergo surgery or chemotherapy, or both, and she was scared. But it wasn't so much the cancer and treatment that had upset her; it was her fear of being cut with a knife. Now, I'm not just talking about the normal fear or apprehension one might have about being operated on. No, she had such a paralyzing fear of being cut that for her, *anything* would be preferable to submitting to surgery.

I told her that Natural Hygiene, my field of study, had an entirely different perspective on lumps in the breast than traditional medicine did. I explained the lymph system to her (which is invariably involved with lumps in the breast), and suggested that she take the Natural Hygiene approach to getting rid of the lump. In four or five weeks, I said, she would have absolute evidence as to whether or not the approach was successful. At that time, she would definitely see whether her lump was the same size, or whether it was larger or smaller. I assured her it would be smaller. Since she would have preferred to do nothing rather than undergo surgery, she was willing to try anything that did not involve being cut. I told her that since her situation would be an invaluable test case for me, I would tell her exactly what to do and supervise her along the way.

The first thing I did was to fill her with a positive feeling about her body and its ability to heal itself. Her doctor's message that she was going to die was not exactly the best jumping-off place for self-healing. I explained to her that success depended upon certain dietetic maneuvering that would allow her lymph system to repair and heal itself. She promised me that she was extremely disciplined and would follow my advice without the slightest variation.

When she left my office she was smiling and filled with hope. I advised her practically every day. She followed my suggestions implicitly. Within the first ten days she was certain that the lump had decreased somewhat in size and it was no longer tender to the touch. In three or four weeks her lump went from the size of a walnut to the size of a dime. In another four weeks, it was gone. *Gone!* She had another mammogram and there was not a trace to be found.

Of course my friend was overjoyed. You couldn't make her stop smiling with a gun. As far as she was concerned, she had been given her life back. One of the very first things she did was to call her doctor with the good news and to get a copy of the original mammogram so I could have the two, one showing the lump, the other showing nothing.

Now, most people would assume that upon learning about his patient's nonsurgical removal of a large breast lump, her doctor would walk barefoot over hot coals and broken glass to find out how she had accomplished this feat so he could share the information with his patients and colleagues. You would think he would want to trumpet the good news from the highest mountain. Well, in fact, my friend's doctor would not even take a phone call from her! *He was angry at her for ignoring his advice!* His secretary told her that it would be best if she were to find another physician. And no, she could not have a copy of the original mammogram.

I lost contact with my friend and did not see her again until seven years later. She was still smiling, and she looked great. In the two months I had worked with her, she had lost about 30 pounds and she had obviously kept it off. More important, there were no more lumps in her breasts. In terms of my goal to educate people about how to ensure their own good health, she told me the greatest thing I could have ever hoped to hear. She said that she no longer felt as if her own body was a stranger to her or that the workings of her body were out of her realm of understanding. She felt in charge and in control of her health. Whenever she put on weight she didn't want or started to feel unwell, she knew exactly what to do to turn the situation around. She thanked me profusely for what I had done for her, not realizing that what her words had done for me was equally as great.

There are millions of women living in fear, biding their time waiting for the axe to fall. They're afraid of their bodies, afraid that their bodies will turn against them. Afraid of cancer. Afraid to get a mammogram for fear of what it may reveal. I know women who for a week or more before they're scheduled for a mammogram are nervous wrecks. By the time they have the mammogram and are waiting for the results, it's everything they can do not to keel over from fright. If the result is negative, the sigh of relief is as though they have just had a death sentence commuted. But that fear sits in the back of their minds, building until the next mammogram or, God forbid, a lump appears in one of their breasts. That is no way to live. It is something that must change. It can change, and if I have anything to do with it, it *will* change.

Prevention versus Early Detection

I wrote this book to empower you, to free you, to put you in charge so that you can live your life with the confidence of knowing that you are not going to become a medical statistic. Worry and fear can be cast aside and become a thing of the past. And I am not telling you this just for effect or to give you false hope. YOU CAN PREVENT CANCER!!

I want you to be very clear on something. Just because the people you have been turning to for answers don't have any, does not mean that there are no answers, or that because *they* don't have any, no one does. There *are* answers and there are plenty of people all over the world who have discovered this for themselves. It is not a closed club; you can join their ranks. The only thing preventing you from learning how to live a life free of cancer, or from the fear of developing cancer, is a lack of information. My sincerest wish is for this book to change that for you.

You are being told from every quarter that early detection is the key factor in combatting breast cancer. Hogwash! Prevention is the key factor in combatting breast cancer, or any cancer. Early detection is defeatist and negative. Buying into the idea that early detection is the most important aspect of combatting cancer is admitting and accepting that there is nothing you can do except wait until *after* you have cancer. Then your fate lies in the hope that you will require the very least amount of disfiguring surgery, and the least amount of brutalizing chemotherapy and/or radiation. *Prevent the problem from occurring in the first place and there is nothing to detect.* That is why this book is first and foremost a book about *prevention*.

Women fall into three categories, as relates to breast cancer. The first is far and away the biggest group and they are my primary audience. This group comprises women who have yet to have any problem whatsoever with lumps in their breasts and they want to do whatever they can to keep it that way. The second group comprises women who have already been through it with breast cancer, have lost one or both breasts, had lymph nodes removed, endured chemotherapy and/or radiation, gone through reconstructive surgery, and the very last thing on earth they want to find out is that the cancer is back and they have to go through the ordeal all over again. The third group are women who have just found a lump in their breast or have been told that a mammogram has detected a mass, a tumour, a lump, something "suspicious" that has to be investigated further. Women at this point are faced with, probably, the most important decision of their lives. They must decide what course of action to take.

Most of the advice and suggestions in this book are directed toward the first two groups—those who have had no problem and those who have been through some form of treatment. Their goal is prevention. You who are in the third group have a more immediate need, and I will address your options later on in the book. You will be shown how to rid yourself of the lump in the least invasive way possible so that you can use the information in the rest of the book to prevent the lump from ever returning.

Regardless of which of the three groups you fall into, one thing I can absolutely assure you of is that this book will confront you with information that will challenge your present beliefs and way of thinking on the subject of cancer. Let me tell you that for there to be a significant change in the incidence of cancer, and a lessening of suffering and decline in deaths from all cancer, a fundamental change in thinking and actions must occur. There is an old saying, short but right on target: "If there is no change, then there is no change." Vibrant health *is* possible to attain, and change is a key factor in bringing it about.

Disrupting the Status Quo—Good for Your Health

Change is a most interesting phenomenon. On the one hand, we all want change. We need it, we cherish it, we demand it. Imagine a world without changes like electricity, airplanes, telephones, computers, televisions, automobiles. Moreover, without regular and significant change, life would become unbearably boring. On the other hand, the new information that heralds these changes we crave is, all too frequently, met with negativity and resistance. Nowhere is this more prevalent than in the sciences, the place where you would least expect it. History is rife with examples to prove this strange irony:

- From Galileo being vilified for pointing out that the sun, not the earth, is the centre of the universe, to Dr. Ignaz Semmelweis being hounded out of his profession for suggesting that doctors wash their hands before surgery.
- From a time when the medical experts of the day warned that washing the entire body more than once a week was harmful, to suggesting that patients spend time in stables where they could inhale the fumes from animal dung to help heal tuberculosis.
- From refusing water to fever patients because it would be hurtful, to suggesting that fresh air would be injurious to the bedridden.
- From the admonition to eat only well-cooked food, nothing fresh, as fresh food would be detrimental, to suggesting that bananas, being such a potent drug, should only be available by prescription.
- And the granddaddy of them all, the idea that blood should be drained from the sick to make them well.

All of the above "established, proven methods" were eventually thrown on the junk heap of history, but not before the new information that brought about their change was obstinately, sometimes violently, resisted. Consider the fact that over *98 percent* of everything that has ever been learned has been replaced with new information, and you can see that resisting that new information is both foolish and futile.

Much of today's barbaric treatment of women who develop lumps in their breasts needs to be thrown on that same junk heap. And you can be certain that there will be resistance to this change as well. But it doesn't matter, because this is a change that is inevitable. When you consider that the only change in breast cancer over the last hundred years is that the problem has become progressively worse, it becomes clear that this situation is screaming out for change. The only sure-fire way to rescue women from what is coming to be known as "the other epidemic" is to stop focusing on early detection and treatment and start focusing on prevention.

I understand what a massive undertaking this is. It will disrupt the status quo. That is never easy. But we can't sit idly by and allow this abysmal situation to continue for another hundred years! There are too many lives at stake. The new approach to breast cancer calls for another way of thinking about your body, how it works, what supports its health, and what undermines it. Respect and admiration for your body has to replace your fear of it. A brand-new awareness of how magnificently capable your body is in ensuring its own well-being is essential. A new understanding is needed of what cancer actually is and the role you can play to avoid it. All of these things are essential to become free of the fear of cancer, and all these things will be made clear to you as you read this book.

Over the years, because we have been systematically conditioned to believe that these issues are far too complicated for us to grasp and are best left to "experts" in the field, we have abdicated all responsibility to them. It may surprise you to learn that cancer is not nearly as complicated as you might think, and you are far more capable of understanding what cancer is and how to prevent it than you might realize.

Natural Hygiene: A Way of Life

Before getting on with it, I need to address some questions that are sure to come up as you read this book. These questions are: "With all due respect, you are not a doctor or cancer specialist. You are the author of a successful diet book. So what qualifies you to give advice on this subject? Why should I believe what you have to say on this?" It's true that my book *Fit For Life* focuses on weight loss, but be clear that it is not merely a book on weight loss; it is a book about health and how to achieve it. In a state of health, one is not overweight, so the book describes how weight can be lost when overall health is achieved. Health is always the goal.

When I embarked on my studies more than a quarter of a century ago, I did not take up the study of weight loss, I took up the study of health: how to acquire it and how to maintain it. I could have studied in the field of medicine, osteopathy, homeopathy, chiropractic or any other specialty, but I chose to study in the field of Natural Hygiene because it is the one that made the most sense to me. Hygiene looks at the body and the pursuit of health differently than the other specialties mentioned. This is not to imply that adherence to one discipline negates the others. All have their place and are appropriate under certain conditions. No one approach to health care has all the answers or is the best choice in all situations or under all circumstances. Those who would tell you differently are looking out for their own interests over yours. As it happens, Hygiene is the approach that helped me recapture my health and allowed me to lose 50 pounds that I've managed to keep off. With such positive results in my life, I just naturally made it my field of expertise.

Compared to other branches of the health services available to North Americans, Natural Hygiene is relatively unknown. But don't let that fool you. It has a 160-year written history and is phenomenally successful in dealing with a very wide range of health problems. This fact is quickly borne out by anyone who adheres to its simple, logical, common-sense principles.

In the early 1980s, after I had been studying on my own for about 11 years, I discovered that there was a highly comprehensive, all-inclusive course on Natural Hygiene being offered by the American College of Life Science in Austin, Texas. I completed this course and was awarded a Ph.D. in Health Science in 1983. So that there is no misunderstanding, the college had no campus, and the course was strictly by correspondence and not accredited. The course did, however, contain a wealth of information that solidified my understanding of Natural Hygiene. In my opinion, the significance of this kind of traditional "book learnin'" is equalled in importance by experience and observation, of which I have more than 28 years' worth. Incidentally, the course I studied has been translated into German, Spanish, Italian and, most notably, French, and was adopted as part of the curriculum of the Department of Medicine, University of Paris. The course is taught as Naturotherapy to the department's medical students.

Actually, what I have studied or not studied is irrelevant. The only thing of relevance and importance is whether the information in this book can help you prevent cancer and experience vibrant health. Where the information comes from and who imparts the information means nothing. The only thing that matters is, does it work? I'm not asking you to blindly follow my recommendations. It must make sense to you. You have to feel excited and confident about it.

About This Book

What I have written is presented in a totally nontechnical way, and is couched in layperson's terms. I feel that too many people have been convinced that this subject is far too complicated, mysterious, and bewildering for them to understand, and they therefore *must* seek the advice and services of highly paid specialists. This is extremely convenient for those making their living selling the advice and services, but know this: You have been blessed from birth with common sense, logic, and basic instincts to help you and to guide you. You are far more capable of discerning what is best for you than you have been led to believe.

There is a tendency in the scientific community to reject anything out-of-hand that is not in line with traditional thinking. I'm not suggesting that my approach should be accepted without question just because it falls under the category of new information. I think that new information should be scrutinized to the fullest extent to determine its viability. It is rejection without investigation, for no reason other than the fact that the new information is in opposition to prevailing thought, that is preposterous and prevents valuable, life-saving information from reaching the very people who could benefit from it the most.

I am telling you that breast cancer does not have to be the killer that it is; that the number of women dying from the disease can be dramatically decreased; that the majority of surgical procedures, including mastectomies, can be eliminated; that the number of diagnoses of breast cancer can be drastically reduced; that there are steps you can take to protect yourself and prevent lumps from developing or from turning cancerous if they do; that you can live your life free of the fear that you may become a breast cancer casualty.

All of this is possible for you and all I want is a fair shot at proving it to you. Read what I have to say and decide if the program I outline makes sense to you. If it doesn't, then don't use it. But if it does, if it rings true to you, if it makes sense, if you can honestly say, "It seems reasonable enough. I can at least try it to see if it can increase my chances of protection," then I assure you, you won't be disappointed.

It is not my intention to underestimate or trivialize the severity of the cancer situation as it exists today. But you are only getting part of the story. There is another whole side of it that has yet to come to light. All you're being told about is the deadliness of cancer, its pervasiveness, and the dreadful statistics that are daily being racked up. The fear! People weren't put on earth to have to live in fear of their own bodies! That is a totally unnatural and unnecessary situation that *can* be changed.

Once again, I'm not asking you to take my word for anything. There is no proof in the world better than personal verification. If you will incorporate into your lifestyle the principles presented in this book, you will not jeopardize or compromise your health one iota. If anything, you will feel better, have more energy, lose or gain weight (if necessary), and be more confident about your overall well-being. You can prove this for yourself. It won't matter who says what about it. Either it will prove itself to you or it won't. All the experts in the world could praise a program or treatment up one side and down the other and it may not work. Or they could ridicule a program or treatment and describe it as useless and it could be just the answer for some individuals. It happens all the time. If you can, with absolutely no risk to yourself, try something that may prove to be a godsend, and there is no downside, why would you *not* try it?

One of the primary reasons *Fit For Life* continues to enjoy such enormous popularity is that I challenged people to try the suggestions in the book for only ten days to see for themselves if they worked for them. They took me up on it and *Fit For Life* has become one of the most popular diet and health books in history. Translated into 29 languages, it has millions of adherents world-wide who have discovered the glory of uninterrupted vibrant health. I want to invite you to join them. Here is an opportunity for you to go on a journey of discovery, of yourself and of your life on this planet—a life that can be devoid of the fear and apprehension associated with cancer. It is, after all, your birthright! As you read the following chapters, I'm sure you'll encounter passages that will challenge some of your beliefs. That's O.K. All I'm hoping for is that after you've read the book in its entirety, you'll be sufficiently intrigued and curious about the program it outlines to at least try to see if it fulfils the promises I make about it. Give it a chance. You won't be disappointed.

I knew that if people took up the challenge in *Fit For Life* and simply followed the book's recommendations, they would lose weight and feel healthier. Well, that has come to pass beyond my most hopeful expectations. I am just as certain now that if you take the challenge here and follow the recommendations in *this* book, your reward will be to live your life with something so valuable no amount of money could buy it: peace of mind.

2

Keeping Abreast

Ask the next ten women whose paths you cross what their greatest health fear is. Don't be surprised if all ten, without hesitation, say breast cancer, which for most women is the health issue of the nineties; so much so that, as mentioned in Chapter 1, it is being referred to as "the other epidemic." If you were to add together all deaths from breast cancer, all deaths from all other forms of cancer, all deaths from AIDS, diabetes and, in fact, all causes of death of women by disease, they would not even come close to equalling the number of deaths from cardiovascular disease alone. But it is breast cancer that women dread the most. Why? That's not hard to figure out. All you have to do is compare the treatment and aftermath of treatment associated with heart disease to that of cancer. It's like the difference between being bitten by a mosquito and being mauled by a grizzly bear.

The Dread of Breast Cancer

If your doctor reports that your cholesterol level is much too high and there is far too much fatty plaque in your arteries, that's not good news, because it puts you at high risk of having a heart attack. Hearing such a diagnosis would certainly alarm you, but the fear or dread you might experience from such a diagnosis is like a stroll on the beach compared to what the words "you have cancer" evoke. After all, the treatment to ward off the heart attack is pretty straightforward. Stop pumping so much fat and cholesterol through your arteries, cut down on your salt, fried foods, tobacco and alcohol consumption, and include a moderate amount of regular aerobic exercise in your routine. That's basically it. Not so with cancer.

For most people, the word "cancer" conjures up the worst of all possibilities. Not only is there the disease itself, which is viewed as a merciless horror that relentlessly eats away at the body, but there is also the treatment, which can be as agonizing as the disease itself. Between the painful, disfiguring surgery, the radiation that can burn holes in your skin, and the chemotherapy which is the most excruciatingly painful treatment ever devised for any disease, the overall impact of being told you have cancer is tantamount to being told you have to pay a visit to hell and duel the devil with burning pitchforks. That's for cancer in general. A diagnosis of breast cancer for a woman is worse yet because it has all the negatives associated with cancer and its treatment *plus* the ordeal of having one or both breasts removed. For some women, this can be the most devastating part of having breast cancer.

We're not talking about the removal of some nondescript organ here. Remove a gall bladder, a spleen, an appendix, or a man's prostate and, yes, these operations are painful, and having surgery, any surgery, is unnerving. But with rest and recuperation, the scars from these operations heal and life goes on pretty much as it did before. Remove a woman's breast and there's another whole set of variables that come into play. The psychological and emotional scars can last long after the physical ones have healed. The removal of a breast goes to the very heart of a woman's self-image.

Let's face it: certainly in North America and a good portion of the rest of the world, there is a fixation on women's breasts. Anyone not aware of that must be visiting from another planet. The female form, of which the breasts are a most significant feature, has been celebrated in art, music, and poetry throughout history. A woman's breasts are deeply and profoundly associated with her femininity, her sexuality, her body image, her feeling of self-esteem and beauty. Women have told me that they felt afraid that their husbands might not think they were pretty after the loss of their breasts. They no longer feel whole and attractive. This is enormously disconcerting to a women in a way I am certain no man could possibly comprehend.

One woman I know was so apprehensive that she said she could hardly look her own husband in the eye, let alone get undressed in front of him. Fortunately, her husband was sufficiently enlightened to recognize that he was in love with *who* his wife was, not what her body looked like, and everything turned out fine for them. But what of single women who have had one or both breasts removed and want to marry and have children?

I was watching a program on CNN[2] about several women who had survived breast cancer and its treatment. One woman's story couldn't help but bring tears to my eyes. She was single, in her late thirties, and had had both breasts removed. She was discussing dating. The fact was, she could not get her situation out of her mind; it was always there. She wants to go out with men and eventually wants to marry. She has no breasts and she has no hair as a result of chemotherapy treatments. She felt as though her femininity had been taken from her. She said that worse than not having breasts was that she had no hair on her head and always had to deal with whatever wig she was wearing. She not only felt conspicuous about that, but constantly anguished over when to tell the person she was dating exactly what her situation was. Instead of thoughts about what a nice evening she would enjoy with a new friend, her thoughts were about whether or not he would be understanding and kind and whether her wig would stay in place. It was impossible to watch this woman and see the sadness in her eyes and not be deeply moved. It is no small wonder that so many women are living in fear of breast cancer. It was this kind of story that filled me with the fire to finish this book as soon as I could, to help ward off such tragedies in other women's lives.

It would probably be the greatest understatement ever uttered to say that women, all women, would do practically anything to avoid ever having to deal with breast cancer, its treatment and aftermath. There is one way and one way only to ensure that: prevention! It goes without saying that if women knew how to prevent breast cancer, they would do whatever they had to do. But, so far, that information has not been forthcoming. It's a complicated subject, no doubt about that, so women rely on the advice of those people who have been designated as "experts" in the field.

"The Other Epidemic"

One of the most important steps in overcoming a problem, any problem, is to know that there *is* a problem. In that regard, I think a brief overview of the present status of breast cancer and what the experts are offering up as an approach to dealing with the disease is in order. Since women are looking to the experts for answers and direction, it may come as a cold, hard shot of reality to learn that the experts themselves are in just as much of a quandary over breast cancer as you. They're stumped! They want to get a handle on the disease, of course, and they *are* trying, but they are virtually incapable of supplying you with the answers you so desperately need and want. Of course, the experts will never openly admit this because such an admission would cause widespread panic. But facts are facts and the truth of what I am saying is absolute and easily proven, as you shall shortly see.

As mentioned in Chapter 1, one of the most disturbing facts is that for the last 30 years *at least*, the problem of breast cancer has done nothing but get worse. Not only here in North America but throughout countries rich and poor, industrial and rural, the incidence of breast cancer is on the rise.[3] Breast cancer is the most common form of cancer in women.[4] Approximately 185,000 women are diagnosed with breast cancer in the United States every year. Of those, approximately 46,000 die.[5] Every 12 minutes, day and night, without stop, another woman dies. During the writing of this book, that fact started to prey relentlessly on my mind. When I went to a movie to relax, what I thought about was that while I was in the theatre watching a film for two hours, ten women died. Overall, cancer claims the life of another person *every minute*. It got to the point where I started measuring what I did, not by how long the activity took, but by how many people died of cancer while I was doing it. I guess you could say I became obsessed with finishing the project. I was so convinced that the book would save lives that I actually started to feel guilty whenever I was doing anything other than writing.

Since 1950, the incidence of breast cancer has increased 60 percent, making it one of the fastest-growing killer diseases in the nation.[6] Since 1960, the number of American women who died from breast cancer is more than twice the number of all Americans killed in World War I, World War II, the Korean War, the Vietnam War, and the Gulf War. Half of these women died in the ten years from 1983 to 1993,[7] which shows the death rate *increasing* as time goes by. In 1962, one in twenty women got breast cancer.[8] In 1982, the number was one in eleven.[9] In 1993, the number was one in eight,[10] and by the year 2000 it is projected that one in seven women will get cancer.[11]

On ABC's "Nightline," Cindy Pearson, program director for the National Women's Health Network, was asked, "Is there a breast cancer epidemic in this country?"[12] Her reply: "What else would you call a condition that has increased in incidence every year for the last 40 years with no explanation and no effective cure? I think there's nothing else to call it but an epidemic."

Documenting Cancer

You will notice that a lot of my supporting documentation comes from common, everyday sources. Not that I don't also use scientific journals. I do. But frankly, the vast majority do not read these journals because they are written in obscure, scientific jargon. I prefer to use the sources that you are most familiar with: television, radio, newspapers, and magazines. Also, when it comes to scientific studies that are published in scholarly journals, it is well known that any premise whatsoever can be "scientifically proven." Depending on who is funding the studies and what outcome is desired, even two opposite views can be proven.

A classic example of science *proving* both sides of an issue is found in the *New England Journal of Medicine*,[13] easily one of the most prestigious and well respected of all medical journals. In one issue, there are two articles on the subject of heart attacks in women. One article "proves" that giving female hormones to postmenopausal women can *substantially protect them against heart attacks*. The second article, equally well substantiated, "proves" that giving hormones to postmenopausal women can *substantially increase their chances of having a heart attack*. Now mind you, these two contradictory studies weren't in the same journal on different dates, two years apart. They were in the very same issue!

How often do you sit down and read scientific or scholarly journals? Probably never for most of the people reading this book. No, the average person will read newspapers or magazines several times a week and never even see a scientific journal. I consider it my role to point out what you may be missing in the articles you're reading or programs you're watching or listening to. You see, you may read an article on cancer and be lulled into thinking that more is being done or more progress is being made than is actually the case.

Frequently, I read an article in the newspaper that is filled with what *may* happen, or what *might* take place, or what is *perhaps* the case, or what outcome is *hoped* for, or what avenues of study *look* promising, or that researchers are encouraged by *prospects* that can and should be pursued further, or that the answer is *just around the corner*, and on and on and on. Buried deep underneath all the wished-for progress are perhaps one or two sentences that reveal the true state of affairs in terms of actual progress being made. The thing is, most people never notice these few sentences. They are not highlighted or embellished, and so get lost amidst the fluff. People just don't have the trained eye to seek out and find these buried jewels that give a more honest and accurate evaluation of the overall situation. When these sentences are scrutinized more closely, an unmistakable pattern emerges. I have been playing this hide-and-seek game for 25 years. Those few sentences of worth jump out at me now like neon lights that are flashing away in rapid fire.

The Experts Are Baffled

To illustrate just how baffled the experts are about cancer, I have extracted some of these statements and present them below. These are revealing statements made by people who are in the best possible position to know the real status of progress being made in the battle against breast cancer. (Although the following are examples of breast cancer, I could just as easily be using any other type of cancer to illustrate my point. As mentioned earlier, cancer, *all* cancer, is woefully misunderstood. Any one of the following quotations could easily be about prostate cancer, for example.)

There are two things we don't know about breast cancer. We don't know the cause and we don't know the cure.[14]

—Nancy Brinker,
Chairwoman,
President's Special Commission on Breast Cancer

Nobody knows what causes breast cancer, nobody knows how to prevent it, and nobody knows how to cure it.[15]

—Linda Ellerbee,
Narrating an ABC special on breast cancer

Despite decades of research, there are still gaping holes in our knowledge of breast cancer. No one knows for sure who is at risk, how to prevent it, or what causes it.[16]

—Host on a PBS special on breast cancer

We don't know what causes it . . . there's no way to prevent it.[17]

—Jane Pauley,
Narrating a PBS special on breast cancer

No one knows how to prevent it, and the mortality rate from breast cancer has not improved for decades. Researchers say it is also disconcerting that the rates have remained so high.[18]

—*The New York Times*

So many questions, one answer: We don't know. Breast cancer, never have so many been given so much conflicting advice and so few definitive solutions.[19]

—Cokie Roberts,
ABC "Nightline"

Throughout countries rich and poor, industrial and rural, breast cancer incidence is on the rise. No one knows what's fueling that increase.[20]

—*Science News*

This continual rise in breast cancer is unexplained. We have some hints at what's causing it, but we don't know the whole story and we also don't know how to stop it or how to cure it when it occurs.[21]

—Cindy Pearson,
Program Director,
National Women's Health Network

We really don't know what causes breast cancer. We don't really even have a clue what causes breast cancer.[22]

—Dr. Susan Love,
breast surgeon, author of *Dr. Susan Love's Breast Book*,
past Assistant Clinical Professor at Harvard Medical School,
Director of U.C.L.A.'s Breast Center

Women are very frightened by breast cancer and there is nothing they can do to prevent it.[23]

—Maryann Napoli,
Associate Director, Center For Medical Consumers in New York

If we knew how to prevent breast cancer, believe me we would have done it. We don't know how.[24]

—John Laszlo, M.D.,
Senior Vice-President for Research,
American Cancer Society

We don't know the natural history of this disease. We don't know whether treatment is necessary and we don't know if it works.[25]

—Dr. H. Gilbert Welsh,
Senior Research Associate,
Department of Veterans Affairs

It's horribly frustrating because I tend to like to look at prevention. If we knew what caused it, we could figure out how to prevent it, but we don't know yet.[26]

—Dr. Janet Osuch,
breast cancer specialist at Michigan State University

Scientists do not understand much about the causes of breast cancer. So while they can detect and treat breast cancer, they do not know how to prevent it.[27]

—Robert Bazell,
NBC News science correspondent

In the above quotations, did you grasp the most important message? Did you notice that every "expert" categorically states that "we don't know," or "no one knows"? Be assured, they would likely prefer not to admit this, but what choice did they have, when the evidence confirming the accuracy of these statements is so overwhelming? It is extremely important that you take the above comments seriously. That is the only way you will be moved to take the actions necessary to protect yourself. I know that many people will be stunned to learn that so little is actually known about breast cancer and that many of the reports of headway made in research have only been what the researchers think *may* be the case, or what they *hoped* would be the case. After all, you have to be told *something*. Imagine your reaction if you asked cancer experts a pertinent question on breast cancer and all they could do was turn their palms up, scrunch up their shoulders, and say, "Sorry, but I just don't know." So instead, they tell you what they think *may* be the answer. What you're getting is conjecture and speculation, nothing concrete. Over time people tend to see what *may* be as what *is*, and they are lulled into complacency.

Let's look at the three most important issues in question.

1) **They don't know the cause.** Without question, there *are* risk factors, but what are they? You're probably familiar with the ones that are mentioned most often: the hormone estrogen, early menstruation, late menopause, pregnancy late in life, never having a pregnancy, birth control pills, heredity and environment (which comprises a lot of factors including pesticides, other chemicals, and diet). Remember, these are guesses. None have been absolutely proven to cause cancer. They may all play a role or none may play a role. They may only be contributing factors . . . or not. On a nationally broadcast program on breast cancer, Jane Pauley states

that, "Most women who get breast cancer do not fit into any high-risk category. There's no way to predict who will get it."[28] Breast surgeon and author Dr. Susan Love states that, "Eighty percent of the women who are diagnosed with breast cancer have no risk factors whatsoever, except being a woman."[29] Based on that, one could say that the only absolute risk factor is being a woman.

It's interesting that most women seem to think that the biggest risk factor is having a family member who has had breast cancer. Equally interesting is the fact that only 5 percent of breast cancer cases can be linked to a family history of the disease.[30] That figure is more a coincidence or the law of averages than a major risk factor.

Also, a recent study found that when a woman moves to a new country, her risk of dying of breast cancer will rise or fall to match the death rate of women in the newly adopted country. This suggests that environmental factors, such as diet, have more impact than family history. The study contradicts current notions that most of a woman's risk of breast cancer is set by the time she reaches puberty or early adulthood. Dr. Noel S. Weiss, professor of epidemiology at the University of Washington School of Public Health in Seattle, says, "The importance of this study is that it reinforces our notion that your risk of breast cancer isn't something you're born with."[31]

2) **They don't know the cure.** Although the bulk of research dollars are spent on the search for a cure, there is no magic bullet for breast cancer, or any cancer, that, once administered, makes the disease disappear, or we would surely know about it. Yet we hear about the "cure rate" of breast cancer patients. If a woman is still alive five years after her cancer is first treated, she falls into the category of "the cured." To put it mildly, it is a great big, humongous stretch of the word. Surviving five years is hardly a cure. Especially when you consider that 20 years after diagnosis, 88 percent of those women who have died, died of breast cancer.[32] In other words, 88 out of 100 died of the disease they were "cured" of.

The five-year survival statistic is completely arbitrary. It is a "line drawn in the sand," its only meaning that the patient has managed to survive five years after diagnosis. It hardly means cure. Every time I hear the five-year survival mentioned, I'm reminded of a movie I once saw, in which tribal warriors capture their enemies and make them run a gauntlet of men who beat them with punches, kicks, and clubs. The prisoners are told if they can make it to the end of the gauntlet they can live. Some did make it, although they were crippled for life. But I guess it was better than being killed. Women who are diagnosed with breast cancer not only have to deal with the progression of the disease itself, but they also have to withstand the treatment, which, as we know, can be horrific. If they submit to surgery, radiation, and chemotherapy, referred to by Andrea Martin, executive director of the Breast Cancer Fund, as "the slash, burn and poison routine of cancer treatment," it *will* take its toll. At the end of the five years, a woman could be disfigured, bald, psychologically crushed, emotionally bankrupt, in constant pain, and on drugs to quell the pain and be declared "cured." I don't think so.

3) **They don't know how to prevent it.** Of the three, this is the issue that is most self-evident. If there were any means in place by which to prevent breast cancer, the problem would not be getting worse every passing year. The irony is that prevention, which without question is the most important aspect of breast cancer, is given scant, if any, attention whatsoever. Yes, scads of lip service is given to the subject of prevention, but that's it. The vast majority of money spent on breast cancer research, which is many billions of dollars annually, is spent on after-the-fact research, such as early detection and treatment.

The National Cancer Institute in Bethesda, Maryland, receives approximately $1.8 billion a year in federal money for research, and a paltry 5 percent is spent on prevention. And only 5 percent ($\frac{1}{4}$ of a percent of the total) of that already pitifully small amount is spent on breast cancer.[34] That's not just peanuts, that's barely pea-nut skins! Why is spending on breast cancer research so low? Why, when no one, and I mean no one, could possibly dispute the fact that prevention is the key to ending, or at least to diminishing, the pain and suffering of breast cancer, is so little attention actually paid to it? It is a troubling question, and the answer, at least in part, is not very pleasant to think about. I know it's going to sound cynical and cold-hearted, but a big part of the reason has to do with money. There's simply more money to be had in chasing cures and selling drugs than in teaching lifestyle changes to prevent disease. Ouch!

I know how much it must disturb you to hear that, but to deny that money is a factor is foolish. I'm not suggesting or even remotely hinting that there are people sitting around saying things like, "The heck with prevention, there's no money in it. Let's concentrate on what will make the most bucks." No way. But when we talk about the money generated by the health care industry in the United States, for example, we're talking about the biggest moneymaking machine there is.

Most people think that the United States spends more money on national defence than on anything else. The U.S. does spend a lot: $300 billion a year. But multiply that by three and you still don't equal what is spent on health care, which clocks in at a mind-boggling one *trillion* dollars a year. That's one thousand billion! This is going to sound heartless as hell, but who stands to lose the most money if cancer is prevented? The cancer establishment! Consider the words of Dr. Samuel Epstein, professor of occupational and environmental medicine at the School of Public Health, University of Chicago Medical Center: "The cancer establishment, the National Cancer Institute, the American Cancer Society, and the pharmaceutical companies associated with them are virtually indifferent or hostile to problems of cancer prevention."[35] Can you think of any legitimate reason why a pharmaceutical company, or anyone for that matter, should be "hostile" toward cancer prevention? I can't either.

Get Angry

So, having acknowledged, admitted, and accepted that the cause, cure, and prevention of breast cancer has eluded them, the experts find themselves in the position of having to offer up *something*. They can ill afford to look perplexed and give us the old "Gee, I don't now what to tell ya'." And what they have pinned all their hopes on, and yours, is what is referred to as "early detection." With nowhere else to turn, all energy is being directed toward early detection.

As part of President Bill Clinton's attempt to provide universal health care, the government asked experts to devise a strategy to deal with the growing incidence of and death from breast cancer. In an address at the opening session of a conference on breast cancer at the National Institutes of Health, in Washington, D.C., Donna E. Shalala, Health and Human Services Secretary, stated that, "The plan must address why the incidence of breast cancer is steadily rising, and what action we must take to detect breast cancer earlier."[36] Discussing breast cancer and women's options, Dr. Timothy Johnson, ABC News medical director, says that "the only thing they [women] can do right now is to try to detect it early through self-exam, physician exam and mammography."[37] (Note the word "only.") Dr. Susan Love was asked by a woman what she could do to lower her risk of breast cancer. Dr. Love's answer was: "The only hope we have right now in terms of dealing with breast cancer is in early detection and that means mammography."[38] The *only* hope. God forbid that should be true. And trust me, it isn't! In fact, not only is early detection not your only hope, it's barely any hope at all. Relying on early detection as your "only hope" is to give up and admit defeat. *Early detection means you have cancer!* Don't accept that.

You know, I read lots of material from many support groups that work with breast cancer patients and also try to bring awareness of the seriousness of breast cancer to both the public and agencies that allocate money for breast cancer research. A theme that seems to run through virtually all this material is a call to arms for women. They want women to speak up and speak out, to fight back, to get angry and *demand* something be done. Good idea! And if you want something to really get angry about, get angry about being told that your "only hope" in dealing with breast cancer is to sit around and wait until you get it, then hope you detect it before it kills you. Because that is precisely what you are being told to do. After all is said and done, after all the talk and posturing about what's been done and what's being done, after all the billions spent and research conducted, all the most highly advanced and technologically superior medical machine in the world can tell you is, in effect . . . nothing! Your last glimmer of hope, your last resort and refuge, lies in a test with the efficiency and accuracy of a coin toss: mammography.

Mammography: Your Only Hope?

All attention and focus as relates to the subject of breast cancer is directed toward mammography. Why? Because there's nothing else to offer. Creating a hubbub around mammography gives the appearance that something is being done about breast cancer. And so now there is what is described in the *New York Times* as "One of the most contentious disputes in medicine."[39] Another article in the *Times* describes the controversy surrounding mammography guidelines as a "wrenching" and "impassioned" debate among the experts.[40] And what is this debate that has captured the headlines? It focuses on this question: Should women under the age of 50 have regular mammograms?

According to a number of studies, if women over age 50 have mammograms every one to two years, their risk of dying of breast cancer is reduced by one-third.[41] But there are no such studies to prove that the same is true for women in their forties. This controversy has flared on and off since the seventies.[42] The United States stands virtually alone in recommending mammography for women in their forties.[43] "The eight-nation European Group for Breast Cancer opposes it on the basis that there is no demonstrated benefit."[44] The "experts" in the United States seem to be equally divided, with opponents saying there is no scientific evidence to support mammography for women in their forties. And since the tissue in a younger woman's breast is far denser than the tissue in the breasts of a woman in her fifties or older, the possibility of high rates of false positives, which can lead to unnecessary treatments, is greatly increased.

Dr. Suzanne W. Fletcher, co-editor of the *Annals of Internal Medicine,* and her husband, Dr. Robert H. Fletcher, write, "Medical scientists and physicians do not do modern women a service by promulgating a screening practice that medical science has not been able to substantiate after so many tries."[45] Proponents of the test for women in their forties acknowledge that there are no good scientific studies to prove the value of mammography for these women, but their argument is that there are no studies proving that they *don't* help either.

And so the dispute rages on. It's interesting that in all other matters of health care, medical experts, across the board, adamantly insist that good, hard data from scientifically sound studies be in place before tests are done. Why the exception here? If you think about it, traditional medicine has always played kind of fast and loose with women's health issues, and this appears to be another example of it. There's another factor to consider that no one *wants* to believe is influencing the decision to push for mammography for women under age 50, but it's pretty hard to ignore. Money!

In keeping with my earlier suggestion that the money incentive is something that should always be looked at when talking about a trillion-dollar industry, I came across an interesting comment from Dr. Howard Ozer, chief of medical oncology at the University of North Carolina School of Medicine. He was being interviewed about the debate over the screening guidelines for women in their forties, and amongst several points he was making, he said that "the mammography business has become highly lucrative and younger women are the best customers."[46] No need to embellish on that, he makes the point better than I.

You know what gets me about all this? It's a smokescreen that clouds the more important issues. Keeping the ongoing controversy of mammography for early detection in the public eye keeps women thinking about the issue, instead of the bigger, more important issue of prevention! Never allow the fact to drift from your mind that the use of mammography for early detection concerns itself with only one thing: finding a cancerous tumour in your breast. Let's not lose sight of your goal here, which isn't to locate a tumour in your breast, but to avoid ever developing one.

Actually, it would be one thing if mammography performed the service it is intended to, dependably and precisely, but there is an unsettling irony in all of this. On the one hand you are being told, in the clearest possible language, that there is no way to prevent or cure breast cancer, so all of your faith and trust should be focused on mammography for early detection, which is being held up as your final bastion of hope. On the other hand, mammography's track record of reliability isn't exactly something that will fill you with confidence. Mammography fails to detect as much as 20 percent of all breast cancers and as much as 40 percent in women under the age of 50,[47] and that is in the best of circumstances when all procedures involved in the test are performed with high efficiency.

Examples of how treatment was either withheld when it should have been given, or given when it should have been withheld could fill this book. Here are a few:

- The television show "Primetime Live" tells the story of a woman who was experiencing soreness in her breast, so she had a mammogram and was told, "Everything is normal." But within eight months, the cancer that was missed grew and spread. The woman's breast had to be removed.[48]
- Another television show—"Good Morning America"—tells the tragic story of a woman who was informed that she had cancer; this diagnosis was based on a laboratory examination of tissue from her breast by a pathologist who had 30 years' experience. The woman had both breasts removed only to find out later that she didn't have cancer.[49]
- In April 1994, a Florida woman whose left breast was removed after a misdiagnosis of cancer was awarded $2.7 million. The jury ruled that *all four* of the doctors who were involved in her diagnosis were negligent. Astonishingly, the mistake was discovered two weeks before her mastectomy, but no one spoke up.[50]

The problem with placing so much reliance on mammography for early detection lies in the fact that there are several variables that come into play at once and influence the ultimate diagnosis. If *any one* of these variables are inaccurate or performed incorrectly, the probability of a misdiagnosis goes way up. There are three factors that are of extreme importance: the machine taking the X-ray picture or mammogram, the technician operating the machine, and the interpretation of the film.

In 1992, ABC's "Primetime Live" conducted a four-month investigation that canvassed the country interviewing surgeons, radiologists, cancer patients, and cancer experts. What they discovered is that "there is a crisis in the quality of mammography in this country [the U.S.]."[51] Unlike Western Europe, where there are federal regulations, the mammography business in the United States has proliferated with virtually no rules. Until very recently, there were no national quality standards. Many of the machines simply do not take good pictures and they are being used every day. In Michigan, it was discovered that 35 to 50 percent of the facilities doing mammographies were doing unacceptable work. Michigan cracked down on these faulty facilities and now has the toughest laws in the country. *But only nine states have tough laws governing mammography.* That means 41 states do not!

The operators (technologists) of mammogram machines should have what can amount to two years of study in X-ray technology; this according to Dr. Ed Hendrick, professor at the University of Colorado and top physicist at the American College of Radiology. A crucial and complicated part of the mammography procedure is the careful placement of the breast. Since each patient is different, a technologist has to know how to compress the breast, not to mention test the machine and check the processing of the film. In one instance, "Primetime's" hidden cameras showed a nurse with only two days' training in mammography doubling as a technologist. In another office, the receptionist did mammographies and she, too, had only two days' training. In 21 states, technologists don't even have to be licensed. Diane Sawyer, the co-anchor of "Primetime," said, "In a lot of states there's more supervision of pizza parlors than mammographies." And this, so you are told, is your "only hope" in dealing with breast cancer.

Here is a rather astonishing piece of information that too few women are aware of and that seriously weakens the premise that early detection is the key in avoiding becoming a breast cancer statistic. Cancer cells grow at a very slow pace. It takes one year for a single cancer cell to become twelve cells. At that rate of growth, it will take six years for the cancer to be the size of a pencil point,[52] and about ten years to even be detectable in a mammogram.[53] At that point, it is one centimetre, about the size of a pea. I want to be sure you see the full import of what I am saying: *You can religiously get a mammogram every year and not have a cancer show up that has been growing in your breast for ten years.*

And then there is the all-important issue of interpretation. A new study has raised serious questions about radiologists' reliability in reading mammograms and making recommendations about what to do when a suspicious lesion is found in the breast. The study, by researchers at Yale University School of Medicine and published in *The New England Journal of Medicine*, found that interpretations and advice given based on those interpretations vary greatly. Where one radiologist might recommend an immediate biopsy, another, looking at the same mammogram might suggest a repeat X-ray in three months, and still another might suggest waiting a year to do another mammogram.[54]

In November 1992, a landmark Canadian study on mammography—the largest study ever conducted in the world—involving 90,000 women, showed "no benefit for women under forty-nine" and it "fails to reduce breast cancer deaths among women between fifty and fifty-nine."[55] Consider the words of physician and best-selling author Dr. John McDougall: "Because most of the years of cancer growth are hidden at microscopic levels, efforts toward early detection are unlikely to ever yield much success in saving lives."[56] And, "To be quite realistic, in most cases the only real beneficiaries from early detection are the health professionals. Early detection gets the patient going to the doctor earlier and, thereby, a longer total time period is available for more expensive doctor visits, hospitalizations and tests. And the patient lives no longer or better from all this well meaning effort."[57]

As more ingenious techniques are developed to detect smaller and smaller cancers, some investigators are voicing their concerns. They point out that studies show that many, if not most, early cancers do not grow large and dangerous and would never be noticed unless doctors with an early detection method went looking for them. Tiny cancers are so common that autopsy studies of middle-aged and older people have found that almost everyone's body contains them. No one can tell which early cancers are dangerous and which ones are not, and no one understands enough about the natural history of cancer to know what it means to find a tumour so small. This led Dr. Barry Kramer, associate director of the Early Detection and Community Oncology Program at the National Cancer Institute, to state, "We have to meticulously avoid the tendency to assume that early diagnosis in and of itself will make a difference."[58] After all the hoopla centred around early detection, this specialist is saying that *early detection makes no difference!*

Do you know what I think of every time I hear about people depending on early detection to save them from dying of cancer? I imagine two people out in mountain wilderness, one of them slips off the edge of a cliff and is stranded on a small ledge jutting over a 2,000-foot drop. The person above throws down a frayed old rope that looks as if it was left over from the Spanish-American War. The person on the ledge yells up that the rope doesn't look as though it will hold any weight and the person throwing the rope down says, "It's all we have, just grab hold and hope for the best." That's what you're being asked to do with mammography and early detection. Fortunately, for the purposes of this book at least, mammography is irrelevant. We're not looking to detect, we're looking to prevent. And mammographies have absolutely nothing to do with prevention. *Nothing!*

Once again, the words of Dr. Susan Love: "What we really need is some kind of prevention of breast cancer, not finding it. We need to prevent it from happening."[59] By using the information in this book, you're taking a giant step toward preventing ever developing cancerous lumps in your breasts. Mammography will go from being a life-raft thrown to a drowning person to a monitoring device to validate your success.

I do not wish to imply that this book is going to wipe out cancer. There are no such guarantees from anyone. There are some people who no matter what they do, and no matter how conscientious they are, *will* get cancer and die from it. That's a cold, hard fact of life. What I am saying is that a lot of people, *a lot*, will be able to avoid that fate by following the recommendations in this book. Moreover, so there are no misunderstandings that may lead to my being accused of suggesting that women stop getting regular mammograms, I want to state clearly and categorically that I am not saying that. I am saying that I want mammography to become something else in your consciousness. I want you to see it, not as a tool to detect an existing cancer, but as a means by which you prove to yourself that you are successfully preventing cancer from getting a foothold.

I could easily understand if you are upset by what you have read in this chapter. After all, it can be disconcerting to find out that the experts you are relying on for direction are as baffled about breast cancer as you are, to put it mildly. But I want you to be very clear about something: I did not share that revelation with you in order to alarm you, but to alert you to the fact that complacent reliance on the experts is not going to serve you well at this time.

I live in South Florida where the danger of a hurricane coming through and wiping me out is a very real possibility. When I'm warned of a hurricane approaching, it is not done to scare me, it's done to give me the opportunity to take the measures necessary to save my life. It's true, I may have given you information that is upsetting, but more important, I am also going to give you the information that you need to save your life.

Dr. I. Craig Henderson is a breast cancer researcher who is chief of medical oncology at the University of California in San Francisco. In an interview with the *New York Times*, he stated that, "Science often made its leaps from unexpected directions, which means that the next great advance in breast cancer may not come from breast cancer research. It is important for us to follow the clues wherever they are and to realize that the answer may not be in breast cancer directed funds."[60]

Thank you, Dr. Henderson, those are my sentiments exactly. And this book is my contribution to proving you right.

The Word No One Wants to Hear

Cancer. The mere mention of the word is unnerving, and understandably so. The only thing associated with cancer is pain, suffering, and death. Former first lady Betty Ford, a breast cancer victor, says, "To hear the word cancer is almost like hearing the word death."[61]

Upon being diagnosed with cancer, one person said it this way: "In the moment of diagnosis, in that one sentence when the doctor says, 'You have cancer,' it's as though everything that matters—every dream, every prayer, every vision, every hope—suddenly has been stomped on and stamped out."[62]

We're all aware of the existence of cancer and all hope and pray that we never have to deal with it. As I said earlier, it's the disease that people fear the most. But very few people know what cancer is. Do you? I mean *really* know. You ask your friends if they know what cancer is and they'll all say something like, "Of course I know what it is, who doesn't?" But when it comes right down to it, people don't know. They know the *results* of cancer and its treatment, but unless they work in the health field in some capacity, they do not know what it actually is. And guess what? *Those* people, the researchers, the scientists, the ones who are supposed to know, don't know either. That's right. Oh, there are suppositions, presumptions, inferences, theories, and hypotheses galore, but when you get right down to it, as mentioned in Chapter 2, the "experts" are still trying to fully understand cancer.

The War on Cancer

In 1971, then-President Richard Nixon inaugurated the "War on Cancer" with the National Cancer Act, passed by Congress on December 23, 1971, as a Christmas present to the nation. The National Cancer Institute's budget was more than doubled for 1972,[63] and it was confidently proclaimed that we would have a cure by America's two-hundredth birthday celebration in 1976. The first major assessment of the "war" came 14 years later. In 1971, one in four developed cancer. Fourteen years later, this statistic increased to one in three.[64] In 1971, two in three families were affected. Fourteen years later, it was three in four.[65] In 1971, the mortality rate, which is truly the most important number of all, was one in six. Fourteen years later, it went to one in five—a 22 percent increase.[66]

Dr. John Bailor, a biostatistician at Harvard, was editor of the *Journal of the National Cancer Institute* and had worked at the Institute for twenty-five years. In 1986, in the *New England Journal of Medicine*, he co-authored a study of the results of the fight against cancer during the years from 1950 to 1985.[67] According to the researchers, the data they reviewed

> [P]rovided no evidence that some thirty-five years of intense and growing efforts to improve the treatment of cancer had much overall effect on the most fundamental measure of clinical outcome—death. Indeed, with respect to cancer as a whole, we have slowly lost ground. Incidence of cancer is also increasing, suggesting a failure to prevent or control new or current causes of cancer.

The researchers summed up their report with, "the main conclusion we draw is that some thirty-five years of intense efforts focused largely on improving treatment must be judged a qualified failure." It doesn't get any clearer than that. In 1997, another article by Dr. Bailor in the *New England Journal of Medicine* called again for more in the line of prevention. In this article, he gave yet another dismal report on the cancer situation in the United States.

Today, more than 20 years later, with over $35 billion spent on research (that's only federal money, much more than that was spent in private money), one trillion dollars spent on treatment, over seven million deaths, and no closer to a "cure" now than we were then, it is blatantly obvious that the best and smartest minds medical science has to offer have been confounded and bewildered by cancer. When Carl Rochelle, CNN correspondent, asked if we are losing the battle against cancer, Dr. Samuel Epstein, at the University of Chicago Medical Center, answered with sobering directness when he said, "Oh, I think we've really lost the fight against cancer. There have been major increases in cancer rates over the last four decades."[68]

Since Richard Nixon declared the war on cancer in 1971, until the end of 1994 more than $23 billion has been spent on cancer research in the United States, and the overall mortality rate is 8 percent higher. This has led cancer experts to tell Congress that the war against cancer has stalled and that without major changes, it will become the nation's *top killer* in five years.[69]

What Cancer Really Is

The seriousness of these grim facts make it all the more essential that we focus on prevention. And since prevention is precisely what this book is about, there is no need for me to go into a long, technical, hard-to-understand explanation of what cancer is. I will briefly describe the nature of cancer, but only to the extent that it will help you understand how and why the principles outlined in this book will help you achieve vibrant health. I promise you, it will be the simplest, most nontechnical, succinct, and easy-to-understand description you have ever read.

Many people might think that demystifying and simplifying cancer is a daunting task. The subject has been buried beneath such an avalanche of jargon that most people perceive it as too complicated, bewildering, and obscure, and they give up on trying to understand it. They decide that the subject is a deep, dark mystery best left to the professionals who can wade through the quagmire and make some sense of it all. Wrong. That kind of thinking may be convenient for the professionals, but it keeps you out of the decision-making process that could affect your very life. It's simply too darned important to be left up to the cancer establishment and the "experts" who, as we have learned, "don't know" and are more baffled by cancer than anything else.

When it comes to health care, your body, and medicine, there are two ways you can be given information. One is in an incomprehensible, convoluted way; the other is with straightforward, unencumbered talk. Unfortunately, the former is the standard approach. Allow me to illustrate. I could tell you that I have antecubital and retropopliteal urticaria with pruritus, or I could simply say my arms and legs itch. I could tell you I'm experiencing orthostatic hypotension, or I could tell you I'm dizzy. See the difference? Guess which approach the professionals have used to tell you about cancer? No wonder you think it's a perplexing subject that you could never understand.

There are people out there who will not accept my contention that cancer, a subject which has been misunderstood and overly complicated, is actually quite a bit more uncomplicated and understandable than we've been led to believe. It all depends on which point of view you choose to consider. The medical explanation, which is likely the only one you have ever been exposed to, is quite different from that of Natural Hygiene, the field of health care I chose to study. Unless you read about it in *Fit For Life,* chances are you've never heard of Natural Hygiene. No matter— you get to learn about it now.

Your body is made up of cells. Lots of them. One hundred trillion of them. (That's a one with fourteen zeros!) Absolutely every part of you is made up of cells, joined together to form skin, bones, muscles, organs, teeth, hair, fingernails, vocal cords, eyeballs—*everything*. All of these cells, right down to the very last one, are under the jurisdiction and direction of the brain. In my opinion, the most astounding fact in all of the universe is that every last one of these hundred trillion cells is constantly sending messages to the brain asking for instructions, as it were, and remarkably, the brain receives and answers each and every message. The trillions of messages are sent up and back 24 hours a day, ceaselessly, and the myriad functions of the body are performed with pinpoint perfection, all *simultaneously!*

Each cell is like a soldier in the army awaiting orders. Every activity, no matter how minuscule, is performed under the direction and supervision of the brain. The process is orderly and predictable. No cell ever does *anything* unilaterally. And, as is the case with most things in life, there are exceptions. The exception here is . . . cancer. A cancer cell is a normal cell so deranged by toxic substances that it loses contact with and is no longer controlled by the brain. It has literally been driven "crazy" by poisoning, and it is "out there on its own." Whereas normal cells divide and stop dividing after a certain fixed time, cancer cells do not. Instead, they proliferate in a disorderly fashion. Two normal cells placed on a slide will stop growing as soon as they touch each other. Cancer cells, in the same conditions, keep on growing; wildly, and out of control. In most cases of cancer, unrestrained cell growth leads to the build-up of tumours which will invade and destroy normal cells.

Obviously, what all the world wants to know is what drives the normal cells crazy. Figure that out and you've figured out cancer. According to the concepts of Natural Hygiene, toxins, or poisons that normal cells are relentlessly forced to come into contact with for years on end, finally drive the normal cells crazy. Our bodies produce toxins from within as a result of metabolism and we take in toxins from the food and drink we consume. Cancer is the end result in a long, pathological evolution that had its beginning long before any chemical signs of cancer showed up. In other words, what is crucially important for you to realize is that *cancer does not attack, it evolves.*

Why Cancer Happens

In all life matters, whether discussing cancer or anything else, we have to operate under the laws of cause and effect. Actions produce reactions. *Cancer will never just happen.* It will inevitably be the result of causes that were not removed over a very long period of time. Traditional therapies of surgery, radiation, and chemotherapy attack the problem at the end stages of its growth, *after the fact.* It is attacking the effect while ignoring the cause. If a person has a tumour or an organ removed and goes right back to the same lifestyle that brought on the problem in the first place without addressing the cause, health will not be restored and this individual's cancerous condition will then "come back." You will hear, "You've relapsed," or "It's returned," or "We must not have gotten it all." It didn't "come back," it never left! Removing a prostate gland, some other organ, or cutting off a breast and removing a bunch of lymph nodes without removing the *cause* of cancer and thinking that the cancer will not return is like thinking that by picking all the apples off a tree, no more apples will grow.

When the toxic conditions that resulted in abnormal cell growth are removed, then and only then will health begin to be restored. This is provided, of course, that the condition has not advanced so far that irreparable harm has been done. Irreparable harm means that negative conditions existed without let-up for so long that the diseased state finally resulted in cancer. If that cancer metastasizes, which means it breaks loose from the original site and spreads to other areas of the body, then, obviously, preventive measures are futile and another course of action must be undertaken. This, of course, is the downside in all of this. There is an upside as well.

Remember my revealing to you earlier that before cancer could even be detected, the disease had to be progressing for some ten years first? You're not well one day and sick the next. You don't go to sleep in health and wake up with cancer. Disease has seven distinct stages (see Chapter 4). They take a very long time to develop, and if the cause of the problem is corrected during any of the first six stages, health will be restored and cancer, the seventh stage, will not develop. In other words, you have years to turn things around and do what is necessary to prevent cancer from ever developing. Plus, your body is always ready to do its part.

The Self-Healing Body

Natural Hygiene teaches us that the body is always, *always* striving for the very highest level of health possible. The human body is self-repairing, self-healing, and self-maintaining, and as a matter of course, persistently martials its forces in a tireless quest to achieve and maintain health. Health is the normal, natural state of your body. Ill health is abnormal and unnatural. When you are healthy, your body automatically directs its efforts toward maintaining that state. When you're in a state of ill health, the body diligently strives to restore health. Every one of the trillions of functions your body performs every day and night without let-up are performed as part of its never-ending effort to procure and preserve health.

The same way a ball full of air will shoot up to the surface if submerged in water and then let go, your body strives for optimum health under any and all circumstances. Once the ball is released when underwater, it can do one thing and one thing only—get up to the surface in as direct a route and as quickly as possible. There's no hesitation, it doesn't move side to side, stay down or stay put, it makes a beeline for the surface. It can do nothing else. Your body, in its quest for health, is the same. It is always trying to achieve health in the quickest, most efficient way. The ball in the analogy can only be kept from rising quickly to the top if it is held down. The only way your body can be prevented from achieving its goal of vibrant health is if it is forced to handle more than it can contend with and its defences are overwhelmed. Even then, it does not give up trying. As long as the body is alive, it is striving for health.

Fortunately for us all, the body has a built-in mechanism that warns us when its health is in jeopardy. The more critical the problem, the more intense the warnings. Unfortunately, most people do not realize that their bodies are trying to get their attention to alert them of impending danger. Because the warnings are not recognized as such, they are either ignored or masked with drugs. What starts out as a situation that could have been corrected before becoming life-threatening is allowed to progress and deteriorate, all too frequently culminating in cancer.

During the first six stages of disease the body initiates these warnings, and it is crucial that you don't miss them by failing to realize what they are and what they mean. If you are able to recognize the warnings for what they are, you can take the appropriate measures to protect yourself and prevent the end result of continued neglect—cancer.

The next chapter describes the seven stages of disease and the warning signs they produce. Read it carefully. More than once if need be. Familiarizing yourself with the information it contains has the potential, not only to save you untold heartache, anguish, pain, and suffering, but also to save your life. It is one of the prime factors in understanding how to achieve vibrant health.

The Seven Stages of Disease

Vibrant Health	1	2	3	4	5	6	Cancer

You are looking at the "two-ended stick" described to you earlier in the opening message of this book. We all wish to be on the vibrant health end of it, obviously. It is the goal and purpose of this book to help you learn how to achieve this.

Have you ever heard someone commenting on the severe illness or death of some person by saying, "I can't believe it, he was so healthy." Or, "I just saw her the other day, she looked so great, so healthy."

Be very clear about something: Disease, especially cancer, never, ever just sneaks up on people and strikes them down. It doesn't happen that way. It takes a long time and a great deal of neglect and abuse of the body for cancer to finally occur. From the first stage of disease to the seventh (i.e., cancer), many years may elapse. At any step, you can stop the disease's progress, and simultaneously end all the aches, pains, and ill health which were the body's warning signs that changes need to be made or the situation will deteriorate further. By familiarizing yourself with the seven stages of disease and their warning signals, you put yourself in control of your health. *You* are in charge, not outside influences.

One   Enervation

The first stage of disease is enervation. The word "enervation" comes from the word "energy." Energy is the essence of all life. Your very existence depends upon how much energy is available at any given time to carry out all of the functions of your body. Enervation is a condition in which the body is either not generating sufficient energy for the tasks it must perform, or the tasks the body must perform are greater than the normal energy supply can cope with. When this occurs, the body becomes impaired and generates even less energy. In fact, all of the body's functions become impaired, and this includes the processes of elimination of the toxic by-products of both metabolism and the residue of foods taken into the body. A certain amount of toxins in the body is totally natural. Problems arise when there are more being produced than are being eliminated. This situation results not only in the further inability of the body to restore depleted energy, it also allows the body to become overladen with toxic material. (This subject is discussed in more detail in the next chapter.) Since energy is restored when you sleep, the first warning sign that you are becoming enervated is that you will become tired and sluggish or require naps during the day and/or more sleep at night. Enervation leads directly to the second stage of disease.

Two   Toxemia

Toxemia (also referred to as toxicosis or autointoxication) occurs when the uneliminated toxic material described above starts to saturate the blood, lymph, and tissues of the body. The body recognizes that this situation must be remedied and, in an attempt to cleanse itself and maintain its health, it initiates a flushing out of the toxins. Expect two results when this happens: first, more recognizable warnings in the form of discomfort; and second, the process places an even greater burden on the body's energy supply. If a person is also overworked, under stress, or getting insufficient rest and sleep—all energy sappers—the feelings of tiredness and sluggishness become more pronounced. At the level of toxemia when the toxins must be forced out, the next stage of disease develops.

Three   Irritation

Whereas with enervation the only recognizable warning sign is a feeling of tiredness or fatigue, toxemia and the resulting irritation create more recognizable warning symptoms. This stage of disease is designed to make you aware of the rising level of toxemia in your body in the hopes that you pay attention to the warnings and take the appropriate corrective steps.

Irritation is a condition in which the body sets its defensive mechanisms in motion and speeds up its internal activities in order to unload stored-up toxins. This process can happen at various points in the body. Although irritation is not so painful that it would lead you to visit a doctor for treatment, it is sufficiently unpleasant to make you look for a way to rid yourself of the discomfort. Irritation is the body's way of prodding you into action.

An obvious example of irritation is the urge to urinate or have a bowel movement. This urge is not painful, unless of course it is ignored for a long time, and then it becomes so painful you can think of nothing else but relieving yourself. The bowels and bladder are clearly a most obvious means by which waste and toxins are removed from the body. Less obvious is when toxins are removed at other sites in the body.

Many warning symptoms produced by irritation will be familiar to you. For example, a common warning of irritation due to toxemia is itchiness. The skin is not only the body's largest organ, it is also an organ of elimination. The body freely and regularly uses the skin's four billion pores to remove toxins from the body, from the top of your head to the bottom of your feet and everything in between. If any part of your skin becomes itchy, that is a classic sign that toxins are being removed; when they reach the surface of the skin, that area becomes irritated. At this stage the condition is not serious or even particularly painful, but it is bothersome, which is the body's way of getting your attention. Only if it is ignored and nothing is done to remove the cause of the problem, does the itchiness progress to something far more troublesome. This will be discussed in stage four (inflammation).

Not everyone experiences itchy skin in a state of irritation. Others feel queasy or nauseated for no apparent reason and at different times of day, but particularly in the morning when the body is in its elimination cycle. Another form of irritation is a persistent tickling sensation in the nose. Yet another is to feel jumpy or uneasy or on edge, so that you "fly off the handle" for no apparent reason. If you find yourself uncharacteristically short-tempered or easily aggravated, those are all signs of irritation. Certainly you've heard people say things like, "She's so irritable all the time," or "Don't irritate him, he's in a bad mood." People feel irritated because their bodies are in a state of irritation. It's that simple.

Other warning signs of irritation include nervousness, depression, anxiety, and worry, especially when those conditions are out of character for you. You may start to experience more frequent headaches or have minor aches and pains in other areas of your body. Difficulty falling asleep or sleeping fitfully are other indications of irritation. So is putting on weight. Other classic indicators are coated tongue, bad breath, increased body odour, and sallow complexion, especially dark circles under the eyes. Women may experience out-of-the ordinary menstrual problems or heavier menstrual flow.

You may be thinking, "Good grief, is anything not a warning signal?" That's pretty accurate. When the body is toxemic it will try anything to get your attention. Unfortunately, some people live years in a state of irritation without ever knowing what's beating them up. The discomfort they experience isn't serious enough to go for treatment so they just "live with it." But when the effects of enervation, toxemia, and irritation are ignored long enough and the toxic residue that started the whole process in motion builds to an even higher concentration, the fourth stage of disease ultimately, and inevitably, results.

Four   Inflammation

Inflammation is the body's most intense effort to cleanse and restore itself. When this process occurs, you become keenly aware that a problem exists, for it involves pain. Pain is not something that occurs haphazardly or without cause. It is not punishment for some indiscretion. *Pain has purpose.*

I told you that this book was going to introduce you to a new way of viewing health and disease. Well, understanding the true nature of pain and the role it plays is a crucial part of that new way of thinking. Pain is your friend. How's that for a new concept? It may not feel comfortable. That's the whole idea. It may not be the friend you would like to have show up on your doorstep, but it is a friend nonetheless. Learning to view pain in a different way will serve you well for the rest of your life. I'm not trying to convince you to like pain; hey, I don't like it any more than you. But I do understand it. And only when you understand it are you going to be able to avoid it.

If you were to accidentally rest your hand on a hot stove, how would you know if it weren't for the pain? If you stepped on a shard of broken glass with your bare foot, how would you know if not for the pain? Pain protects us. It not only warns us that we need to put our hand on something other than a hot stove, it also warns us when our health, our very lives, are at risk. Pain is the body's most effective warning signal. It is specifically designed to alert you to the fact that without corrective measures you are endangering yourself. But because we have not been educated to know this, we fail to recognize that pain is a friendly messenger. When pain is chronic and unrelenting, it is a sign that the body is more desperately attempting to get rid of an ever-increasing level of toxemia before it causes devastating damage. Pain is the means by which the intelligence of the body brings the situation to your attention. Does pain get your attention?

Precious few people realize that pain is a cleansing, healing mode of the body as it tries to fix itself. Instead it is looked upon as an "attack" against your well-being, so it's off to the doctor in search of relief. And sure enough, the doctor will find signs of pathology, which, more often than not, will be treated with drugs. Of course there will be pathology; after all, *that's what the pain is trying to alert us to.* The drugs do nothing to *remove* the cause of the problem. They serve only to lessen the pain of the problem. Unfortunately, they are also adding to the body's level of toxemia, while giving the false impression that the problem is being handled. Pain, discomfort, and ill health are the first, faint warning signs of what will ultimately develop into cancer if it is not immediately addressed.

With inflammation the toxins in the system have usually been concentrated in a particular organ or a particular area of the body (the breasts or prostate perhaps) for a massive eliminative effort. The area becomes inflamed due to the constant irritation from toxic material. When inflammation exists, we are diagnosed with one or more of the "itises." "Itis" at the end of a word literally means "inflammation of." So tonsillitis means inflammation of the tonsils. Appendicitis—inflammation of the appendix. Hepatitis— inflammation of the liver. Nephritis—inflammation of the kidneys. Arthritis—inflammation of the joints. Colitis—inflammation of the colon. A cold with inflammation of the sinus cavities is rhinitis with sinusitis. The list of "itises" goes on interminably. When a lymph node becomes inflamed, it enlarges and becomes tender. This condition is called "lymphadenitis."[70] A swollen lymph node or gland is one of the body's most obvious warnings that a cleansing of built-up toxins is long overdue. (The lymph system is discussed more fully in Chapter 6.)

When irritation of the skin (see stage 3) is allowed to progress, it results in dermatitis—inflammation of the skin. Eczema, psoriasis, and a certain type of lupus that affects the skin are particularly severe types of dermatitis and are most obvious and recognizable examples of the body using its reparative powers to forcibly push toxins right out through the skin. At this juncture corrective measures that lower toxic levels in the body will invariably clear up these conditions. I have seen this happen firsthand on numerous occasions.

Sadly, however, people often do not take action at this point. Rather, they suppress the painful symptoms with drugs. The pain may temporarily go away, but the problem doesn't. When the cleansing efforts of the body are suppressed with drugs, the level of toxicity increases until other organs become affected as well, not only with the toxins already in the body but also, as mentioned above, with the added toxicity of the drugs that are administered.

The most obvious examples of the body in an advanced state of inflammation are fibromyalgia and lupus. Anyone who has ever suffered from either of these two inflammatory maladies will tell you in no uncertain terms that they're no fun. Generally speaking, fibromyalgia mostly affects the muscles of the body, while lupus mostly affects the deep connective tissue in the body. One study points out that 55 percent of fibromyalgia patients also suffer from lupus. In both instances, sufferers will tell you that they "hurt and ache all over." Everything hurts—a lot. Although medical science doesn't know the reason for this unrelenting, debilitating pain, I can tell you with the utmost confidence that both fibromyalgia and lupus are classic examples of the body in an advanced state of toxemia and inflammation. By the time you have finished reading this book, and have absorbed the information in Chapter 6 and understand the principles that teach you how to clean the lymph system, neither fibromyalgia or lupus will ever be a problem in your life.

Stage four is a most pivotal juncture in that actions taken at this point determine whether or not you are going to recover your health and return to a state of vibrancy, or fall deeper into the diseased state. You are right in the middle of the seven stages and your actions now are crucial. If the body's general toxification is unceasing, it will result in the next stage of disease.

Five   Ulceration

The fifth stage means that the body has been under assault for such a long time that massive amounts of cells and tissue are being destroyed. This condition is often intensely painful because there are exposed nerves. Lesions or ulcers can occur inside or outside the body. An example of an ulcer on the inside is the classic stomach ulcer—a hole in the stomach is literally opened up. Those who have experienced this type of ulcer know all too well how much pain is associated with it. An example of an ulcer on the outside of the body is a canker sore on the mouth, or an open, oozing sore on the arm or leg. While the body may use an ulcer as an outlet to rid itself of toxins, it will heal the ulcer if the level of toxemia is sufficiently lowered. Following on the heels of ulceration is the process the body goes through to seal these wounds.

Six   Induration

Scarring is a form of induration, which is a hardening of tissue or the filling in of tissue where it has been lost, such as with an ulcer. But this hardening has real direction and purpose. The toxic material that is threatening the well-being of the body is encapsulated in a sack of hardened tissue. This is the body's way of quarantining the toxic material, holding it in one place so it will not spread freely throughout the body. The sack is what is referred to as a tumour and is very often diagnosed as cancer when, in fact, no cancer exists.

Induration is the last stage during which the body is still in control of its cells. If the destructive practices that brought matters to this stage are allowed to continue, cells will start to "go crazy." They will become parasitic, living off whatever nutrients they can obtain, but contributing nothing to the body in return. The constant poisoning has finally altered their genetic encoding and they become wild and disorganized. When cells go wild in this manner, the condition is called cancer.

Seven   Cancer

This is the end point in the long evolution of disease, and if the causes that brought it about are continued it is usually fatal. At this stage, body vitality is at a very low level, cells are no longer under the control of the brain, but are multiplying wildly in an unorganized manner. Although in the best of circumstances, with a most healthy regimen, cancer can be arrested and reversed, it would take a diligent, concentrated effort. The entire purpose of this book is to show you how to prevent this stage from ever occurring.

Contrary to what a staggering number of people think, especially those who have been diagnosed with cancer, your very best friend, your greatest ally in your quest for vibrant health and the prevention of cancer, is your body. *Never, ever doubt that.* I cannot tell you how many times I have heard people describe a part of their body as their enemy. As though it were somehow separate and apart from their bodies and acting on its own. Consider the following statement made by a woman interviewed on a television program on breast cancer aired on PBS: "I had a feeling of wanting very much to get rid of my breasts—they had become my enemies. I wanted rid of them, they were something that was going to kill me."[71] Nothing in all of the universe could be further from the truth. Nothing!

People may view the human body as a lot of different parts that are separate from one another, but the body does not see it that way. Every part of the body is as sacred and important and cherished and protected as any other. One organ is just as important and receives just as much healing attention as any other part of the body, be it the breasts, prostate, heart, lungs, teeth, skin, eyes, or intestines. No part receives more or less attention than any other. It's just like when the sun shines, it shines on everything equally. There are no favourites. If something is amiss somewhere in the body, energy is sent to that area in an attempt to correct the problem. And as part of the wisdom inherent in every cell, the body sends messages to us to alert us of any impending problem.

Throughout the first six stages of disease, the body uses pain to give us incessant warnings. If the warnings are understood and corrective measures are taken, the warnings stop and the pain goes away. If the warnings are not understood and the individual persists in the same habits, the warnings become progressively more acute. The pain continues or becomes more intense. This built-in mechanism is as automatic as the eyes blinking when necessary or blood flowing through the veins. This warning system is yet one more beautiful example of the magnificence of the human body. But all the body can do is warn us to make a change; it can't make the changes for us.

Have you ever been driving down the road and all of a sudden you notice a red light flashing on your dashboard indicating a problem of some sort? What do you do when you see that red light? Do you ignore it in the hope that it will just go away? Do you cover it with tape so you don't have to see it? Or do you take the car into the repair shop as soon as possible to see what the problem is? Car manufacturers have figured out how to put a warning system into automobiles to prevent the destruction of the vehicle. In your wildest imaginings do you think that God forgot to do the same for us? No! God didn't! No way that God, infinitely wise and intelligent, would forget to give our bodies such a crucially important component as a warning system to protect us from harm.

Keep in mind that health is natural and illness is not. The body always strives to maintain a healthy state. If its health is threatened and warnings appear, it means that the body has not been provided with the best circumstances for maintaining its health and is trying to deal with an overload of toxins. At this point, if corrective action and a healthy lifestyle is adopted, illness will progress no further, the warnings will cease (pain will go away), and health will again return. On the other hand, if the warning signals are suppressed or ignored, the toxic overload will not be removed. More serious illness will ensue with the final end point being cancer.

Make it a priority to become sensitive to the warnings described above and to the steps you need to take to remove them, and you are well on your way to learning how you can prevent pain, ill health, and cancer.

5

The Clean Machine

Everybody wants to be healthy! And of late there has been an encouraging surge in the number of people taking personal responsibility for their health. It's not what science or medicine has done for them, it's what they have done for themselves.

The last decade has produced an army of people who have discovered the benefits of upgrading their diets and participating in some regular form of exercise. If you have not yet joined them, this is your time, your opportunity. You can have control over your level of health. You can have a say in the length and quality of your life. You can experience vibrant health. You can! And more and more people are becoming aware of that fact every day. The beauty of this revelation is that taking control and being in charge of your health is not all that complicated. Oh, I know you've been conditioned to believe that it is, but it isn't! And you can turn the tide in your favour almost immediately, depending upon how long it takes you to finish reading this book.

I know that the subject of disease has been complicated to the point of mass confusion and frustration, so I can easily relate to those of you who are skeptical of my claim that you can prevent it just by reading one book. No problem. I can handle skepticism. It's apathy I have to conquer. But if you will give it a chance and just try the suggestions contained here, I will succeed, as will you.

You are going to learn not only *what* you need to do and *why*, but also *how*. There is a component in the quest to live in health that is absolutely essential, possibly more crucial than any other, but that has somehow, astonishingly, been overlooked. What is this certain something, this special ingredient that will make it so much easier to attain your goal to live free of the fear of ill health? To introduce it to you, I will use a car analogy once more. (Since practically everyone either has a car or relies somehow on cars, it is likely you will have no difficulty relating to the analogy.)

The Key to Vibrant Health

In one respect, understanding the intricacies of the engine of a car and how all the parts interact to make the car run can be a real challenge. On the other hand, a car's basic operation is rather simple: put in fuel and the car will continue to run and serve its owner in an endless number of ways for a very long time. Your body is like a car in that you give it fuel (food) which it converts into energy it uses to perform the myriad functions necessary to accomplish all the activities of life.

In order to keep the car in good running condition, you *must* periodically change the oil. If you didn't, the inner workings of the vehicle would quickly become silted up with sludge and break down. Neglected long enough, the oil would ultimately become so thick with this sludge that it would become solid. The car cannot operate under these circumstances. The dirty oil must be replaced with clean oil on a regular basis. There is no amount of *external* cleaning that will substitute for this *inner* cleaning. You can wash, shine, polish, paint, or detail the car until it is the best-looking car on the block. But it won't run if the inside of the engine is filthy.

The same scenario holds true for the human body, and understanding this is the key to vibrant health. *The inside of your body must also be cleansed regularly or it too will become silted up.* The result can be not only cancer but all manner of ill health. Just as the oil in your car's engine becomes dirtier and dirtier as time passes, a certain amount of toxic residue is continuously generated in your system as a normal and natural result of the body's biological processes and your daily living habits. This waste *must* be eliminated from every part of the body.

Fortunately, your body *does* have the mechanism to expel it. But the body *can*, under certain commonly experienced circumstances, be overwhelmed. The result is a dangerous and harmful build-up of toxic matter. Where exactly does the waste come from? Some is produced inside the body by the replacement of billions of old cells with new ones every day. The old cells are toxic, highly poisonous, and they *must not* remain in the body. The rest is produced from the food and drink that is consumed daily. The residue that is not incorporated into new cell structure is waste that must be cleansed from your system.

The cleaner the body is, the better it works. We clean our houses, our tools, our closets, our garages, our stoves, our offices, our clothes, our cars, and we fanatically, in some cases, clean the outside of our bodies. It is peculiar in the extreme that such a simple and essential prerequisite of a healthy life, that of cleansing the *inside* of the body, has so consistently been ignored. It's not taught in school. It's not taught in college. *It's not taught!*

Hundreds of billions of dollars are spent annually on health care, but the entire expenditure revolves around expensive screening tests, expensive drugs, and other exorbitant treatments, all of which are designed to address problems after they occur. Sadly, the subject of prevention is given lip service; and the importance of detoxification is completely ignored.

This is a tragedy of considerable proportion, because detoxifying the body, or "cleansing," the word I prefer to use because it is easier to relate to, will do more to lay the groundwork for prevention than practically any other measure you take. *If there is, in fact, such a thing as a "secret" or a "key" to health, the cleansing of the inner body is surely it.* That is one of the reasons why organizations that attempt to help people overcome drug and alcohol addiction call their programs "detoxification programs." They are literally eliminating their patients' dependence on drugs by cleansing the drugs from their bodies.

My goal is to help you understand that until the inside of your body is cleansed and rejuvenated, you remain at risk of developing cancer. Once this cleansing has been accomplished and you start to enjoy the rewards it brings, you will wonder how you could ever have missed a tool of such inestimable value.

Cleanse And Rejuvenate

Isn't it fascinating that whenever the subject of caring for the body comes up, it's *always* in the context of what should or should not be put into the body? Put in more fibre. Don't put in so much fat. Put in pure water. Don't put in chemicals, additives, and pesticides. Put in this or that nutritional supplement. Don't put in refined salt or sugar. Ever notice that there's never a discussion about what should come out?

The missing link in experiencing the vibrant health that we all strive for and that still eludes so many, is yours for the asking. You merely have to grasp the value of doing what is necessary to cleanse and rejuvenate the *inside* of your body. To return to the car analogy, interesting, isn't it, that I used the analogy of the car and the letters C-A-R are the first letters of—*Cleanse And Rejuvenate*. Whenever you use your car, let the fact that the old, dirty oil must be periodically replaced with clean oil be a reminder that your body deserves at least as much attention. And don't worry, by the end of the book you'll have all the tools you need to show you what steps you can take to minimize the harmful build-up of waste in your body. You will see exactly how to accomplish the regular Cleansing And Rejuvenation I so emphatically suggest.

Energy-The Essence of Life

In order to accomplish the goal of cleansing, or in order to accomplish any goal, for that matter, there is one decisive element that must always be present. It is the one commodity that everyone knowingly or unknowingly wants, the one that will allow you to do everything you wish to do in life, the one that you can never have too much of. No, it's not money. It's energy! As stated in Chapter 4, energy is the very essence of life. When it is plentiful, all things are possible. You feel you are omnipotent. When it dwindles, life becomes an ordeal, and you find yourself at the mercy of all the forces around you. When energy is completely absent, life is over.

Amazing stuff, this energy. You can't see it or hold it in your hands, but you sure as heaven know when someone around you has it. And you certainly know when you have it. As human beings, we literally are energy systems. The truth is, there is not one activity or process of the body that can or will be performed without energy. Everything that you do and everything that your body does requires energy.

Back to the car analogy. What good would your car be to you if it had no engine? What good would the engine be to you if you had no car to put it in? Cleansing and energy levels are that inter-related. So much so that we are practically dealing with a catch-22 in that we must have energy to cleanse and we must cleanse to have more energy. Just as in its unfathomable wisdom the body allots energy to circulation and the constant beating of your heart, it is also acutely in tune with the need to regularly cleanse itself of deleterious waste and it automatically allots or conserves a certain amount of energy to do this.

"CARE"

Throughout nature, all forms of life herald the spring season with signs of rebirth. Flowers bloom, hibernating animals awaken, new life appears everywhere. And spring also invokes the age-old tradition of "spring cleaning," when we go from the attic to the cellar getting rid of the old and starting fresh. This commendable industriousness must also be extended to the most precious possession of all: your body. I am sure that at some time you have thought of a real spring cleaning for your home. Care about your body in the same way. When you care for your body, it cares for you. Your caring is best exemplified by allowing your body to function at its greatest level of efficiency. And that is only possible when it is cleansed of anything that might interfere with its smooth operation.

Isn't the word "care" a beautiful word? It can be used to express so much feeling or concern:

"I care about what you are feeling."

"My mother shows such care to everyone."

"She took such good care of me."

"I care for you."

"He sure does take good care of himself."

There is something about the word "CARE" that brings to mind positive feelings: help, empathy, compassion, concern, love.

I now wish to introduce you to a brand-new meaning for the word "CARE," and this meaning is a major reason why this book was written. I have expressed how crucial it is in your quest for vibrant health to cleanse and rejuvenate the inside of your body. I have also touched on the pivotal role energy plays in the cleansing process. Remember the car analogy and the observation that C A R are the three first letters of Cleanse And Rejuvenate? Now take the "E" from the beginning of the word "energy" and put it at the end of the word "car." You have CARE—CLEANSE AND REJUVEN-ATE ENERGETICALLY. That is the new meaning of the word "care" that will ensure for you a long and healthy life. CAREing for your body is the best possible health insurance you'll ever have. This process that I call CARE—Cleansing And Rejuvenating Energetically—is the ultimate tool in preventing disease while invigorating your entire life. Understanding the dynamics of how toxins are stored up and removed from your body is the key to understanding the importance of making CARE an integral part of your lifestyle.

Waste Management

The accumulation and elimination of a considerable amount of toxic waste matter in the body is a physiological fact of life. The question of the moment is: Where does all this waste come from? And, more important, When more is built up than removed, where does it go?

There are two sources that produce toxins in the body. The first is generated entirely from internal sources; the second from external sources. The body is essentially a machine that requires fuel, turns that fuel into energy in order to carry out its many functions, and generates waste in the process. Just like a car.

When I speak of internal waste, I am referring to the regeneration of the trillions of cells in our bodies. Literally hundreds of billions of old cells are replaced with new cells every single day! The worn-out, spent cells are toxic and must be eliminated, and the body, knowing this, uses the eliminative organs—the bowels, bladder, lungs and skin—to get rid of them. This cell replacement process is an automatic phenomenon. It is as spontaneous a process as the circulation of blood or the digestion of food. We have no control over this internal waste production. What we do have the most control over is the waste generated as a result of what we put into our bodies. This waste is the end product of all the metabolic activities occurring in every cell of the body. Every cell is a miniature "body" in its own right, taking in what it requires and excreting its wastes. Problems arise only when the build-up of toxins exceeds that which the body can eliminate via the eliminative organs. It's very simple. If, on a daily basis, more toxins are produced than are removed, the excess remains in the body where all manner of problems can develop because of it.

How sad that the prevailing opinion of traditional medicine ignores the need for inner cleansing. This tragic oversight results in all the clogged, choked-off, and self-poisoned bodies that are unnecessarily treated with drugs and surgery. If only it were true that our bodies do not get dirty, and that cleansing is not an issue! But it is an issue and the proof is all around us.

It is an undeniable fact that millions of people are walking around with distended abdomens due to a build-up of waste that has not been eliminated. They spend a fortune on laxatives each year because they cannot have something so natural and basic as regular bowel movements without drugs. Millions of others suffer from skin problems or high blood pressure. Others have sinus and respiratory problems. All these conditions are the result of dirty bodies.

It is terribly naive to think that all wastes are removed from the body. The body can only get rid of so much. It can be overburdened. Think of a bathtub full of water. If you pull the plug but leave the water running and more is going into the tub than is leaving it, what is the only inevitable result? The tub will overflow. When this happens inside the body with toxins, it spells disease. If it were true that the body always rids itself of harmful or inappropriate substances, it is unlikely that nearly a million people a year would be losing their lives due to *clogged* arteries. These arteries are not clogged with good intentions! They're clogged with sticky, toxic waste matter that the body *wanted* to get rid of and *should* have gotten rid of but couldn't.

If you lived in a house in which you did not clean the floors, did not empty the garbage, did not wash the bedding, did not wash the dishes or the windows or periodically dust, you could survive there, but what would it be like? Perhaps you are saying right now, "Who in their right mind would ever let a house go like that?" Right! But you must understand that far too many people are unknowingly allowing this kind of neglect right inside their own bodies. The principles of CARE presented in Part Two are going to make sure that you are not one of those people. The program is designed to allow your cleansing mechanism to operate at optimum efficiency so you will not suffer from cancer, one of the dire consequences of a body overwhelmed by toxins.

6

Your Very Best Friend

I sincerely hope you realize how exquisite you are, how magnificent your body is, what wisdom it possesses. It is capable of performing tasks in such prodigious numbers, and with such perfection, that even to try to comprehend the extent of the intelligence of your body is fruitless. You are a marvel of creation.

There are those in the biological and physiological sciences who are convinced that we will never fully fathom the depth of the intelligence of the human body. The brain alone is beyond comprehension. Indeed, the most sophisticated computer ever devised can't compare to the intricacies of the brain. Joined with its other components, your body is unmatched in power, capacity, and adaptability.

As you learned earlier, the human body comprises 100 trillion cells all working in perfect harmony. Each organ is a marvel in itself. The heart pumping 6 quarts of blood through 96,000 miles of blood vessels. The digestive tract turning food into flesh and blood. Balance always being maintained, temperature always being kept stable. Lungs supplying oxygen to the cells. More than 200 bones and more than 600 muscles working together to enable you to move in any direction anytime you wish. Ears that allow you to enjoy music. Eyes to behold the glories of a sunset. Sense of smell to marvel at the scent of a rose. Taste buds to take pleasure from food. And more activities, too numerous to list, all proceeding with extraordinary precision, simultaneously, for a hundred years or more, if need be. It is staggering to try to grasp the infinite intelligence necessary to coordinate the activities and precision of the human body. We can only stand in humble awe of it.

The Magnificent Human Body

There is a force, an energy, that resides in each of us that directs and governs all of the functions described above and more. That energy was what transformed you from an infinitesimal bit of protoplasm into the astonishing being you are today. It is that energy that "knows" instantly what to do if you cut your finger. Without any stimulation on your part, the blood coagulates, a scab forms, the wound seals itself, the scab falls off and presto, no more cut. What heals a broken bone after a fracture? Is it the cast and sling? Of course not. A complicated process creates new bone. It is the wisdom and power of the body that heals. The body heals itself automatically as part of its never-ending quest for self-preservation. A substance more powerful than any glue is secreted by the bone at both points of fracture, and the two segments are reunited as strongly or stronger than before the break. This process is neither chemical nor physical (i.e., man-made). It is biological! Even if you were to fall and break several bones and sustain several cuts, *all* of them would be healed simultaneously, while all the other myriad functions of the body were also being performed. Such is the power inherent in the energy that directs the activities of the human body.

This energy, this force that has been with you since the beginning of your life, *never leaves* you as long as you are alive. It is an integral part of your very existence. This energy that miraculously heals wounds is always there to carry out other, even more serious healing. From this point on you can be totally confident that whether you are in a state of exuberant health or failing health this energy is automatically striving for your highest possible level of health under all circumstances. *It can do nothing else as this is why it exists!* It is with you *fully* at this very moment and always will be. My goal is to create in you a sense of reverence for this powerful energy, reverence that will lead you to support your body in its ability and effort to provide you with vibrant health.

It is precisely in this area of acknowledgment of and appreciation for the remarkable power of the body to protect and heal itself that the "experts" have somehow managed to commit the most astonishing oversight in all the history of the healing professions. Do you recall the statements in Chapter 2 in which the experts declare: "We don't know, we don't know, we don't know"? *This chapter is what they don't know!* What is mind-boggling is that what they have missed is so glaringly obvious that there's really no accounting for why it has been missed. It's just one of those unexplained mysteries.

The Lymph System—The Body's Garbage Collector

I wonder if you happen to have a recollection similar to one I have that goes something like this: As a youngster I was asked by my mother to get the butter from the refrigerator and bring it to the dinner table. "Sure, Mom," I said as I jumped up from the table and headed for the fridge. After opening the refrigerator door, the following conversation ensued between me in the kitchen and my mother in the dining room:

"It's not here, Mom."

"It certainly is, I put it there myself."

"I'm looking all over. It's not here."

"Open your eyes. It's right in the front."

"I'm tellin' you, Mom, my eyes are open. It's not here!"

"Don't make me come in there and get it myself."

"Mom! Somebody must have taken it already."

At this point she strode into the kitchen, walked up to me and the open refrigerator and, without so much as a glance, reached in and picked up the butter dish, which was on the middle shelf *right in front!* I couldn't believe I was looking right at it and didn't see it. If it were any closer to me, it would have stained my shirt.*

---

*I don't think I'll ever forget the look on my mom's face when she picked up that butter dish. She gave me the kind of look that was a cross between annoyance and disgust that she might give if she saw someone pick his nose and wipe it on his sleeve.

What the authorities in cancer research have missed should have been as obvious to them as the butter dish should have been to me. The only difference is that my oversight has not resulted in the unnecessary loss of life.

By now you must be asking, "My God, what is it? What did they miss?" Only the single most important factor we have in the prevention of not only cancer, but also the years of pain and ill health that led up to it. It falls under the category of "the dynamics of the human body." Herein lies the most fundamental difference between the standard medical approach and that of Natural Hygiene. Hygiene looks at the human body as dynamic and capable, always aware of problems that may exist and constantly on top of dealing with them. Traditional medicine looks at the human body as a hapless victim, forever at the mercy of any and all malevolent beasts that may attack it.

Specifically, I am talking about the body's lymph system. This magnificent system's purpose has been misunderstood and its activities have been misinterpreted. As part of the incredible intelligence of the human body there are several systems that perform seemingly miraculous functions: the nervous system, cardiovascular system, respiratory system, digestive system, reproductive system, musculoskeletal system, and the lymph system which is an integral part of the body's defence system.

Your body is infinitely capable of defending and protecting itself. Our creator thought of absolutely *everything* when making our bodies. God didn't forget something as critically important and essential as a mechanism to protect against disease. That is the defence system, erroneously referred to as the "immune system." There is no such thing as an "immune system." It would be lovely if we could be made to be "immune," but it doesn't work that way. And you may think I am merely splitting hairs by calling it the "defence system" rather than the "immune system." Not so.

If you hold a loaded gun to your head and pull the trigger, there is no immunity to blowing your brains out. And there is no immunity to violating the laws of nature for years on end and not having to pay the price for doing so. People have been convinced that they can regularly live a life, the only possible consequence being ill health, and then run to the doctor for a pill or shot that will make everything O.K., as if miraculously, all past transgressions can be swept away by some potion. That's delusionary thinking that ultimately leads to one's demise. So throughout the book, whenever I refer to what is traditionally called the "immune system," I will be calling it the "defence system."

As far as preventing cancer and creating vibrant health is concerned, your success in doing so lies in understanding the lymph system, which is the heart and soul of the body's defence mechanism. The lymph system is not at all complicated. You already know something of it. Most of what you know about the "immune system" is actually the work of the lymph system. And I am sure you are well aware that whenever there is a discussion of breast cancer, for example, lymph nodes are invariably involved. You can be certain that is no coincidence.

I have mentioned the word "toxins" or "toxic waste" or "toxicity" so often already, you may be getting tired of reading them. But they have been mentioned so often for a very good reason. Recall our discussion of the seven stages of disease (Chapter 4): from the second stage (toxemia) on, it was made abundantly clear that toxins are a major contributing factor in the development of cancer. There is just no getting around this fact. No understanding of disease will ever be reached if the role played by toxemia is not also understood.

If toxins are allowed to build up and remain in the body, they will eventually cause harm to some degree, anything from general aches and pains all the way to cancer. If, however, they are removed from the body on a regular basis so that what is being built up is not allowed to exceed what is eliminated, your system will be kept sufficiently clean to prevent cancer from ever getting started. Does it not, therefore, make all the sense in the world to do whatever you possibly can to assist and facilitate the mechanism in your body responsible for removing toxins?

How fortunate we are that our bodies are equipped with such supreme intelligence. You may not have ever thought specifically about it before, but isn't it absolutely amazing that your body knows how to turn an apple into blood? It's really quite a remarkable feat if you think about it. In this technologically advanced world, there is no scientist anywhere on earth that can go into a laboratory and turn food into blood. Yet the body accomplishes this formidable task as a matter of course right along with all of the other equally impressive feats it performs. It is with the same intelligence, ability, and precision that the body performs all of its functions, *including the removal of toxins from the body*. Enter the lymph system.

Do you remember a few years back when the New York City Department of Sanitation went on strike and refused to pick up any garbage? I don't recall how long the strike lasted, but I do know it was long enough to become an abominable situation for New Yorkers. The mere sight of huge piles of garbage everywhere you looked was depressing enough, but such a prodigious amount of garbage accumulated that it actually blocked sidewalks for pedestrians and, in some instances, spewed out into the streets, impeding traffic. Worse yet was the sickening stench, horrendous enough to take the enamel off your teeth.

Every day the news on television brought us pictures of the ever-worsening crisis and the comments of frustrated and disgusted New Yorkers. It was, in no uncertain terms, a great big ugly, stinking mess that if not corrected would have eventually shut down the city. Guess what I'm getting at? *The lymph system is, quite literally, your body's garbage collector.* Although it can be overwhelmed and forced to try to contend with more than it possibly can, fortunately for us, our garbage collector never goes on strike. It is hard at work 24 hours a day in its relentless effort to keep the inside of the body clean and healthy.

I hope I have succeeded in giving you a sense of the magnificence of your body, of the incomprehensible wisdom by which it is governed. You can be totally confident that the incomparable intelligence with which the lymph system carries out its many functions is no exception. The lymph system is an astounding network of fluid, organs, nodes and nodules, ducts, glands and vessels that continuously and aggressively cleanse the system of waste matter. Millions upon millions of nodes, some minuscule, some large, guard the passages into the body against the intrusion of destructive substances. Placed end to end in a straight line all the lymph vessels in the body would cover a distance in excess of 100,000 miles. They would circle the globe four times![72] There is three times as much lymph fluid in your body as there is blood.[73] That should tell you something of its importance.

Unlike the circulatory blood system, the lymph system carries fluid only *away* from the tissues.[74] It picks up wastes from all the cells and, through an intricate series of processes, breaks them down and arranges for their elimination from the body. The lymph system is also involved in the production of white blood cells (lymphocytes) that seek out, capture, and destroy foreign substances such as bacteria and other "invaders," and remove them from the body as well.

Physiology of the Lymph System

Except for cartilage, nails, and hair, your entire body is bathed in lymph. If you could somehow see a picture of the network of glands and nodes inside your body, you would see what looked like an extremely fine sheath of lace totally covering and saturating everything. You can actually feel some lymph nodes where they are close to the surface of your skin. You can most easily feel lymph nodes on the sides of your neck, under your chin, under your arms, and where your legs meet your torso.

If you would like to see some unusually large lymph nodules, open your mouth and look at your tonsils. This, of course, will not be possible for a huge segment of the population, because before it was realized how extremely important and beneficial the tonsils were, they were unceremoniously removed willy-nilly as though they were some mistake of nature. Now that it is known that the tonsils are an integral part of the lymph system, forming a protective ring of lymph tissue around the opening between the nasal and oral cavities that provides protection against bacteria and other potentially harmful materials,[75] they are allowed to stay where God put them.

The traditional attitude that the tonsils are expendable demonstrate how this marvel of creation—the lymph system—has not been given the understanding and respect it deserves. Indeed, it has been entirely overlooked as the protector of our health.

I remember traveling through London in 1988 and, while reading the local newspaper there, I saw an article with the headline "Tonsils Bargain." Evidently, in an effort to facilitate the removal of these troublesome and obviously useless organs, physicians gave their time free and set up an assembly line so that over two weekends children could have their tonsils removed at a very low cost. According to the head of the health department who arranged the Tonsil Bargain: "We did 128 operations last Easter and it was such a success we thought we would repeat the exercise."[76] I had my tonsils summarily removed at age three. In those days (late 1940s), having them taken out was almost automatic. Tonsils were considered a kind of practical joke that God stuck in our throats. They were an affliction. The attitude to their removal was good riddance. Tragic, really.

When the tonsils enlarge, swallowing becomes very uncomfortable. It's almost as though the body is trying to tell us something like, "Hey, will you stop eating for a while so I can catch up and clear things out?" And instead of being educated to understand the message our tonsils are sending us and taking the appropriate action, we tear them out at the roots and get a big bowl of ice cream as a reward for being cooperative while they were being removed. It makes me sad.

You do not need an in-depth, highly technical understanding of all the physiological functions of the lymph system. In fact, for the purposes of preventing ill health in general, and cancer in particular, you practically know all you need to know about it. The main thing is to know that toxins build up in your body. If they are not removed, they will cause you pain, make you sick, and eventually drive certain cells crazy, making them cancer cells, and that is the explicit function of the infinitely capable lymph system: to break down and remove toxins from the body before they can cause harm.

Lumps and Lymph Nodes

There is an area that I do want to be more specific about so that you both fully understand it and also feel comfortable implementing the three principles of CARE that are given in Part Two. It's this: finding a lump in your breast is no reason to panic.

I am not trying in any way to minimize the seriousness of any aspect of breast cancer. Far too many women have suffered far too much for me to do that. No. What I mean is, because of the nature and dynamics of the lymph system, it is likely that you have had many lumps in your breasts come and go without your ever being slightly aware of them.

Lymph nodes fill up and empty all the time, and not only in a woman's breast, but in all areas of the body. The frequency with which this happens depends upon the level of toxemia in your body and the amount of vital energy your body has to empty them. That is why Dr. Susan Love says, "If you feel a lump [in your breast], the first thing you should do is take a deep breath. There is no rush. Even the diagnosis of breast cancer is not an emergency. And certainly the diagnosis of a lump is not an emergency. There are twelve benign lumps for every cancer."[77]

I find it criminal that women have been whipped into such a frenzy of fear over searching out and finding lumps in their breasts. Women have actually been taught to fear the normal activities of their bodies rather than to understand and appreciate them. We fear the unknown. Once you know what the lumps are, however, why they have appeared, and how simply you can facilitate their removal, fear will no longer have a hold over you. This, I might add, is true not only for swollen lymph glands in a woman's breast, but also for lumps and swollen glands anywhere in the body.

As I am a devoted fan of the analogy as a learning tool, I will use one here to explain a few things about lumps and lymph nodes. Think of a fountain that has water forced up its center. When the water reaches the top, it cascades onto a series of shallow, bowl-shaped ledges. The fountain is like a Christmas tree in shape in that the top ledge is small in diameter and all the ledges below increase in diameter. As the water fills the top bowl-like ledge, it spills over into the next ledge below it. As the ledge fills, water spills over into the larger one below it and so on until all the ledges are filled and the last one at the bottom spills over into the pool and a pump sends the water back up the center of the fountain. I've seen miniature versions of this type of decorative fountain at parties, used to dispense fruit punch. To fill your glass, you simply hold it under one of

the ledges where the punch is overflowing. It is a simplistic com-
parison, perhaps, but the activities of the lymph system with its
network of lymph nodes work similarly to that of the fountain: the
waste matter in your body is the water and the lymph nodes are the
ledges that fill and overflow.

Now remember, waste matter—toxins—are constantly being
produced and built up, picked up by the lymph system, and
removed from the body. Lymph nodes are truly amazing little
processing plants. As an indispensable component of the body's
defence system, lymph nodes filter out bacteria and other foreign
material from lymph fluid which constantly flows through the
nodes. This waste material is broken down, degraded, and sent on
its way for elimination. When the level of waste in the body builds
at a greater pace than it is eliminated, the lymph nodes are overburdened and they enlarge. They simply cannot keep up. As
lymph nodes swell and fill to capacity, the waste moves on to the
next available node. Frequently, these swollen lymph nodes are
surgically removed, especially if cancerous cells are detected in
them. *But removing the nodes is not removing the problem.* The
problem is the ever-increasing level of toxemic waste, not the
nodes that are trying to contain it.

Let's return to the fountain analogy for a moment. Do you think
for one fleeting moment that removing one of the ledges near the
top of the fountain that is filling with water would prevent the water
from getting to the other ledges? Even the removal of all the ledges
would not impede the water's progress one iota. The only way to
prevent the ledges from filling with water is not to remove them, but
to stem the flow of water. So, the only way to prevent lymph nodes
from enlarging is not to remove them, but to stem the flow of wastes
flowing into them. Imagine the dire consequences of removing all
the lymph nodes in the body because they'd become enlarged. The
defence system would be so severely impaired that premature death
would inevitably follow as poisons flowed freely through the
"undefended" body. Your body is your citadel of life. Your lymph
nodes are your warriors, your guardians, performing an indispensable service protecting you from harm. *You can't live without them!*

Road to the Truth

There is something I wish to share with you. During the writing of this book, whenever I needed some bit of information or some help, as though by divine grace, I got exactly what I needed when I needed it, in the most unusual fashion. I don't want to sound airy-fairy here, but what I needed came to me in totally unexpected ways so many times that I simply can't help thinking that it was more than mere coincidence. For example, this book was one of three that I was contemplating writing. It was going to be either a book on weight loss, AIDS, or cancer, and I was having difficulty deciding which topic I should focus on.

Just when I was trying to decide which to do, and I was looking for some sign to direct me, ABC-TV aired a most provocative show on breast cancer. Less than two weeks later, "60 Minutes" aired a great segment on breast cancer. Two weeks later, PBS aired an equally thought-provoking show on breast cancer, and five days later PBS aired yet another information-packed show on breast cancer. I taped all those programs, watched each of them twice, and my head was so full of what was happening with breast cancer that I couldn't think of anything else.

Right then, I met and had the conversation with the woman whose story is related in Chapter 1. My course was set, no doubt about it. This kind of "coincidence" kept happening. I won't relate all the instances because they are simply too numerous to mention. Suffice it to say, if I needed a certain piece of information, it would show up in the mail, sent to me by someone who was merely sending me an article that he or she thought I would be interested in. Or I needed a certain quote and I would see what I was looking for on the cover of a magazine in a bookstore.

Once I was anguishing over the fact that I didn't have enough information on a certain aspect of my subject and that very day I happened to call someone on a completely unrelated issue and wound up with a phone number for a service that screened television talk shows for various subjects and provided transcripts. I wound up with a four-inch-high stack of precisely what I was looking for.

I remember thinking that it was all too much. They were the most remarkable string of coincidences of my life. That very day that I was ruminating on whether it was coincidence or divine intervention, a friend told me about a book that she thought I would enjoy. It was called *The Celestine Prophecy* by James Redfield. I wasn't doing a lot of reading outside of the subject I was working on, but I picked up the book to take a look at it because I was beginning to get the hint that these *coincidences* weren't coincidences. The book describes nine key insights into life that will help readers experience a deeper spiritual awareness. The first of the insights describe how everything happens in life on schedule, with purpose—*that there are no coincidences*. You could have knocked me over with a feather.

I knew from the very beginning of this project that this particular chapter was going to be one of the most important and pivotal chapters in the book. Important for two reasons. First, it explains what lumps in the body are, why they appear, and the incredible lymph system that governs the coming and going of lumps and swollen lymph nodes. Understanding the body's dynamics is crucial to your understanding how the three principles of CARE (see Part Two) will help you prevent disease and achieve vibrant health. Second, it is no small matter to state that the experts in charge have somehow missed something as significant as the lymph system's role in *preventing* cancer rather than being victimized by it.

I also knew that I would have to build a very clear, logical, unassailable case to prove my point. Of course, the most convincing evidence is the frequency with which lymph nodes are routinely removed from a woman's chest, side, and arms, and how little provocation is needed for this procedure. I know many women whose physicians convinced them to allow the removal of lymph nodes from under their arms as a "safety measure." That would be like tearing out your alarm system at home as a safety measure against burglary.

Anyway, one day I was at my desk working on *this* chapter and I received a phone call from a friend to whom I had not spoken for some time and who lives far away. After I told him about my project, he mentioned, almost as an afterthought, that he'd been looking through a really first-rate physiology book that was used as a textbook and was beautifully written and illustrated. He said he remembered reading some interesting material on the lymph system. After all of the similar experiences I'd had, I realized that his call and the book my friend mentioned as another of these "coincidences." Because it's more of a teaching book, it was not available in any bookstores in my town. But I found a store in the state willing to FedEx it to me.

I received the book the next day, and I immediately sat down and read the chapter entitled "Lymphatic Organs and Immunity." Have you ever been watching a movie, a taut suspense-thriller in which someone is trying to find some lost or hidden piece of evidence to solve a mystery? After following numerous leads, that elusive piece of evidence is finally found. The suspense has built to a nerve-wracking crescendo and at the moment when the hero finds what he's been looking for, the camera moves in for a close-up of his face, a fanfare sounds, and the person who has been searching so long and hard pumps a clenched fist in the air and yells, "*Yes!*" I came to a passage in the chapter I'd been reading on the lymph system that made me feel that same surge of excitement, and I looked around for the movie camera, fully expecting to hear the fanfare. At that moment, I would not have been the least bit surprised if Steven Spielberg himself stood up behind me and said, "Cut! That's a wrap!" The short, simple passage spoke volumes. At first I couldn't believe my eyes, so I read it over carefully again and again. It was as if all my work and effort had been rewarded with one simple sentence found in the last place on earth I would expect, or even hope, to find it: in a textbook used to *teach* the subject.

The passage reads:

> Cancer cells can spread from a tumor site to other areas of the body through the lymphatic system. At first, however, as the cancer cells pass through the lymph system, they are trapped in the lymph nodes, which filter the lymph. During cancer surgery, malignant (cancerous) lymph nodes are often removed, and their vessels are cut and tied off to prevent the spread of the cancer.[78]

So what is so momentous about this? you may well ask. Let me highlight the sentence that jumped off the page at me like a pit bull going after a steak, and explain why it is of such significance:

> At first, however, as the cancer cells pass through the lymph system, *they are trapped in the lymph nodes,* which filter the lymph.

This sentence confirms what I have been stating. How? First, it shows that although there may be a masterful understanding of the *technical* functions of the lymph system, there is no understanding of the *practical* functions it performs. Earlier I stated that Natural Hygiene sees the body as dynamic, as the actor. Traditional medicine sees the body as passive, as a victim. We so often hear about how cancer spreads and works itself into a lymph node, requiring the node's removal. But it is made very clear, totally clear in the passage from the textbook, that cancer cells don't work their way into a lymph node, the cancer cells are "trapped by" the lymph nodes.

Lymph Node Removal

A cancer cell works its way into a lymph node in the same way a piece of dirt "works its way" into a vacuum cleaner. The lymph node is doing something to the cancer cells. It's not the other way around! No wonder "they don't know." They have reversed the entire order of things. (Talk about not seeing the butter in the refrigerator, how about not even seeing the refrigerator in the kitchen?) It would be like describing our solar system, noting that the sun is at the centre with the planets circling it, then stating that the sun actually does move across the sky because you can see it do so. It only looks as if the sun is moving; in fact, it isn't. It only looks as if cancer cells are attacking lymph nodes; in fact, they aren't.

As cancer cells are carried by the lymph fluid, they are *brought* to lymph nodes where they are trapped. Let's look at this more closely. I have made the point over and over how magnificently intelligent the human body is. It "knows" what it's doing. It performs trillions of actions and reactions; no activity is wasted, none are superfluous, all have an absolute reason for taking place.

The body has far too much to do to busy itself with activities that don't directly contribute to its own survival. So you can be sure beyond even the most infinitesimal shadow of a doubt that if the body traps cancer cells in its lymph nodes, it has a damn good reason for doing so!

The lymph nodes contain phagocytic cells. *Phago* means eat and *cytic* means cell. Eating cells gobble up and degrade foreign substances. Cancer cells are trapped there as the body's last line of defence. Remember, cancer is the seventh and last stage of disease. During the first six stages (see Chapter 4) when cancer could have been prevented by certain lifestyle changes but wasn't, the next stage kept inevitably following the previous one until cancer appeared. As a last-ditch effort to deal with the cancer that had obviously broken away from its original site and started to spread through the lymph system, the body traps them, to deal with them.

There is no other possible reason that the body would make this effort. The body never gives up the fight no matter how bad things are, no matter how serious the situation, no matter how ongoing the neglect. As long as it is alive, the body strives for homeostasis— balance. Like water in a jar that seeks its own level no matter what position the jar is in, the body seeks to normalize, correct, and maintain balance no matter what the circumstances. Even in the face of such long-standing abuse and neglect that cancer finally develops, the body still has the wherewithal to call to arms its last sentinels guarding the health of the body: those amazing, cancer-trapping, protective lymph nodes.

And how are these precious lymph nodes treated by those who "don't know?" *They are cut out!* And why? *For performing the very function they were created and intended to perform!*

Nothing, and I mean nothing, could be more backwards. Would you allow your bladder to be cut out because of the presence of urine? Would you allow your colon to be cut out because of the presence of faeces? Would you allow your lungs to be cut out because of the presence of carbon dioxide? Can you imagine a more preposterous suggestion than that? The removal of one of your vital organs for doing the very job it was put there to do? It is every bit as preposterous to remove a lymph node for doing its job as it is to remove the bladder, colon, or lungs for doing their job.

We look back in amazement and disbelief that our ancestors were so blind to the dynamics of the body that they routinely drained blood from the sick. Bleeding patients was a standard, universally accepted practice. It was believed that as the blood ran out of the body, so would the sickness. Removing lymph nodes for doing the job they were created to do, at the very moment when what they are doing is most needed—preventing the wild, uncontrolled spread of cancer cells—makes bleeding look like the cornerstone of scientific wisdom.

And just where, pray tell, will the waste and cancer cells go when these lymph nodes are removed? To the next available lymph nodes, that's where. Removing one of the ledges in the fountain won't stop the water from going to the next available ledge, and removing a bunch of lymph nodes won't stop the cancer from going to the next available node. That's why it is so common to hear the two famous statements, either, "You've relapsed," or "We didn't get it all." Because until the build-up and flow of wastes and toxins in the body are curtailed, you can excise every lymph node in the body and it will be to no avail. That is because the swollen lymph node is only the symptom of a cause that is not being addressed. Under those conditions, "relapse" is inevitable.

I must say I was enormously encouraged in late 1996 when I read an article published in the journal *Surgical Oncology Clinics of North America*[79] that said, "Lymph node removal in an increasing number of breast cancer cases is done as a matter of tradition and history, not medical necessity." Some women, the authors said, "are needlessly enduring a lifetime of swollen or numb arms and a high risk of infection because doctors have been indiscriminate about removing lymph nodes." This is because, "It was once thought that cancer from the lymph nodes could be spread to other organs or tissue through the lymph fluid. It has since been proved that the lymph nodes don't spread cancer—they merely tell doctors if the cancer has already spread." They went so far as to state that, "Even with some invasive cancers—it might be possible, or even advisable, to forgo lymph node removal." That change could, they suggest, "spare many women from the disabling side effects of lymph node removal." I was pleased that the authors stated, "One should have the courage not to do lymph node removal as a routine." As encouraging as all this is, there is still a long way to go before there is a full understanding of the lymph system, as evidenced by the following.

When O. J. Simpson was in custody awaiting trial, he had a lymph node removed from under his arm to determine if it was cancerous. It turned out that it wasn't. The attending physician diagnosed the swollen lymph node as "benign reactive lymphocytic hyperplasia." Translated into English, that is the abnormal growth of normal white blood cells that results in the increased size of the node.

Now, even the most elemental understanding of the role lymph nodes play in the lymph system's job of keeping the body clean tells us what was happening in this case. The body increased production of white blood cells to deal with an overload of toxins in the body that had started to accumulate in the lymph nodes. It's the body's defence system in action. Simple. Obvious. Elemental. But the media stated that "further studies" were going to be conducted to try to "determine the cause of the swelling" of the node.[80] Studies? That would be like pulling a floundering person out of a swimming pool and then doing "further studies" to determine why the person was soaking wet.

Poisoned Back to Health: Radiation and Chemotherapy

I was deeply saddened by the passing of Jacqueline Kennedy Onassis. Not so much because she was the widow of one of the presidents of the United States or that she was a woman of great courage, style, and dignity who had gone through so much in her private and public life. I was saddened by the fact that she became yet one more victim in a long and heart-rending line of victims to lose their lives because of a lack of understanding of the basic needs of the human body. History will record that Jacqueline Kennedy Onassis died of cancer. And most assuredly the cancer in her body contributed to her demise. But I believe that ignorance of the dynamics of her lymph system hastened her journey to the grave.

There is a simple, obvious, logical, common-sense axiom in Natural Hygiene. It is so obvious that one might think it is ludicrous even to mention. Here it is: You cannot be poisoned back to health. Does that seem reasonable to you? But lo and behold there is also a medical axiom. In Latin it is *Ubi virus ibi virtus*. Translation: Where there is poison there is virtue. If you were in a bookstore, would you be captivated and sufficiently interested to spend your money on a book entitled *How to Poison Yourself Back to Health*? Probably every fibre of your being would revolt against such a suggestion; yet, by some inexplicable fluke of reasoning, medical treatment dictates that those who are sickest be poisoned the most.

Radiation and chemotherapy are poisons. They poison and kill both cancer cells and healthy cells. Moreover, these treatments are themselves carcinogenic. That's right, the treatment for cancer *causes* cancer. Back in the early eighties, health care workers who were involved with the preparation and administration of anti-cancer drugs were warned to take special precautions when handling the drugs because of the risk of developing cancer from being in contact with them. An article published by the American Cancer Society states that the increased risk "should be of great concern to those handling anticancer agents."[81]

Now, get this: Those *handling* the drugs should be greatly concerned. What about the people having it injected directly into their veins! No need for concern there? If a strong, healthy, fit, and vibrant person were to be given intense radiation and chemo-therapy, that individual would quickly become debilitated, devitalized, and sick. How then could the same treatment given to someone who is already sick be expected to make that person well? Where's the reason? The logic? The common sense? If something will make a well person sick, it will surely make a sick person sicker. How could it possibly be otherwise?

As I read articles describing the cancer treatment given to Mrs. Onassis, I was filled with sorrow and dread. In the midst of the assault she was under, I commented to a friend that Mrs. Onassis couldn't possibly live out the week. She died the next day.

Although it was not breast cancer that Jacqueline Onassis had, it was cancer so very similar that I cannot resist using her case to make my point here. Mrs. Onassis had lymphoma. "Oma" means tumour, so what she had was a tumour in her lymph system, meaning one or more of her lymph nodes were found to have cancer cells in them. *Trapped there,* no doubt, by her body as it struggled as best it could with the results of years of toxemia within her system. Had the affected lymph nodes been in her breasts, she would have been told that she had breast cancer. If cancer is diagnosed in a lymph node, it is described as a lymph-oma. In fact, a tumourous lymph node in the breast could be called lymphoma as well.

Newspaper accounts of Mrs. Onassis's cancer and treatment said that her cancer "attacked" the lymph system and that "tumors can arise anywhere there are lymph nodes and lymphatic channels."[82] She became acutely aware of her problem when in December 1993 she "noted a swelling in her right groin."[83] A physician diagnosed a swollen lymph node. A few weeks later she developed a "cough, swollen lymph nodes in her neck and pain in her abdomen."[84] She flew to New York to be examined and her doctor found "enlarged lymph nodes in her neck and in her armpit."[85] A CAT scan (a computerized X-ray) showed that "there were swollen lymph nodes in her chest and in an area deep in her abdomen."[86]

To a Natural Hygienist, in tune with the dynamics of the body and the knowledge of the important role the lymph system plays, these signals could not have been more clear. Mrs. Onassis needed to allow her system to be cleansed of toxins and waste and she needed it fast. Unfortunately, she did not have the benefit of that point of view. If she did, she could very well be alive today.

Instead of realizing that cancer cells had been trapped in lymph nodes as an attempt to cordon them off from the rest of the body until they could be dealt with, traditional medicine looked upon them as helpless victims under attack by marauding cancer cells. In response to that view, a course of very aggressive radiation and chemotherapy was undertaken and the former first lady's fate was sealed. She was bombarded with drugs. Lots of powerful, virulent, energy-sapping, life-diminishing drugs. The *New York Times* stated that she "initially responded to therapy, but it [cancer] came back in her brain and spread through her body."[87]

For the unrelenting pain in her neck, Mrs. Onassis received more drugs. For the acute pneumonia she developed in her weakened state, she received more drugs. Steroids were part of the mixture in her chemotherapy, which caused a perforated ulcer in her stomach. In the middle of her ordeal, she had to be operated on to sew up the hole in her stomach. She went from bad to worse and, as a final assault on her body, she was subjected to even more radiation and chemotherapy, only this time it was shot directly into her brain. The cancer spread to her spinal cord, her liver, and throughout her body. She became weak and disoriented, lost weight, developed shaking chills, her speech slowed, and she had difficulty walking.

How Mrs. Onassis held on for as long as she did under such a barrage of poisonous chemicals is a testament to her strength and will to live. The fact is, her body was already weak from her own internal struggle to deal with the cancer in her lymph system. Add to that a relentless attack with the most virulent poisons on earth and she didn't stand an ice cube's chance on the sun. After the assault on Mrs. Onassis's body culminated and it was apparent that all hope of recovery was gone, the headline in the *New York Times* read: "Doctors Told Mrs. Onassis That There Was Nothing More They Could Do." I'd say!

How ironic that the constant contact with toxins—poisons—is what turns cells cancerous in the first place and it is *more* poisons that are then used to try to destroy those cells. It is the elements of health, not poisons, that will produce good health, recapture it if it is lost, and maintain it once found.

I watched the same scenario unfold in 1963 when my father was only 57 years old. He'd been diagnosed with cancer. It was bad, but nothing compared to the aftermath of the radiation and chemotherapy he endured. I was only 18 at the time and had not yet learned what I know now, so obviously I couldn't exert any influence on the decisions being made on his behalf. He is one reason that my life's work is to help people avoid a similar fate to his.

A few days after Mrs. Onassis's death, there was a big article in the *New York Times* with a headline that made me shake my head in exasperation. It read: "Lymphomas Are On the Rise In U.S., and No One Knows Why."[88] In the article, there were statements like, "No one knows precisely why." "Experts are stymied." "Doctors know little." "Reasons are poorly understood." It always amazes me that whenever medical scientists don't know something, they immediately declare that "no one knows." It's not true.

I am very fortunate to have several friends who are doctors who are not threatened by the fact that although I am not medically trained, I can sufficiently challenge their thinking on certain aspects of traditional medical treatment to make them stop and think. One of these friends, who I have known for more than a dozen years and with whom I am very close, asked me what approach I was going to take in telling people how to prevent cancer from invading their bodies. I told him my approach focuses on an understanding of the lymph system, how it works and how to keep it sufficiently clean so as to prevent tumours from appearing. After explaining to him the Natural Hygiene view of how the lymph system operates, I asked him point-blank, "How is it that medical doctors, including you, can go to school for 12 years and come away with no understanding of the crucial role the lymph system plays in preventing cancer?" He thought for a few moments and said, "You know what, Harvey? I don't know why. It's just not stressed. We learn the mechanics of it, but not its practical application." And it is this epic oversight that is the very reason that so many of the experts "don't know" how to prevent cancer.

Here is my message to you, dear reader: Don't worry! By applying the three principles of CARE (see Part Two), you will know how to deal with cancer, because by understanding and respecting the activities and needs of your lymph system, you will be taking the appropriate steps to prevent it from ever occurring in the first place.

Too Fat or Not Too Fat

I love to eat. I love food and I love to eat. Always have, too. I love everything about food. I enjoy thinking about it, looking at it, talking about it, preparing it, smelling it, tasting it, and eating it. Going to a new restaurant and sampling its cuisine is as exciting an adventure for me as going to a thrilling sports event may be for someone else. So I am not the least bit surprised that my life revolves around the study and teaching of the effect of nutrition on the human body. I don't mind telling you that I feel blessed to have been given the ability to grasp the important relationship between nutrition and good health. Frankly, had I not grasped the concept, considering the road I was on, I would probably be dead or as close to it as one can be and still be breathing.

In terms of my health, the difference between the first 25 years of my life and the second 25 years is like the difference between a barren strip-mine site and a lush rainforest. My first 25 years of life was an ongoing battle against pain, excess weight, and lethargy. I suffered from excruciating stomach pains, frequent headaches, including migraines, numerous colds and sinus problems, a perennial lack of energy and ultimately reached a weight of just over 200 pounds. This sorry situation occurred because my love for eating knew no bounds. I was never raised with or taught anything about the effect of food on my health. My only prerequisite for what I would eat was, could I get it down my throat?

In 1970, at age 25, I had the immeasurable good fortune to be introduced to Natural Hygiene, and since that time, I have had no stomachaches, headaches, or sinus problems. I have an abundance of energy and the 50 pounds I quickly lost have stayed off. And the really *good* news, for me anyway, is that I achieved all this while still revelling in the joys of eating. The difference is, I learned how to fully enjoy the eating experience *and* maintain my health.

Nutrition and Vibrant Health

There are many factors involved in the development of disease, be it cancer or any other illness. The most prominent factors are quality of food, air and water, exercise, rest and sleep, sunshine, loving relationships, self-love and inner peace, and our mental processes. I know that all of these variables, and more, play a role in whether or not we become ill, but I am certain beyond any possible doubt that far and away the number-one factor affecting our health and well-being is the food we eat. This is a conviction based on my own extensive experience and on both mine and others' observations.

If we were to compare all foods that we consume, everything, to measure its worth, obviously something would have to be the very best food for our health and something would have to be the most detrimental, with everything else falling somewhere in between. Later on I'm going to talk about the very best, but right now it is essential that I talk about the one at the other end of the scale: food which, if eaten in excess, will do more to increase your chances of developing cancer than any other.

Animal Products

The greatest threat to your health are animal products. Animal products comprise all meat, chicken, fish, eggs and dairy products. I am convinced that the overconsumption of them is the leading cause of a clogged lymph system, excess weight, pain, ill health, disease, suffering, and death.

Of course, these are words that make organizations like cattlemen's associations and dairy councils have apoplectic fits. After all, the animal products industries take in over a quarter of a trillion dollars a year, so they hardly want you to find out the truth about their products. One major strategy they use is to call out their hired "experts" to scare the blood out of the veins of anyone who would even contemplate investigating a diet that contains little or no animal products. The people making the trillions of dollars selling animal products would have you believe that the next three generations of your offspring will be condemned to all manner of deficiencies and disease if you skip meat or milk at even one meal. A slight exaggeration, but they do get a bit carried away when our quest for health starts to interfere with their profits.

Actually, their attempts to dissuade us from eating less of their products are becoming increasingly more difficult because of the vast amount of data consistently coming forth that proves our love affair with animal products has been and remains a major contributor to ill health. To clarify my position and head off any campaign by the animal products industries to label me as something I'm not, I wish to spell out precisely where I stand in relation to vegetarianism.

Vegetarianism

Vegetarianism is *ideally* the healthiest way to eat, but vegetarianism is not for everyone. I know vegetarians who have had their lives saved by eliminating meat and dairy from their diet. I also know strict vegetarians whose health suffered until they reintroduced some animal products into their diets. Anyone who insists that vegetarianism is the *only* truly healthy way to eat is just as off base as someone who insists you can't be truly healthy if you are a vegetarian.

There are those who understand intellectually that cutting meat and dairy from their diets is best, but because they were raised on those foods and have eaten them for years, they're up against a tremendous amount of physical and emotional conditioning. Being a vegetarian is an exceedingly personal choice and depends on many variables that relate to each individual's characteristics and unique circumstances. Just because a vegetarian diet works well for some people does not automatically mean it will work for everyone. It is as objectionable to demand that people embrace vegetarianism as it would be to tell them to change religions.

There is, however, something that everyone can do, and that many people are already doing, to take advantage of the most up-to-date research on the subject: *cut back!* For decades we have been overeating animal products. Research on the effect of this over-consumption is overwhelmingly conclusive: It is killing us!

In *Fit For Life*, and especially in *Fit For Life II*, I discussed in great detail the full extent to which animal products contribute to every major disease. I challenged several dietary myths: the four food group mentality (see Chapter 11); the daily need for huge amounts of protein; the idea that meat is the best source of protein; and the notion that dairy was essential for calcium intake and for protection against osteoporosis.

Today, discussions no longer revolve around whether or not we should reduce our intake of animal products, but on the *extent* to which we should reduce it. As with other matters of such import, opinions on extent vary from a conservative cutback of 15 percent or 20 percent to abstinence from all animal products. What you as a person motivated to achieve vibrant health must decide is what extent would be most comfortable and work best in your life. One thing is certain: lowering your intake of animal products is going to have a beneficial effect on your health commensurate with the extent to which you reduce these foods in your diet. Why? What has happened to so dramatically alter the landscape of nutritional studies that would have so many people agreeing on this issue?

The Killers—Cholesterol and Fat

Do the words "cholesterol" and "saturated fat" sound familiar? One short decade ago, you hardly, if ever, heard these terms. Today it is nearly impossible to go through a single day without hearing or reading something about them, and with good reason. They kill people! Lots of people. In fact, the argument is very strong that, together, cholesterol and fat kill more people than any other single cause of death in the United States.

Where do these killers come from? Absolutely all cholesterol comes from animal products. Cholesterol is produced in the liver and cells of animals and nowhere else. It is impossible to ingest cholesterol from the plant kingdom. However, there are still people who are confused about this fact. They will ask, "What about avocados, nuts, and oils? Don't they contain cholesterol?" Since none of these have a liver, they contain no cholesterol. If you have any concern or problem with cholesterol, it is the result of the animal foods in your diet. Reduce them and you reduce your level of cholesterol. A simple formula.

The vast, vast majority of fat, including saturated fats, comes from animal products as well. And although cholesterol is an important contributing factor to ill health, it is now well understood that fat in the American diet is as much or more of a cause for concern.

Saturated Fats and Heart Disease

Before revealing to you how animal products contribute to ill health, I would be remiss if I didn't briefly comment on the impact animal products have on the biggest killer we have ever known. Cardiovascular disease, which includes heart disease, all atherosclerotic diseases of the blood vessels, and stroke, kill more people than all other causes of death combined![89] It kills nearly one million people a year, two and a half thousand every day! When blood is constricted and unable to get to the heart, a heart attack is the result. When the blood is prevented from reaching the brain, a stroke or "heart attack of the brain" occurs.

What causes the veins to be blocked? Plaque. What is plaque? A thick coating of cholesterol and fat trapped in the arteries which the body has been unable to remove. And you can be sure that if these substances are overburdening the cardiovascular system, they are doing the same to the lymph system, as you will see shortly. Certainly many other factors contribute to cardiovascular disease, and animal products are not the exclusive cause, but they are unquestionably the major cause. The abundance of research corroborating the direct link between fat and cholesterol levels and heart disease is irrefutable. It is the leading predictor of athero-sclerosis (clogged arteries) and subsequent heart disease.[90]

Let me introduce you to Dr. Marc Sorenson, the incredibly fit and healthy founder of the National Institute of Fitness in Ivins, Utah, where he is known as "Doctor Fit" and where thousands of people from all over the world go to recapture their health. The author of three highly comprehensive and informative books, he has this to say on the subject of heart disease:

> Heart disease is an insidious and unnecessary malady which is caused explicitly by the consumption of animal products and saturated fat. It is predictable, preventable, reversible and wholly unnecessary.[91]

And yet about 50 percent of Americans die from heart disease,[92] while $12 billion is spent on bypass surgery annually[93] which, amazingly, is actually worse than doing nothing![94] What is imperative for you to know and never lose sight of is that while animal proteins definitely raise cholesterol levels, vegetable protein can reduce them![95]

Cancer and Lifestyle

The second leading cause of death in the United States is cancer. There is a widespread misconception about cancer which I must clear up right now: cancer is cancer—regardless of what part of the body it affects. A cancer cell is a cell gone crazy and that can happen anywhere in the body. The area of the body in which cancer develops is incidental to the fact that it did actually develop. People talk of breast cancer or colon cancer or prostate cancer or cancers in other areas of the body as though they were all separate and distinct diseases. They aren't. That's why I have told you over and over that it doesn't matter which type of cancer I use to bring all of this information to you. Again: *Cancer is cancer regardless of where it appears in the body.* If people live their lives in such a way that the cells in their bodies are forced to contend with a relentless barrage of toxins for years on end, then there is a strong likelihood that some cells somewhere in the body will go crazy.

Where that happens isn't the most important thing. *Why* it happens is the issue. That is why it's such a tragedy for some women to have their healthy breasts removed with no sign whatsoever of cancer or even swollen lymph nodes present. If a woman has her breasts removed, she won't have cancer of the breasts, it is true, but the possibility of developing cancer hasn't been removed. Only a lifestyle built around a cleansed and healthy lymph system will do that.

To say that breast cancer is a different disease than prostate cancer, which is a different disease from colon cancer, would be exactly like saying that rain, snow, ice, sleet, frost, dew, and hail all have separate and different essences when, in fact, they are all water in different degrees of consistency. Rain and snow may be different in appearance, but they are both water in different forms. Breast cancer and prostate cancer may be different in appearance, but they are both cancers in different forms.

In my local newspaper there was an article describing the experiences of three people who had cancer. One woman spoke of her "three kinds of cancer."[96] She lost a lung to cancer in 1983; she lost a breast to cancer in 1986; and she had a skin cancer excised in 1992. The article stated that she took responsibility for getting the lung cancer because she'd smoked for 34 years. However, in her words, "But my breast cancer—what did I do to get breast cancer? What did I do?"

Earlier in the article she also said that "Smoking was probably the cruelest thing she ever did to her body." That is the key, although she didn't realize it. *What she did to her body.* Smoking, which in my opinion is singularly the most toxic offence against life and health in existence, and which contains hundreds of toxic substances, affected her whole body, not only her lungs. Of course, the lungs would be the most likely area of the body to be affected by smoking, but it is a person's entire lifestyle that determines whether or not cancer will develop. Something as inherently poisonous as smoking affects all the cells of the body, not only cells of the lungs. The woman's smoking was a factor, a major factor, in her cancer of the lungs, cancer of the skin, and cancer of the breast.

Because of smoking, together with other negative lifestyle habits, her body simply started to break down at its weakest points.

It's been my experience that people who smoke also indulge in dietary indiscretions that contribute to their ill health. By the way, a study conducted by the American Cancer Society on more than 600,000 women, concluded that smoking escalates a woman's risk of dying from breast cancer by at least 25 percent. The more cigarettes a woman smokes and the longer she smokes, the greater her risk. The study also said that the risk is eliminated by quitting.[92]

The Case Against Animal Products

Right behind lung cancer, colon cancer is the second leading cause of cancer deaths. In 1990, two major studies were published that dealt with diet and colon cancer. Both looked at large numbers of people over a long period of time. Both studies reached similar conclusions. They indicated meat eating as a major risk factor in colon cancer.[98] One of the studies reported in the *New England Journal of Medicine* followed more than 88,000 subjects for six years. Its findings indicated that the more animal fat eaten, the more likely it was that colon cancer would result. Those eating the most animal fat were nearly twice as likely to develop colon cancer as those eating the least animal fat.

Dr. Walter Willet, who directed the study, concluded: "If you step back and look at the data, the optimum amount of red meat you eat should be zero."[99] That's not a lot of red meat. Typical of the research I see, this study made no mention of the importance of cleansing the colon. That is the most effective measure an individual can take to prevent all cancers, including that of the colon. Animal products, which are very high in fat and devoid of fibre, serve only to block and toxify the colon. High-fibre plant foods (all fruits and vegetables, grains) are the colon's best protection against cancer. It is noteworthy that women who consume the highest amount of vegetables have one-tenth the rate of breast cancer as those who eat the least amount.[100]

In the late 1980s, the case against animal products really took off. In October 1988, the Surgeon General's Report on Health and

Nutrition exploded on the front page of newspapers all over the country. After reviewing more than 2,500 scientific studies on the subject, the nation's top medical doctor removed any hope the animal products industry might have had of not being incriminated. In the report, and in interview after interview, the message from the Surgeon General was clear: *Cholesterol and fat (animal products) are wreaking havoc on the nation's health.* His advice: Cut back on these foods and add more fibre to your diet in the form of fruits, vegetables, whole grains, and legumes. Although he did not label them as such, these, of course, are the *cleansing* foods.

In 1989, the Surgeon General's report was followed up by recommendations from the National Academy of Sciences. After taking three years to review 6,000 research studies, the academy released what it called the "most definitive dietary recommendations in the history of the organization."[101] It was the Surgeon General's recommendations all over again.

Then the National Institutes of Health released their recommendations. Same again. Plus there were the recommendations of the Senate Select Committee on Nutrition and Human Needs in 1977 (see Chapter 11), the American Heart Association in 1979, the National Cancer Institute in 1979, the American Cancer Society in 1984, and at least 20 other authoritative agencies and organizations in the United States and abroad. All said the same thing: *Animal products are wreaking havoc on the nation's health.*

When you have that kind of unanimity among top authorities, it's time to pay attention. For so many in the medical community to now so strongly and so unanimously concur with the very findings they denied as recently as the late 1980s sends the clearest possible message: The amount of evidence supporting the recommendation to reduce our intake of animal products has to be titanic. And when they finally link the case for reducing animal products with the individual's ability to prevent illness by cleansing the body, they will have the whole picture and we will begin to enjoy an approach to health care that is truly grounded in prevention.

Whenever I attempt to impart information that may be new for some people, I have always asked them to rely as much on their common sense as on the so-called "scientific proof." Because, frankly, under the right circumstances and with proper funding, scientists can "prove" anything they want. Medical libraries are rife with examples of "scientific studies" that have proved one premise only to be replaced by other studies that prove the opposite.

I already gave you the example earlier of the two studies in the same journal "proving" estrogen to both prevent and cause heart disease. As another quick example, consider the incredible, terrible egg. Eggs contain one of the highest concentrations of cholesterol of any food. Data abounds showing that this is so. Eggs are the choice of researchers when they want to study their subjects' staggering increases in cholesterol levels.[102] In fact, eggs will increase blood cholesterol levels more effectively than pure cholesterol dissolved in oil![103] Yet the egg industry is quick to cloud the issue by constantly referring to five "scientific" studies that "prove," of all things, that eggs don't raise blood cholesterol levels.[104] The five studies, by the way, just happened to be funded by the egg industry.[105]

These examples demonstrate why it is so difficult to rely solely on scientific studies and scientific experts, and why observation and common sense have to be given equal weight when making decisions about what actions you're going to take in your own behalf. This is particularly important with regards to fat as a major risk factor in the development of cancer. There is at present a controversy raging in the scientific community about this very subject. Once again, the "experts" are divided; half think there is conclusive evidence and half think there is inconclusive evidence. How this can be absolutely boggles my mind. To me, there is about as much doubt that fat is indeed a risk factor in the development of cancer as there is doubt that the world is round, not flat. I will do my best to prove this to you using both scientific data and common sense.

Reduce Fat Intake Now!

Those who are convinced that fat is a risk factor feel that there is sufficient evidence incriminating fat to reduce intake of it now so as not take any added chances. Those who are not convinced agree that there is evidence pointing to fat as a possible villain, but since there are no studies that absolutely and definitively prove that to be so, they want more research to be conducted before they can feel certain that it is so and make recommendations accord-ingly. Since I am one of those who need no further proof, I am going to give you all the reasons I think you should reduce your fat intake now. Then you can decide for yourself.

There are numerous studies that make a compelling correlation between breast cancer and the consumption of dietary fat.[106] And fat intake also has an impact on a couple of the other suspected risk factors. One of those suspected risk factors is the female sex hormone estrogen. According to *Science News*, "Scientists don't understand exactly how estrogen fosters breast cancer,"[107] but the consensus is that the more estrogen there is in the blood, the more likelihood of developing breast cancer. High-fat diets cause high levels of estrogen in women.[108] Comparisons reveal that women who eat meat have significantly higher levels of estrogen in their blood than vegetarian women.[109] And when women switch to low-fat diets, the levels of estrogen drop sharply.[110]

Another suspected risk factor in developing breast cancer is late menopause. A correlation has been shown between late meno-pause and excessive fat in the diet.[111]

One very convincing piece of evidence incriminating dietary fat as a risk factor that promotes breast cancer is the incidence of breast cancer in Japanese women who either come to North America and change their diet or stay home and change their traditional diet (plant-based) to a North American diet (animal-based). An article in the *FDA Consumer* states that, "The death rate from breast cancer is the highest in countries like the United States, where the intake of fat and animal protein is high."[112] Further, it commented that Japanese women historically have a low risk for breast cancer, but that risk has been rising dramatically, concurrent with a "westernization" of eating habits, that is, from a low-fat to high-fat diet. Other research that has studied fat consumption of women living in Japan or Japanese women who come to the United States and increase their fat intake also confirms that the more fat eaten, the higher the incidence of breast cancer in these women.[113] An article in *Newsweek* magazine commented on the hazard of a western diet (beef, dairy and other fat-laden foods) to Japanese women. The article was titled "Death By Fried Chicken."[114]

Japanese women are not alone in this. The chart below illustrates clearly the correlation between fat intake and breast cancer in various countries. It is no accident that the incidence of breast cancer increases commensurately with the increase in fat consumption.

Relationship of Dietary Fat Consumption to Death from Breast Cancer, by Country

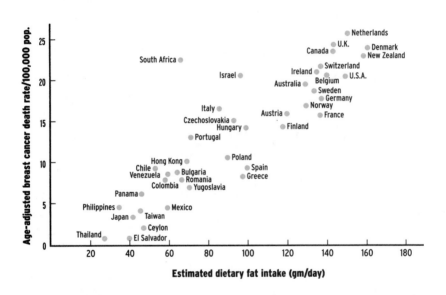

Source: Marc Sorenson, Mega-Health, (Utah: Sorenson, 1993).

Researchers at the National Cancer Institute reanalyzed 100 animal experiments pertaining to fats, calories, and breast cancer, and concluded that each excess fat-derived calorie posed 67 percent more risk than calories from other sources.[115] A study of Finnish women found that the participants who later developed breast cancer showed a "consistently higher" average percent of fat-derived calories.[116]

The Glorious Plant-Rich Diet

As important as it is to become aware of the foods that put you at risk of developing cancer, such as animal products, it is every bit as important to know what foods contain compounds capable of retarding cancer. The more researchers understand about the ingredients in fruits, vegetables, and other plant-based foods, the more impressed they are with the power of these compounds to retard the bodily breakdown that results in cancer.[117] Consider the following comment from an editorial in the *New York Times*: "Nutritionists and epidemiologists have long observed that people who eat a plant rich diet suffer lower rates of cancer than do meat loyalists."[118]

I guarantee that you will not see headlines proclaim that some special ingredient in a pork chop or a hamburger has been isolated and has been found to fight cancer. The compounds of food that are becoming increasingly familiar to people all come from plant foods, not animal foods. Compounds like flavonoids, carotenes, antioxidants, and fibre, and many, many more are all derived from plant foods. Every time you hear about some newly discovered multisyllablic compound that fights disease, it is derived from fruits, vegetables, grains, or some other plant food.

Have you heard of sulforaphane? Its discovery resulted in a headline that read, "Broccoli Extract Shown to Block Breast Cancer."[119] Researchers at Johns Hopkins University made the discovery and reported it to the media. Sulforaphane is a substance that is found in cruciferous vegetables: broccoli, cauliflower, Brussels sprouts, and cabbage. They didn't find any in steak.

Or how about this headline that jumped off the page at me: "Orange Juice Fights Breast Cancer."[120] New research at the University of Western Ontario shows this to be so. And what component in the orange juice accomplishes this feat? Small molecules found in all citrus fruits known as flavonoids.

Dr. Gladys Block, of the University of California at Berkeley, reviewed approximately 90 studies relating Vitamin C intake and cancer. She indicated that, "There is overwhelming evidence of the protective effect of Vitamin C and other antioxidants against cancer of the breast."[121] Fruits and vegetables such as citrus fruits, tomatoes, green leafy vegetables, and potatoes are rich sources of Vitamin C and other nutrients. Additionally, Dr. Block reviewed 170 studies from 17 nations and concluded that people everywhere who eat the most fruit and vegetables, compared with those who eat the least, slash their chances of developing cancer by about 50 percent![122] The evidence is so overwhelming that Dr. Block views fruits and vegetables as a powerful preventive that could substantially wipe out the scourge of cancer, just as cleaning up the water supply eliminated past epidemics such as cholera.

Dr. Peter Greenwald, director of the Division of Cancer Prevention and Control at the National Cancer Institute, Washington, D.C., says, "The more fruit and vegetables people eat, the less likely they are to get cancer, from colon and stomach cancer to breast and even lung cancer. For many cancers, persons with high fruit and vegetable intake have about half the risk of people with low intake."[123]

Dr. David Kritchevsky, in the journal *Cancer*, states that, "Breast cancer might be prevented if more women were to get sufficient amounts of Vitamin A, beta carotene and the other carotenoids."[124] Carotenoids are found in parsley, carrots, winter squash, sweet potatoes, yams, cantaloupe, apricots, spinach, kale, turnip greens, and citrus fruits.

Geoffrey R. Howe of the National Cancer Institute of Canada reviewed 12 case-controlled studies of diet and breast cancer and reported that fruits and vegetables provided a protective effect. Vitamin C showed the most consistent statistically significant inverse association with breast cancer risk in all women.[125]

In *Medical Tribune*, two studies indicated that nutrients, fibre, and antioxidants in fruits and vegetables protect women from cancer. One study found that of 310 women with breast cancer and 316 women without breast cancer, those without cancer ate more fruits and vegetables.[126]

Dr. Bruce N. Ames is a member of the National Academy of Sciences. He is a biochemist and molecular biologist at the University of California at Berkeley, where he is the director of the National Institute of Environmental Health Center. Dr. Ames is one of the two dozen most-often cited scientists in the world.[127] His colleagues refer to him as "one of the most innovative thinkers in the world of science."[128] Dr. Ames states that the antioxidant nutrients in fruits and vegetables "can suppress all stages of the cancer process," and that "diet is at least as important as smoking as a cause of cancer."[129]

A recent study on cancer prevention was conducted at the Memorial Sloan-Kettering Cancer Center in New York, and appeared in the *Journal of the National Cancer Institute* in October 1995. Dr. William R. Fair, at Sloan-Kettering said, "What we found was astonishing to us."[130] And what was it that Dr. Fair found so astonishing? It is that human prostate cancer tumours grew only *half* as fast in mice eating diets that contained about 21 percent fat as those eating diets that contained about 40 percent fat.

Are you starting to see the picture here? Could there be any doubt in anyone's mind that it is at the very least probably a good idea to minimize intake of fat and maximize intake of plant foods? How much proof is enough?

Once again, here are a few comments from people involved in cancer research on one level or another.

Women on low fat diets have less breast cancer than women on high fat diets, and women on high fiber diets have less breast cancer than women on low fiber diets.[131]

—Dr. Lawrence Power,
author and syndicated food and fitness columnist

If I were to blame anything for the modest increase in breast cancer that is not related to early detection, I'd point to dietary fat.[132]

—Dr. Ernst Winder,
President of the American Health Foundation

In terms of fat in the diet, there are several different types of evidence—none of them completely conclusive, but all of them pointing in the same direction—that link a very low fat diet, really about half of what the average American woman eats now, 20% of the total calories, to a lower incidence of breast cancer.[133]

—Cindy Pearson, Director, National Women's Health Network

As far as diet is concerned, while various investigators have looked into the question of fat in relation to breast cancer, none of them have examined the very much more important question that fat and fatty meat contain high concentrations of pesticides and sex hormones, steroids, which are clearly known to induce cancer, including cancer of the breast.[134]

—Samuel Epstein, M.D.,
professor of medicine, University of Chicago Medical Center

There is no such thing as a 'Cancer Personality,' although certain life-style choices—choosing to smoke or eat a fatty diet, for instance—do make a difference.[135]

—Jimmie Holland, M.D.,
Memorial Sloan-Kettering Cancer Center

One study monitored more than 14,000 women for six years, focusing on their consumption of meat, fat, protein, and other animal products. Paolo Toniolo, of the New York University Medical Center, who headed up the study, said, "It seems that frequent meat consumers are at more of a risk for breast cancer. I don't know if it's fat or other elements of one's diet. But I know it's diet."[136]

And this final statement made on the nationally televised show "Nightline" by Dr. Timothy Johnson—truly the voice of common sense and reason:

You can probably lower your risk (of cancer) by cutting down on the fat in your diet. And even if we can't prove that either way, it makes sense to do it for all kinds of other reasons, so why not do it?[137]

Hear, hear. Why not, indeed?

Michael Sporn, director of a new National Cancer Institute laboratory devoted to intervening in precancerous stages of the disease using a combination of new therapies, states that, "Over the next twenty-five years, breast cancer will disappear like the Cheshire cat."[138] I'm all for positive thinking, but breast cancer is not going to just "disappear." There is no magic bullet. It may very well be gone in 25 years, but that will be because of the actions women take now to protect themselves and prevent the disease.

The China Health Project

Over the years, there have been thousands of studies supporting what is now becoming common knowledge about the negative impact of animal products in the human diet. There are various requirements that are taken into consideration when determining whether a study will be established as credible and reliable; for example, the size of the study, the length of the study, the number of people studied, the preciseness of the data collected, the means by which data is classified, the exactness with which the entire study is conducted and to what extent each variable impacts the overall outcome.

Because it is so difficult to meet all the above prerequisites in one study, for decades researchers have hoped for one study that linked diet to health that was so large-scale and definitive in every aspect it would be viewed by everyone as absolutely precise and unquestionably accurate. The days of hoping are over. Just such a study was inaugurated in 1983, and in mid-1990 the first seven years of its data were released. It is called the Cornell Oxford China Project on Nutrition, Health and Environment, known simply as the China Health Project (CHP).[139] In the many reviews of this extraordinary study, it has been referred to as the "Grand Prix of Epidemiology,"[140] "The Champion Diet,"[141] and in one it was hailed as "one of the most rigorous and conclusive studies in the history of health research."[142]

At my seminars, I always ask my audiences how many people have heard of the China Health Project. Even in audiences of more than a thousand people, only a smattering of hands go up. What an injustice! What a tragedy! How deeply saddened I am by this state of affairs. Considering its importance and potential benefit to people everywhere, this study should have been headlined on the front page of every newspaper in the world and been the lead story on every news program for at least a week, or for however long it took to be certain that every global citizen was aware of it.

If there is a true hero in the area of research linking diet to health, it is surely Dr. T. Colin Campbell, a nutritional biochemist at Cornell University, and mastermind and coordinator of the

China Health Project. Dr. Campbell has been studying diet and health for more than a quarter of a century. He was instrumental in producing the National Academy of Sciences' landmark 1982 report Diet, Nutrition and Cancer, which was the first "official" recommendation to reduce fat intake some 25 percent and which led to the guidelines adopted by the National Cancer Institute, the American Cancer Society, and the American Institute for Cancer Research. Although Dr. Campbell's innovative and ground-breaking research into the link between diet and health frequently met with opposition, his perseverance and commitment never wavered. Those traits brought him to the forefront of this area of research and made him one of the world's leading nutritional experts.

One of the factors that makes the China Health Project unique is the sheer scope of the study. Dr. Campbell, together with researchers from Oxford University and researchers commissioned by the Chinese government, observed 6,500 Chinese citizens for six years to obtain the widest possible range of data on death rates for more than 50 diseases, making the CHP the most complex study ever conducted of a single large population.

Undoubtedly the most striking aspect of the study and the element that has made it so reliable is the lifestyle of the study's Chinese subjects. Chinese people have two very interesting traits that helped make the research as exacting as it was. First, they generally do not move around. They are born, live, and die in the same locale. Second, their eating habits rarely vary. They eat essentially the same foods their entire lives with very little, if any, variation. Their diets are simple and basic, determined by the season. These factors allowed researchers to study a human laboratory on a very large scale for a very long time.

Perhaps you are familiar with the term "diseases of affluence." These include heart disease, cancer, diabetes, osteoporosis, and obesity. Throughout the world, wherever enough wealth allows people to move away from their basic needs, the prevalence of these diseases increases. In the United States, diseases of affluence are rampant. In China, they are either practically nonexistent or notably uncommon.

It is not a secret that the more affluent and industrialized a society, the more animal products and refined foods its people consume. Americans consume 16 million animals, 165 million eggs, 11 million pounds of fish, and 345 million pounds of dairy products every single day![143] The United States leads the world in diseases of affluence. In contrast, the Chinese primarily eat the cleansing foods: vegetables, grains and legumes, some fish, and no dairy. What is of inestimable importance is that they obtain 7 *percent* of their protein from animal products, while Americans obtain 70 *percent* of their protein from animal products. Ten times as much!

The major reason Americans eat so much animal protein is that over the years they have been effectively conditioned to believe that protein every single day—indeed, every single meal—is absolutely essential for their health, and that animal products are the very best source of that protein. It would be as though a car manufacturer were to somehow convince you through false advertising that you couldn't get a safe car unless you bought one of theirs. And the propaganda works so well that you're actually scared to buy a car from another source, even though you might be able to buy a vehicle as safe or safer than the one you are conditioned to buy.

The idea that it is difficult to obtain sufficient protein from the plant kingdom is an outright falsehood perpetuated by the industries that make money selling animal products and by their hired "experts." Millions of dollars have been spent over the years to condition you to automatically think of meat and other animal products whenever you think of protein. One of the most frequently asked questions of a vegetarian is, "Where do you get your protein?" As if by not eating animal products the nutrient can't be obtained. The conditioning has worked all too well.

The China Health Project rather soundly obliterates that particular profit-driven nutritional myth. In *Eat For Life: The Food & Nutrition Board's Guide to Reducing Your Risk of Chronic Disease*, published by the prestigious National Academy of Sciences, Dr. Paul R. Thomas writes, "There is nothing nutritionally unique about meat products that other foods cannot supply."[144] Dr. William E. Connor, author and head of the Division of Endocrinology,

Metabolism and Nutrition at Oregon's Health Sciences University in Portland, sums it up well by saying, "The public has been sold on the idea that protein from animals is best and doesn't realize that plants contain high quality protein. Everything that grows has protein."[145] After all, isn't that where the animals we eat get theirs?

Heart disease in China declines to an almost negligible level when fat and cholesterol levels are low. The China Health Project shows that low fat and cholesterol not only protects against heart disease, but also against cancer of the colon. The more animal products eaten, the greater the risk to human health.

Obesity is a rarity in China. Although the Chinese consume 20 percent more calories than North Americans do, North Americans are 25 percent fatter! I have long maintained that calories are not a significant factor in whether you get fat or not. I was even attacked for saying so. The China Project and other data (see *T-Factor Diet* by Dr. Martin Katahn) certainly substantiate my point. After all, a calorie is nothing more than a measure of heat. Heat does not make you fat. Fat makes you fat. Unfortunately, it is being consistently shown that fat can also make you dead! Researchers show that as obesity rate increases, so does the death rate.

Another area of great global concern, especially for women, is osteoporosis, the loss of calcium from the bones until they become so porous and weak that a rib or hip can be broken merely by driving over a bump in the road. In the same way that we have been conditioned to think of meat whenever the word "protein" is mentioned, we have also been taught to believe that dairy products are the finest source of calcium, and the best means by which to prevent osteoporosis. That is precisely what the dairy industry, which makes billions of dollars selling dairy products, wants you to believe and once again it is patently untrue. It is a well-established fact that the high protein content of meat and dairy products turns the blood acidic, which draws calcium out of the bones. This causes the body to lose or excrete more calcium than it takes in. The deficit must be made up from the body's calcium reserve which is primarily the bones. Result—osteoporosis. This is not new information. It's been known since 1920 that protein from meat consumption causes a net loss of calcium.[146]

Fortunately, protein from vegetable sources does not cause a negative calcium balance and, in fact, can actually have a protective effect against bone loss.[147]

Women who are eating dairy products to prevent osteoporosis must pay attention to this well-documented fact: The countries of the world that consume the greatest amount of dairy products have the highest incidence of osteoporosis! The countries that consume the lowest amount of dairy products have the lowest incidence of osteoporosis.[148] The United States is among the world's leading consumers of dairy products and has the highest incidence of osteoporosis affecting between 15 and 20 million people and taking at least 20,000 lives a year as a result of hip fractures alone.[149]

The Chinese don't even have a word for osteoporosis in their language! It simply isn't a problem in their country. And how much dairy products do the Chinese people eat? According to Dr. Tierry Brun, an agricultural and nutritional scientist from the National Institute of Health and Medical Research in France, "The Chinese consume no cow's milk or dairy products, yet they have among the lowest rates of osteoporosis in the world."[150]

Dr. T. Colin Campbell points out that, "Dairy calcium is not needed to prevent osteoporosis. Most Chinese consume no dairy products and, instead, get all their calcium from vegetables. The Chinese data indicate that people need less calcium than we think and can get adequate amounts from vegetables."[151] As mentioned above, isn't that where the animals we eat get theirs?

For how many years have you been subjected to the aggressive propaganda by the dairy industry and their paid "experts" to frighten you, especially if you are a woman, into consuming dairy products lest you suffer the horror of osteoporosis? How much more sinister do those deceptive advertisements turn out to be now that it is becoming more obvious every day that the protein and dairy products sold contribute to osteoporosis?

Yet another scare tactic employed by the animal products industry is its claim that red meat and other animal products are the best source of iron and that without animal products, one risks developing anemia. The truth is that even in vegetarians and vegans, iron deficiency anemia is rare. In fact, studies reveal that they have iron levels as high or higher than those who eat an animal-based diet.[152] Moreover, Vitamin C, which increases iron absorption from food, occurs in plant foods, not animal foods.[153]

The China Health Project sheds much-needed light on this subject as well. Those in the study "with the highest fiber intake also had the most iron rich blood."[154] You must understand that red meat, or any animal product for that matter, contains no fibre. The CHP also shows that "consumption of meat is not needed to prevent iron deficiency anemia. The average Chinese who shows no evidence of anemia consumes twice the iron Americans do, but the vast majority comes from the iron in plants."[155]

Results of the China Health Project

The results of this extraordinary study could not be clearer. The massive amount of industry-initiated, profit-driven propaganda that we have been inundated with over the years extolling the virtues of a diet laden with animal products has been instrumental in the toxification of your body and the deterioration of your health. The animal products industry has been well served. You haven't. The relationship is clear: The more animal products you eat, the more ill health ensues. Dr. Campbell reveals that:

> "[I]n those few regions in China where meat and dairy consumption has begun to increase—notably the heavily westernized cities—it has been closely followed by a higher incidence of cancer, heart disease and diabetes. Once these people start eating more animal products, that's when all the mischief starts.[156]"

What has been demonstrated most clearly by the meticulously conducted China Health Project and what cannot be altered by the animal products industry's posturing and propaganda is that those who eat the least amount of animal products have the least risk of disease. Those who eat the most animal products have the highest rate of diseases of affluence. It is interesting to note that complex carbohydrates, which are only to be found in plant foods and never in animal foods, are the only food category not in some way linked to dread diseases.[157]

Today, the recommendations we are receiving from every quarter are to *decrease* our intake of foods high in cholesterol and fat (animal products) and *increase* our consumption of foods high in fibre (fruit, vegetables, legumes, and whole grains). Remember that animal products are extremely high in cholesterol and fat, which clog you up, and are virtually devoid of fibre, which cleans you out! In other words, animal products could not be in more direct opposition to what researchers the world over are recommending we eat.

Having masterminded the China Health Project, having spent seven years in close contact with the accumulation and deciphering of its data, and having seen firsthand the result of this project, what does Dr. Campbell suggest we do to best prevent disease and preserve our health? As relates to diet, he recommends, "Change the diet so that 80% to 90% of protein comes from plant products, only 10% to 20% from animal products. Build meals around plant foods such as fruits, vegetables, grains and pasta. The idea is to use animal products to flavor and as an accompaniment, not as the main focus."[158]

As relates to exercise, Dr. Campbell recommends, "Exercise more. Chinese people are more physically active than people in the United States. They ride bicycles every day."[159] These are the basic guidelines of the program you will soon be following (see Part Two).

Dr. Campbell sums up what he learned from the China Health Project as follows:

> We must come to realize that we are basically a vegetarian species. The study suggests that whether industrialized societies such as ours can cure themselves of their meat addiction, may ultimately be a greater factor in world health than all the doctors, health insurance policies and drugs put together.[160]

Another reason it is so important for you to understand the findings of the China Health Project is what it says about breast cancer. Remember, Chinese women obtain 7 percent of their protein from animal products, while North American women obtain 70 percent of their protein from animal products. The breast cancer death rate for North American women is not double, triple, or even quadruple what it is for Chinese women, but a whopping *five times* the number of deaths. That is a 500 percent higher death rate. It is not time to sit around and wait for further evidence. It is time to take action and take the steps to protect yourself now!

As part of the National Institute of Health's Women's Health Initiative, some 4,000 women will be tested to see if cutting dietary fat by half can lower breast cancer rates. They expect their results in the year 2006.[161] YOU CAN'T WAIT THAT LONG! The time is now!

All you have to do is ask questions of those around you to find out that a change in thinking and habit as relates to the eating of animal products is taking place. Many of you are already cutting back. Whether it's due to an instinctive "knowing" that you should eat less meat and dairy, or the fact that more progressive physicians are now regularly encouraging it, or that news from the numerous studies supporting such a change is filtering down to the public, it is clear that people are consuming a less animal-based diet. How often do you hear others say, and how many of you can yourselves say, "I have definitely cut down on red meat and I'm eating more fish and chicken"? That is part of the trend, and that trend is validated and encouraged by a rapidly growing number of authorities both outside and inside the medical community.

If you have not yet joined this trend because you feel the issue is not quite settled or that the "experts" are still at odds, your time has arrived. It would be a formidable challenge to find anyone other than those making money from their sale not to agree that reducing animal products in the diet is a wise decision. When it comes to diet, many people choose to follow the direction of the American Dietetic Association. In its position paper on vegetarianism, the organization makes it clear that even if you wanted to become a strict vegetarian, you could do so confidently by eating from a wide range of non-animal foods.[162] If the journey all the way to vegetarianism is safe, obviously only cutting back would pose no problem.

Comments on vegetarianism from places where not even ten years ago you would never have expected to hear them are beginning to surface. Where do you think the following statement comes from?

> Although we think we are one, and we act as if we are one, human
> beings are not natural carnivores. When we kill animals to eat them,

they wind up killing us because their flesh was never intended for human beings who are natural herbivores.[163]

Are these the words of someone clinging to the "sixties"? Are they the words of the head of one of the many animal rights groups in America? Wrong on both counts. They are the words of Dr. William C. Roberts, professor of clinical medicine at Georgetown University and chief cardiology pathologist for the National Institutes of Health. He also happens to be the editor-in-chief of the *American Journal of Cardiology*, a conservative, mainstream medical journal. The above statement appeared in an editorial in that journal and it should prompt us to wonder how we could have ever been so misled.

Sometimes change is difficult. It certainly is when the change runs counter to what we have been used to doing for years, *decades*, but the change of reducing the overall amount of animal products in your diet can have only one long-term effect: a longer, healthier, disease-free life. That is why one of the principles of CARE deals with how to accomplish this in the most effective and convenient way possible (see Part Two).

As discussed in Chapter 6, the lymph system plays an invaluable role in the prevention of all disease. That being so, make the following two things priorities. First, strive to do whatever you can to reduce the burden on your lymph system; and second, strive to do whatever you can to optimize the lymph system's functionability.

As regards the first point, one of the major, basic functions of the lymph system is to absorb fats from the digestive tract.[164] The more fat you eat, the harder your lymph system has to work, the more clogged it becomes, and the less energy it has for the cleansing and removal of wastes. It is no accident that a primary function of the lymph system is to remove fat, so the less it has to remove, the better.

As regards the second point, there is something you can do to directly assist and support your lymph system's optimum operation and effectiveness. It is an ingredient that is indispensable to a healthy lifestyle and imperative for the activities of the lymph system. That ingredient is, of course, exercise—the subject of the next chapter.

Exercise

Hold it! Before you pass up this chapter with something like, "Yeah, yeah, I should exercise. I know. I'll read this later," just read a little of it now, please. Later has a funny way of turning into never, and I promise not to beat you over the head with a celebrity workout tape. I know darn good and well that if you're not exercising, one more admonishment that you'd better start is probably not going to get you out huffing and puffing.

So what I'd like to do is tell you something about exercising that you are probably not aware of and offer you such a simple, effective means of supplying your exercising needs, that you just *couldn't* stay sedentary. Besides, I could hardly write a book on health care and *not* include exercise. The relationship between a healthy life and regular exercise is irrefutable. Consider the fact, for example, that exercisers have an all-cause mortality rate that is less than one-third that of non-exercisers.[165] Moreover, some form of regular physical activity, even if it's a very mild form of activity, is crucial for vibrant health. Here's why: Exercise helps your lymph system function at an optimal level.

Unlike the cardiovascular system, that has at its centre the heart which acts as a pump to keep the flow of blood going, the lymph system has no such pump. But lymph fluid must constantly be flowing throughout the body, in the same way that blood must constantly be flowing throughout the body. Remember, there is three times more lymph fluid in your body than blood. What is it that does for the lymph system what the heart does for the cardiovascular system? Physical activity. *Exercise!*[254] The flow of lymph through the body is also helped by the muscles in the walls of lymph vessels and by respiration (breathing in and out), but the important contribution of exercise cannot be minimized in any way. This information should put the need for regular physical activity in a whole new light.

Most people, whether they exercise or not, are aware of the value of exercise in supporting a healthy lifestyle. One of the most important and convincing studies supporting this fact and reported in the *Journal of the American Medical Association* by a group of highly respected researchers, including exercise guru Dr. Kenneth H. Cooper, studied the exercise habits of more than 13,000 men and women for more than eight years. Their physical fitness was measured by a treadmill exercise task. The study showed that the all-causes death rate of the least fit men was three times that of the most fit men; with women, this rate was five times higher. The data showed that an unfit man could reduce his risk of death from all diseases by nearly 37 percent by becoming fit, and an unfit woman could reduce her risk by about 48 percent![167] Those are figures that are hard to ignore.

Yet, with this and so many other studies proving the life-extending benefits of exercise, at last count, *less than 10 percent of the nation's adults exercise vigorously at least three times a week.*[168] Why not? It's not simply a communication problem, to be sure. Non-exercisers know they need to exercise.

How often have you heard, or even said yourself, "I know I need to exercise, but . . ." Let's face it, there are probably many reasons, physical, emotional, and psychological, that people don't exercise. It's not necessary to delve into all the reasons. What is important is to somehow get those people who are the most seden-tary sufficiently motivated to do at least something.

If you are already doing some form of exercise, no matter how little or how much, that's fine. What I wish to accomplish here is to get those of you doing practically nothing up and moving. You see, it doesn't take that much. There's no reason to feel intimidated. You don't have to join a gym or take aerobics classes. Really, I'm not suggesting you become a world-class athlete. But I will tell you this, and I won't soften what I'm about to say. Are you serious about doing what you can to live a vibrantly healthy life free of the pain, anguish, and suffering disease can wreak? If your answer is yes, and you are serious, and I mean *really* serious, then you must do everything you can to keep your lymph system operating at its highest possible efficiency, and some form of regular physical exercise is a major contributing factor in that effort. Period! There's no way around it: Exercise is the key.

Walking

The one vigorous, physical activity that can bring you all the benefits afforded by exercise, can be done practically anywhere at any time, by nearly anyone, regardless of physical condition, doesn't require elaborate facilities or equipment, is convenient and easy, is walking! According to the National Sporting Goods Manufacturing Association, walking is the fastest-growing participation sport on the continent.[169]

What is it about walking that has captured the interest of between 70 and 100 million people? Probably the single most important factor is that walking produces results in short-term training and in long-term health benefits equal to any other aerobic exercise. Including jogging![170] When you jog, you land with three or four times your body weight. When you walk, you don't leap, you always have one foot on the ground and, therefore, land with only 1 to $1\frac{1}{2}$ times your body weight. As joggers age, they increasingly experience knee, ankle, and back injuries. Walking is far easier on the joints and bones.

All around the world, walking has been a popular and recognized means of keeping fit. At the turn of the twentieth century, in the United States, one of the most gruelling, competitive events of the day was the "six day race." Edward Payson Weston was, arguably, the most popular walking champion of the day. He would regularly cover more than 400 miles in those competitions and his fans lined the route and cheered him on all the way. In 1904, at age 71, he walked across the United States from San Francisco to New York in 104 days, walking on average over 40 miles a day. Mr.

Weston passed away at age 91, leaving the legacy of the "evening constitutional" as a part of the American way of life.[171]

At that same time, Theodore Roosevelt, the president of the United States, was considered to be one of the fittest presidents ever. Vigorous exercise helped him overcome serious childhood health problems, and he exercised regularly and encouraged exercise throughout his life. In 1909, at the end of his presidency, he demonstrated his physical fitness by walking 50 miles in three days.[172]

At the beginning of the twentieth century, heart attacks became increasingly prevalent. This devastating health problem was so thoroughly misunderstood that doctors actually thought physical activity made the heart wear out and, astonishingly, discouraged heart attack victims from physical activity.[173] Those afflicted were told to rest and remain inactive, the very worst possible advice. The heart, which is a muscle, requires regular exercise to keep it strong and make it stronger. But more than 50 years would pass before this understanding would take hold.

In 1924, Dr. Paul Dudley White founded the American Heart Association and is considered to be the "father of American cardiology." He stunned his colleagues by saying that not only was walking *not* dangerous, it was, in fact, absolutely beneficial and people should be encouraged to take daily walks. This statement was made at a time when cardiology patients were forced to lie flat on their backs with as little movement as possible for six weeks! Doctors theorized that it would take that long for the heart to heal.

This bed-rest theory was disputed by Dr. White because he noticed too many complications from such prolonged inactivity. After all, the human body is beautifully designed for activity and does not deal well with six weeks of forced inactivity. Another three decades would pass before changes were actually made in medical treatment for heart attack patients. Dr. White, of course, was already encouraging his patients to get out of bed and start a program of walking.

Probably the most well-known studies on risk factors involved in heart disease are the Framingham studies started in the 1950s in Framingham, Massachusetts. There, researchers studied approximately 10,000 people for more than 30 years and amassed a wealth of information that began to reveal the important role of activity in preventing heart disease. Many more studies have been subsequently conducted and today the inescapable fact is that the need for regular physical activity to ensure good health and prevent heart disease, the country's number-one killer, is acknowledged by virtually everyone. After all, as one study conducted by the Center for Disease Control, Atlanta, Georgia, revealed, people who do not exercise have twice the risk of developing heart disease as those who do.[174] In this regard, walking has emerged as one of the most convenient exercises to guarantee good health.

Walking is the ideal aerobic exercise, one that oxygenates the blood which, in turn, supplies oxygen to all cells of the body. The number-one prerequisite of life is air. Weeks can go by without food, days without water, but only a few minutes without air before you die. The literal meaning of the word "aerobic" is "in the presence of air." The heart, lungs, and blood vessels work in harmony to carry this life-giving oxygen to every part of the body.

When you walk, you use your body's large muscles, which allow the entire aerobic mechanism of your body to work harder than when you are at rest. If this exercise is done consistently, over time, the system becomes stronger and ever more efficient and capable of performing the functions it was designed to perform. Over a lifetime, walking is the best possible means of reducing the risk of cardiovascular disease. Add to that the fact that walking will stimulate the activity of your lymph system, and you have a real winner in this exercise.

Truly exciting and encouraging are the recent studies showing that even the most moderate, unstructured walking program will reap substantial benefits.[175] Of course, common sense should tell you that the more you do, the more vigorously, the more benefit you will enjoy. But the good news, the *great* news, is that even low levels of activity are beneficial. For example, in one of the first clinical studies of its kind, as reported in the *Journal of the American Medical Association*, it was shown that regular hour-long strolls will reduce a woman's risk of heart disease.[176] Mile for mile, walking is actually the best fat burner.[177] Walking four miles burns more fat than running the same distance in less time![178] An editorial in the same journal points out that a brisk 20-minute walk three times a week would produce many benefits.[179] Dr. James Gavin, author of *The Exercise Habit*, maintains that, "Ten minutes of extra activity per day can reduce an individual's risk of heart disease by 80%."[180]

Considering the subject of this book, and this chapter, imagine my excitement when I was looking through the *New York Times* one morning and the following headline jumped off the page: Study Links Exercise To Drop In Breast Cancer. The results of the study were published in the *Journal of the National Cancer Institute* and stated: "A thorough new study has found that moderate but regular physical activity can reduce a woman's risk of developing premenopausal breast cancer by as much as 60%.[181] Sixty percent! In a discussion of the study on the "NBC Network News," it was stated that "the researchers are saying that exercise is the most important step a woman can take to reduce her risk of breast cancer."[182]

This study and these comments were made in September 1994. In May 1997 there was yet another major study in the *New England Journal of Medicine* that followed 25,000 women for 14 years. The study stated the following: "Compared with sedentary women, those who exercised at least four hours a week had a 37% lower risk of developing breast cancer, and the more women exercised, the less likely they were to develop the disease." The executive director of the Center for Cancer Prevention at Harvard University said, "This is a new, quite powerful piece of evidence."[183] There simply is no longer any reason not to do *some* walking.

Get Walking!

I suggest a program of walking that is very unstructured, quite easy and will satisfy your body's need for exercise and support your efforts to achieve vibrant health. This is not a contest, you are not being graded on your effort, and no one will be "looking over your shoulder" to check up on you. This is your chance to do what you know in your heart is so important, without pressure and without guilt. You do as much or as little as you choose for your own comfort. Anything helps!

All that is required is an agreement with yourself that you *will* do something. Your goal should be to build up to a 30- to 45-minute easy walk three or four times a week, *at your own pace.* That's it! Perhaps in the beginning you will find it easier if you make your walks functional. Turn them into an errand to pick up some lightweight odds and ends at the store or to mail a letter. Sometimes getting used to walking is easier if you have a purpose and destination.

There are other ways to integrate walking into your lifestyle. On occasion, you can leave early enough for work in the morning to park a mile or so from your place of employment and walk the rest of the way. That walk, coupled with the return walk at the end of the day, will not only fulfil your daily exercise requirement but will also allow you to feel invigorated when you arrive at work and perked up when you return home. Or you can incorporate a walk into your lunch routine, especially during the winter, when extreme cold in the morning and darkness after work might keep you indoors.

In addition, whenever you can, walk upstairs instead of taking an elevator. Stair-climbing is an excellent workout that also helps keep your legs in good shape, and you will benefit from even brief stair-climbing efforts. Drive to a park for the sole purpose of taking a walk in fresh air and pleasant surroundings. Any way or at any time that you can walk, no matter how much or how little, do it! It all adds up physically, and psychologically the feeling of accomplishment will be immeasurably worthwhile.

Walking Hints

To optimize your results, consider the following hints to make your walking experience the most enjoyable and productive it can possibly be:

1) At the top of the list, and possibly the most important factor for successful walking, is wearing the proper footwear. Contrary to what many people believe, walking is not merely running at a slower speed. The motion of walking is very different from that

of running. The transfer of weight is not at all the same. It's a much slower rolling motion versus landing on your heel quickly, with more weight. Running shoes need to be softer; walking shoes need to be firmer. Just as running, tennis, soccer, and other sports require specifically designed shoes, so does walking. Take your walking seriously, and please buy the proper shoes! Cutting corners will be a big mistake. *This is very important!* Purchase a good pair, of which there are many brands, and they will pay for themselves many times over in comfort, enjoyment, and benefits.

I have found walking shoes made by ASICS to be the best. Although they are relatively new to the walking market, ASICS' shoes are the most innovative. Not only are these shoes particularly comfortable, they also have an exclusive, patented gel system in the soles and heels that make them unique.

What really sold me on the uniqueness and efficacy of ASICS shoes was the experience of the great basketball hall-of-famer Rick Barry. Between his playing days and several operations on his knees, Rick was left with absolutely no cartilage in his knees. None, just bone against bone. He is very athletic; he plays basketball and tennis, and enjoys jogging. Due to the absence of cartilage in his knees, however, he could only engage in his favourite activities for very short periods of time and even that caused him considerable pain, requiring rest and ice packs. He told me that he had resigned himself to the fact that he was not going to be able to be as physically active as he would like. But then along came the ASICS gel shoes and Rick can now play for hours without discomfort or the need for ice packs.

The gel in ASICS shoes disburses vertical impact into a horizontal plane, absorbs shock, and dissipates vibration. No pain. No damage. Amazing, and in Rick Barry's words, "a real miracle" for him.

2) Walk either in the early morning or late afternoon. Walking in the heat of the day is not a good idea because you not only absorb the heat directly from the sun, but also from the pavement. Heat also tends to tire you out faster. It has been shown

that when exercise is performed in the morning, 75 percent of participants stick with it versus 75 percent who drop it when exercise is scheduled for any other time of day.[184]

3) Don't push it. Take it easy at first. Start slowly and build up strength, especially if you have not been exercising regularly. Perhaps the first week or two, or the first month, you may not even go for 30 minutes or only walk twice a week. You don't have to prove anything to anyone. Remember, less than 10 percent of the nation's adults exercise vigorously three times a week!

The mere fact that you're doing it at all puts you in a very elite group, and you are to be commended. Your muscles are there to be used. It will not take long before they accustom themselves to the new activity and normalize. Yes, you may feel sore muscles at first, but this is a "good" soreness. You are using muscles that have been deprived of activity and are being "broken in," so to speak. Warm baths do wonders to alleviate initial strain.

4) If it is windy out, start your walk with the wind in your face and return with it at your back. This prevents your getting a chill as a result of the perspiration you've worked up.

5) Swing your arms. This helps circulate the blood and strengthen the heart. Ever notice how long music conductors live? When I hear of a music conductor passing away, he's usually in his eighties or nineties. Music conductors spend their lives swinging their arms, and heart disease is rare amongst them.*

6) It is best if there is no food in your stomach when you are exercising. Digesting demands energy and detracts from your ability to exercise well. The exception is fruit, which requires very little energy to digest.

---

*Leonard Bernstein died in his sixties a few years ago, but he was hopelessly addicted to cigarettes, which killed him.

7) Dehydration can be a real problem in any form of exercise. You must drink water to replenish yourself. Your body is approximately 70 percent water and, as a normal course of events, you lose about 2 to $2\frac{1}{2}$ quarts a day. That can go to 4 quarts if you exercise. Do yourself a favour, drink water, not soda, Gatorade, or any of the other fluids that contain chemical substances that undermine health. Drink a glass of water before you walk and after you finish your walk. Drink more if you feel the need. It would be better to take in a little more than you need than not to take in enough.

8) Stretching is an excellent practice to develop before and after walking. Stretching can prepare muscles for exercise, relieve stiffness, increase the range of motion of your muscles, and prevent injuries. Stretching should be performed very slowly and should never go to the point of causing pain. Stretching can itself be of enormous benefit, and there are dozens of stretches. Here are three to try:

- Stretch your hamstrings on the back of your legs by bending over and touching your toes. If you can't touch your toes, just go as far as you can. Hold it for 15 to 20 seconds and come back up. As far as you can go is fine. By doing this stretch regularly, you will be amazed at how soon you will be able to touch your toes with ease.
- Stretch your thighs by holding on to something for support with your left hand while, with your right hand, you pull your right foot up behind you towards your lower back. Then reverse.
- Stretch your calves by standing on the edge of a stair with only the front half of your foot on the stair, then sink your weight down on your heel.

Each of these three stretches can be repeated. You can't stretch too much, so do as much as you like.

One of the most attractive aspects of walking is the convenience of it. You can walk anywhere—on the street, around your house, near your office, in the woods, park, or country trails. When you're on vacation, at work, no matter where you are, with no more than a good pair of walking shoes, you're always able to take advantage of this life-extending practice. Sometimes, depending upon where you live, it may be too hot or too cold to walk. If you're committed, even this obstacle can be overcome. Over the last decade or so, more and more people have been walking in shopping malls. Most malls open their doors quite early, hours before the stores are open. The temperature is always just right. The walking surface is flat and smooth, and malls are well lit and safe. It's almost as if they were *designed* for walking.

Benefits of Walking

Any way you look at it, walking is an enormously positive activity and can influence your life in many positive ways. The list of benefits you can reap from walking is definitely impressive. Consider:

1) It helps increase the strength and efficiency of your heart and muscles.[185]
2) A recent study indicates that walking lowers cholesterol.[186]
3) Walking, like other exercises, increases both energy level and stamina.[187]
4) Walking actually increases bone mass.[188] Bones, like muscles, become stronger with regular exercise. It has been well established that the risk of osteoporosis is lowered with regular exercise.
5) Overall strength, flexibility, and balance are improved.[189]
6) Together with a healthy diet, walking can be instrumental in helping you lose weight. A 45-minute walk every other day for a year can burn 18 pounds of fat.[190]
7) According to Dr. James Rippe, walking reduces the condition associated with hypertension (high blood pressure) and aids diabetics.[191]
8) Walking, like other exercise, promotes better sleep.[192]
9) One study at a medical centre in Salt Lake City showed that mild exercise such as walking after eating moved food through the stomach more quickly, helping to relieve minor indigestion.[193]

10) A study at Appalachian State University showed that women who walked 45 minutes a day recovered twice as fast from colds as women who did not exercise.[194]

11) According to the Berkeley Wellness Letter, walking is the perfect exercise for promoting a healthy back.[195]

12) Walking relieves stress. Researchers at the Center for Health and Fitness at the University of Massachusetts found that people who took a 40-minute, brisk walk, experienced a 14 percent average drop in anxiety levels. Walks are part of the therapy at the Betty Ford Center for Drug and Alcohol Rehabilitation.[196]

13) A study at the Exercise, Physiology and Human Performance Laboratory at the University of California at San Diego showed that healthy men age 35 to 65 who started a regular exercise program hugged and kissed their wives more often and had more sexual intercourse and more orgasms than those who did not exercise.[197]

14) A growth hormone administered to people over the age of 60 reduces fat, increases bone mass, improves skin condition and reverses many other apparent symptoms of aging. The artificial hormone is very expensive and has serious side effects, but walking as little as 20 minutes a day has been shown to stimulate this growth hormone production.[198]

15) Walking lowers blood pressure.[199]

16) Walking reduces the risk of colon cancer.[200]

17) Walking boosts the defence system.[201]

18) Walking stimulates the lymph system, which, as you have learned, is essential in the prevention of breast cancer.

One of the greatest rewards from a program of regular exercise such as walking is the mental and emotional lift it provides that spills over into the other areas of your life.

We all know the importance of exercise, and when we don't do any, not only do we suffer physiologically, we also suffer psychologically. Somewhere inside, we berate ourselves for not doing the right thing. That all changes when you start to walk. Instead of having a negative feeling every time you are reminded that you don't exercise sufficiently, you feel a surge of pride that you do. Your level of self-esteem grows steadily and a positive message resounds through you instead of a negative one. You start to exude happiness and healthfulness because you truly *are* happier and healthier. On every possible level, you are improving your health. The richest person in the world can't buy this feeling of well-being for any amount of money because its value transcends money. You can have this feeling starting right now for the price of a pair of shoes. Make the effort. You're worth it!

With walking or any other form of exercise, consistency is the key. Do it at a pace that suits you and doesn't put pressure on you. Don't let it be something that hangs over you as a kind of onerous responsibility. If you start slowly and engage in it moderately, walking will gradually become as normal and natural a part of your life as putting on clothes in the morning. You'll look forward to it. You'll miss it if you don't do it. Discover walking. Make it a part of your life, and you will never regret it.

Other Exercise

There are two other noteworthy ways in which you can assist the stimulation of your lymph system. The first is a technique called Lymphatic Drainage Massage. Seek out a qualified massage therapist familiar with this technique. There are several areas of the body, on the legs, arms, torso, and neck that can be massaged to directly assist the lymph system in its effort to cleanse the body.

The second approach is Rebounding, discussed in great detail in *Fit For Life II*. Rebounders, or "mini-trampolines" as they are commonly called, can be purchased very inexpensively. I have seen perfectly adequate ones for around $20. Considering the extent to which Rebounding can help you prevent cancer, that's the greatest deal on Earth.

Rebounding is extremely easy. All it calls for is a slight up-and-down bounce, which subjects the body to a change in velocity and direction twice with each jump. At the bottom of the bounce, all the one-way valves of the lymph system are closed because of the pressure above them. At the top of the bounce, the valves are open, allowing the lymph to flow up as the body starts down. Every valve opens at the same time, allowing and stimulating the flow of lymph.[202] As little as five or six minutes a day can be of immeasurable value.

Anything you can do to assist your lymph system should be done. A little effort goes a long way.

Start now! Your body will thank you with renewed, good health.

Part Two

....

THE CARE PROGRAM

9

An Introduction to "CARE"

No matter how great-sounding a program for disease prevention is, no matter how convincing the argument to follow it is, no matter how promising the results will be if it is followed, if there is not a way to easily implement it and see results, all the swell-sounding promises are for naught. For decades, there have been numerous admonitions telling us over and over again *what* we have to do, and *why*, to experience the highest level of health. And although knowing what and why is of extreme importance, both are unhelpful, if not useless, unless accompanied by the how that will bring about the desired results.

The CARE program *is* the new path to vibrant health! At the heart of this approach are three principles which, if implemented regularly, will quickly prove their worthiness. Your health will change for the better and the evidence of this bold statement will make itself apparent in no uncertain terms. You will *feel* better, you will *look* better, and your lymph system will be clean and operating at a highly efficient level.

Bear in mind, however, that there are no magic formulas, although sometimes when the body is cleansed of wastes and toxins the positive results do appear to be miraculous. But your body automatically brings about these "miracles" when you make the changes to facilitate them. As I said earlier, for change to occur, changes must be made. It's like the old saying goes: "If there is no change, then there is no change." We are talking about simple logic here. If you want your health to be different from what it has been, then *there must be some changes made* to make that a reality.

More often than not, I have found that people wanting change in their lives put far too much pressure on *themselves*, especially when the change calls for dietary modifications. For some reason, people put themselves in an "all-or-nothing" mode, diving into new behaviours with great resolve, restricting themselves too severely and burning themselves out in a few weeks, quickly reverting to the old habits that weren't working. The only thing different in their lives is some new guilt to deal with from not succeeding in this latest fling with health.

Some of you may conform to the above scenario when you try to apply the three principles that are set out on the following pages. So before going any further, let me try to prevent as many of you as possible from falling into this trap: *These principles are guidelines to help you, not edicts to hinder you. They are tools to assist you, not rules to enslave you.*

Your effort to improve your health and prevent becoming sick needn't be a stress-filled journey. It can be a joyous one. *This is not a race! The prize does not go to the one who gets there first. The prize goes to all who join the race! That is because the prize is the journey itself!* It's not how *fast* you travel, it's that you even make the trip at all. You have time. More time than you need. You see, even if you make use of the three CARE principles in a very conservative way until you are comfortable with them and they become an integral part of your lifestyle, you will have changed your *direction*, and in so doing, disease will become less and less of a possibility in your life. Rather than stagnating or becoming a little unhealthier every day, allowing the disease process to progress, you will, with each passing day, know what it means to become a little healthier. *Direction is everything. Speed is nothing.*

Imagine you and your family pulling through the entrance gate at Yellowstone National Park. You could spend a week taking in the beauty of this awe-inspiring national treasure and still not see it all. Or you could race through it in half a day as though you were being chased by hungry bears. In either case, you could boast to your friends, "Yeah, we did Yellowstone." But which trip do you do? Which trip do you think would be most uplifting? The one in which you leisurely drink in the natural beauty that feeds your spirit and soul, or the one in which you screech through at breakneck speed throwing yourself and everyone with you into a panic of apprehension?

The principles I am about to share with you should not be viewed as a forced march, but rather as a light along your path. When it is convenient and comfortable to use them, do so. When it is not, don't. Know that to whatever degree you use these principles, however often you choose to implement them, that will be right for you, and they will serve you exactly as well as they will serve those who embrace them to a fuller or even to a lesser degree than you. It's always better to do a little less at first and then do more as you start to see results than to try to do too much and have to cut back and feel as though you failed.

One thing you can count on if you use the three CARE principles: they will work! I have seen them do so for many people for many years. I'm one of them. So ready is your body, so well equipped and capable is it to acquire and maintain a consistent level of vibrant health when given the opportunity, that even with the most moderate adherence to these principles, you will start to experience the benefits that they can so effectively bring about.

The Healing Power of the Body

Throughout the book I have praised the nearly unfathomable magnificence and intelligence of the human body. I wish to return to this for just a moment before presenting the CARE principles. Earlier, I made the point that all of the endless activities of the body are sourced and monitored by the brain. It's amazing when you think about the fact that all of the incredible advances made by the human species, from electricity to air travel, from automobiles to computers, all had their beginnings in the brain, and *we only use about 10 to 15 percent of our brain*. Wow! So, what is the remaining 85 to 90 percent of this spectacular gem of creation doing? You can be sure it's not merely there to take up space in our skulls.

The body's—the brain's—number-one priority at any and every given moment, is self-preservation. If the part of the brain used to figure out how to go to the moon at 17,000 miles per hour, play hopscotch, and come back is so small, can you even begin to imagine the power working for your well-being in the vast majority of your brain? Awesome! Your body will *never* give up on you. All you have to do is not stand in its way. In other words, all you have to do to benefit from its unparalleled power is support its natural inclination to seek out and maintain its highest level of health possible. The three principles of CARE, which are the subject of the next three chapters, provide that support.

Naturally, you want some kind of proof that these principles will indeed do what I claim. I could tell you about plenty of people who use the three CARE principles and have not developed cancer, but someone could easily say, "Well, how do you know it was the three principles that prevented it? Maybe it was because they liked to garden, or because they took vitamins, or because of any number of other activities they participated in." So, about the only proof I can offer is how the principles fare in either stopping, reversing, or banishing cancer once it has taken hold.

Case Study

Over the years I have received hundreds of thousands of letters from people who have made truly remarkable recoveries in their health. I want to share with you a most extraordinary story that clearly demonstrates the indomitable spirit of one woman and the unparalleled healing ability of the human body. Her name is Anne Frahm. She wrote a book about her experiences. Here is her story.

Anne Frahm is a 40-year-old wife and mother of two. In her mid-thirties she started to experience an excruciating, unrelenting pain between her shoulder blades. X-rays showed "hot spots" on the bones of her shoulder which her doctor diagnosed as bursitis. The doctor also told her that her condition was being complicated by a kidney infection.

She was given cortisone shots, and was told to apply daily ice packs to her shoulder. She was also given heavy doses of antibiotics both orally and intravenously for the kidney infection. All that happened was that the pain became progressively worse. In fact, it became so bad that she could not roll over in bed or even hug her own children without experiencing unbearable pain.

This situation went on for seven months, at which time she went to a hospital emergency room to seek another doctor's opinion. This doctor conferred with Mrs. Frahm's family doctor and they wondered if all this pain wasn't really just in her head. She was given a shot of muscle relaxant and a prescription for Valium, and sent home.

Still in pain, she demanded more definitive answers of her doctor. She was sent for a CAT scan. A young doctor came into her room with the results and told her she had advanced breast cancer to such a degree that she had to have a mastectomy the very next day! When she asked how bad it was, the doctor answered, "I'm not going to pull any punches, most people who have cancer so advanced die within two years."

It wasn't only hearing that she had breast cancer that so shocked her, it was also the fact that several months before the pain even began she found a small lump in her breast during a self-examination. Since her grandmother had died of breast cancer and her mother had had both breasts removed because of ongoing, troubling cysts in her breasts, Anne had wasted no time in getting a mammogram. She was told that there were indeed two tiny lumps but they were benign, noncancerous. An additional ultrasound test also confirmed that they were benign. The doctor said, "Nope, no cancer here."

Not only *were* they cancerous, but the cancer had spread and tumours were found covering her skull, shoulder, ribs, pelvis, and up and down her spine.

Her breast was removed along with a tumour that was beneath it, the size of her entire breast. For the next year and a half her body was subjected to varied treatments including high doses of chemotherapy and radiation. She went bald, developed severe pneumonia, and her skin from head to toe broke out into itchy, red splotches.

After all of her pain and suffering from the cancer, the chemotherapy, and the radiation, she was told that the cancer was steadily progressing and that her situation was becoming ever worse. She was told that her last possible hope was a bone marrow transplant. I don't even want to begin to tell you what a horrendous experience such a procedure is. Suffice it to say that it is something you never want to experience.

A couple of months after the bone marrow transplant, monitoring of her white blood cell count indicated that there was still a lot of cancer in her bone marrow. Further chemotherapy was out of the question, as it would have killed her outright.

When she inquired about a new experimental drug being tested on some patients to stimulate the growth of white blood cells, she was given the most stunning, mind-numbing response imaginable: Since there was only a limited amount of the drug available, it had to be held in reserve for patients with a more favourable chance of survival. Sorry!

With sadness and regret, she was sent home to die.

It is impossible to read Anne's account of her husband, her children, and herself huddled together, mourning her impending death, without weeping.

But Anne Frahm did not know the meaning of the words "give up." They weren't in her vocabulary. She loved her family and her life and was not ready to leave. Her last-ditch effort was to turn to a nutritionist for help. She was counselled, given books to read, put on a very strict, detoxifying diet, and never lost her positive attitude. She knew she was going to win. A mere five weeks later, in the most remarkable instance of self-healing I have ever encountered, not even the slightest trace of cancer could be found in her body. It was gone! Her doctor, noticeably flabbergasted, said, "When you returned from the transplant with cancer in your marrow, I honestly thought you were doomed!"

As word of Anne's miraculous recovery spread and doctors and laypeople alike kept contacting her to hear her story, she decided to put it all down in a book. That book is called *A Cancer Battle Plan*, and it was published in 1993.

Before I heard of either Anne, or her book, she wrote me a letter and sent me a picture of herself. Looking at her smiling face and her full head of lush, black hair filled me with joy, as did her letter, which read:

> Dear Harvey,
>
> Thank you! Thank you! Thank you! You have helped save the life of this 40-year-old wife and mother—me! Four years ago I was dying of cancer. After $1\frac{1}{2}$ years of chemotherapy, radiation, surgery and even a bone marrow transplant, nothing worked and I was sent home to die. Instead, I consulted a nutritionist. FIVE WEEKS later at my next checkup, tests revealed NO TRACE of cancer in my body!! I've been cancer free and HEALTHY for four years!*
>
> One of the first books my nutritionist recommended was FIT FOR LIFE. The simple, common sense approach you use helped me and my husband form a basis of understanding that helped me overcome cancer. THANK YOU for standing up in the face of overwhelming opposition to tell the truth!!
>
> Your greatest fan,
>
> Anne Frahm

In order to overcome this severely advanced cancer, Anne detoxified her body through dietary regimentation (Principle One in the CARE program); entirely removed animal products from her diet (variation of Principle Two); and filled her mind with positiveness and prayer (Principle Three). The implications of this should be blindingly obvious to anyone interested in preventing cancer. If this woman, who was brought to death's door with no hope of survival, was able to use information similar to the information contained in this book to reverse and banish the cancer from her body, do you fully realize the power and ability you have to prevent cancer from ever developing in the first place? I hope you do. I sincerely hope you see the control over your health the concepts in this book give you. *If cancer can be reversed, it can be prevented.* You *can* prevent cancer! You can live in vibrant health!

---

*As of this writing, it has been nine years of cancer-free health for Anne.

Now I want to ask you a question—a question that you need to ask of yourself. What are you willing to do to support your body's effort to attain the highest level of health available to you? Knowing that your body, with the brain at its helm, is tirelessly working for you, doing everything and anything it can to keep you in health, are you willing to also make an effort to help? Or, are you of a mind that you want to just go your merry way and leave it all up to fate? I think when you see how simple the three CARE principles are and how easy they are to incorporate into your lifestyle, your answer will be a resounding, *"I'm ready to do my part!"* Well . . . turn the page and I'll show you how you can do exactly that.

10

The First Principle: Periodic Mono-Dieting

All three CARE principles, each working in concert with one another, are important, and all will help you immensely in your effort to live a life free of pain and disease, which is the automatic result of living a lifestyle that prevents cancer. But the first principle, *periodic mono-dieting*, if practised intelligently, will do more to cleanse and strengthen your lymph system than any other action you could take besides fasting.*

More than any other factor, periodic mono-dieting is, without question, responsible for my recaptured health and my continued well-being. I have benefited immeasurably from the practice for more than 25 years and continue to reap the rewards of its effectiveness in helping me maintain the level of health I enjoy. The beauty of periodic mono-dieting is its simplicity. *Anyone* can make use of this tool to bring about an immediate improvement in health and to ensure long-term health. It is the key element in preventing ill health while nurturing vibrant health.

---

*The subject of fasting is far too complex and deserves far more space than can be allotted here. Suffice it to say, however, that there is no health routine that is more thorough, effective, or beneficial than a properly conducted fast, and no other area of healing that is more neglected, misunderstood, or unfairly maligned. Those who call fasting and starvation the same thing are sorely ignorant of the physiology of the human body. It would be like calling swimming and drowning the same thing.

What Is Periodic Mono-dieting?

Periodic mono-dieting is the eating of fresh fruits and/or vegetables and their juices, uncooked, for a length of time that ranges from one day to several weeks. Before explaining the rationale of mono-dieting and the benefits that can be expected from it, let me give you three examples of possible mono-diets.

1) Drinking only fresh fruit and vegetable juice for *1 to 3 days*.
2) Drinking only fresh fruit and vegetable juices and eating whole fruits and vegetables for *3 to 5 days*.
3) Drinking only fresh fruit and vegetable juices and eating only fresh fruits and vegetables and salads for *1 day to a week to 10 days*.

In other words, periodic mono-dieting is the taking of any combination of any raw, fresh food or juice for whatever length of time you wish.

The reason that all food during a mono-diet must be in its natural, raw state is quite simple, and crucial to the cleansing of the lymph system.

Purposes of Mono-dieting

The purpose of mono-dieting is twofold. The first purpose is to use as little energy as possible on digestion so that energy can be freed up and directed toward the cleansing and rejuvenation of the lymph system. The second purpose of mono-dieting is to obtain the maximum amount of fuel and nutrients from the food being eaten. Raw food fulfils these two purposes of mono-dieting better than cooked or processed food. Raw food demands less energy to digest and provides the most nutrients because it is in its purest state, its natural state. And *any* cooking of food removes or denatures *some* nutrients. Bear in mind that human beings are the only species that eats cooked food, and humans lead all species in degenerative diseases. Obviously our superior thinking and reasoning abilities have not served us in this area.

Periodic mono-dieting should not be used as a diet in a crisis to empty out a swollen lymph gland or to deal with an existing cancer, although in both instances the approach can be beneficial. To gain the greatest benefit from periodic mono-dieting, *make it a regular part of your lifestyle and use it as a means of long-term prevention and long-term wellness.* Remember: the extent to which you use periodic mono-dieting is up to you; there are an unlimited number of ways to use it, and there are no specifically prescribed regimens. Some people have an all-juice or all-fruit day once a week. Some eat only raw food one day a week. Some have three straight raw days every month. Author and lecturer Dr. Gabriel Cousens suggests that every six months you drink only fresh juices for a week.

The object of periodic mono-dieting is, of course, to *use it!* If you must discipline yourself by marking on your calendar exactly when you are going to mono-diet for a day or three days or five days or a week, then do it. Or if you wake up one morning and just feel like only having juice that day, then that's your day. Mono-dieting is a flexible tool; it's regimented only if you function better that way.

If I seem to be harping on this one aspect it's because whenever food is discussed, people tend to look for restrictive rules they must follow as punishment for past dietary indiscretions. I encourage you to cultivate a different viewpoint. See periodic mono-dieting as a dynamic and integral part of your lifestyle that will bring you to a state of vibrant health and keep you there.

With periodic mono-dieting, the eating experience itself also becomes much more liberating. Moreover, one of the most rewarding results of mono-dieting, besides preventing disease, is the incredible surge of energy and well-being it produces. You will feel renewed and positive, and this feeling will spill over into every area of your life. Once you incorporate mono-dieting into your life, you never abandon it. Even if you mono-diet only three days a year, you never get it out of your mind. You will look forward to mono-dieting with great anticipation *because periodic mono-dieting is not a punishment, it is a joy!*

Throughout the book I have made the point that the traditional approach to healing is all involved with after-the-fact treatment. But, the only way to *prevent* disease depends entirely upon what you do *before* such treatment is necessary. Periodic mono-dieting is the cornerstone of a vibrant, healthy life.

When I embarked on my journey down the path to health, mono-dieting proved to be invaluable. At a time of desperate need, it gave me my first glimpse of how good I *could* feel. After starting with short mono-diets of one, two, and three days, as my health steadily improved I began increasing their duration until I was going ten days or two weeks, two or three times a year. My health problems dramatically improved, and I am convinced that periodic mono-dieting was the major reason for my recovery. To this day, it remains my most important tool for health maintenance.

The rationale behind periodic mono-dieting is simple as simple can be. The message of this book is that you can take charge of your health by cleansing the body of wastes and toxins. The means by which that is accomplished is to CARE—Cleanse And Rejuvenate Energetically. Periodic mono-dieting specifically and dramatically does just that. It greatly facilitates cleansing and skyrockets energy levels. And let's face it. Energy is everything. Without it, nothing is possible and nothing happens. A car without fuel goes nowhere; neither does a body without energy.

Freeing Up the Digestive System

There is no way on earth to discuss energy and energy levels without discussing digestion. When you take into account the full extent of the digestive activities involved in taking in food, processing it, and extracting nutrients and delivering them to the cells, the elimination of wastes and all the interactions of the organs, stomach, intestines, pancreas, liver, and kidneys, and the metabolic processes that turn food into blood, muscle, and bone, it is no wonder that the digestive process takes such an enormous amount of energy.

There is precious little you can do that requires more energy than digestion. You likely have evidence of this fact. After eating a big meal of many kinds of foods, for example, which do you look for, a mountain to climb or a sofa to climb onto? Knowing the extreme importance of energy to the cleansing process, what better place to free some up than from the vast amount required for digestion.

There are two ways to free up energy from the digestive process for use in other areas of activity. The first is to streamline digestion, have it work more efficiently. In my previous books I introduced the concept of food combining for just that purpose. The second way, the way that has the potential to free up huge amounts of energy, is *to give the digestive tract less to do*. With less work to do, energy that is routinely spent on digestion is automatically used by the body to cleanse itself of waste. The body always works on priorities, and removing impactions and silted-up waste that is interfering with the smooth operation of the system is right up on top of the list. Lymph nodes in the breast or anywhere else in the body will not become swollen with waste if wastes in the body are kept to a minimum.

Thus, by giving the digestive tract less to do, periodic mono-dieting becomes probably the most compelling and potent tool you can use to prevent ever becoming sick. I know what a provocative and bold statement that is. Indeed, many people would immediately demand proof. Therefore, although the greatest proof of all is in the doing, let me offer a couple of exhibits, one scientific, the other observational.

Roy Walford is a medical doctor. He has been a UCLA professor since 1966 and is one of the world's eminent gerontologists. The director of a 16-member research laboratory at UCLA for the study of immunology and the aging process, he was also a member of the White House Conference on Aging and the National Academy of Sciences Committee on Aging, as well as chairman of the National Institute on Aging Task Force in Immunology. He has written five books on immunology and aging and is a world-renowned expert in his field.

Dr. Walford has conducted numerous long-term experiments on aging. Based on the results of those experiments, he is convinced that he is going to live *healthfully* to about age 120—in his opinion the life span within the reach of us all. To be sure, his experiments have not focused on periodic mono-dieting. That is a term I have coined. But his experiments *have* studied the effect of less work for the digestive tract, over a long term, on health and longevity. Dr. Walford's findings fully substantiate my premise that the less work the digestive tract has to do, the healthier you will be and the longer you will live.

Dr. Walford puts his experimental mice on what he refers to as "the restricted diet," which means they fast two days a week. Whereas most mice live about two years, his mice live *more than twice that long*. They not only live much longer, they also show significantly lower rates of heart disease and cancer. Moreover, the small number of mice that *do* develop these diseases, do so at a much later age than mice that are allowed to eat without restrictions. These experiments have consistently shown this improvement in health and longevity. Dr. Walford is in his seventies and vibrantly fit. He fasts two days a week.[203]

The doctor's experiments support what practitioners of Natural Hygiene have known for a long while: that during our lifetime, we will each consume approximately 70 tons of food, and the metabolic activities involved in processing that food, using what is needed and ridding itself of the rest will take more energy from the body over a lifetime than any other activity. Learning to channel some of that energy toward cleansing that will ultimately result in vibrant health is a gift of immeasurable value. That is the gift of periodic mono-dieting.

The practice of giving the digestive tract less work to do in order to free up energy for the healing process is common throughout nature. Anyone who has worked a farm or spent time working with animals has seen this over and over. A horse that is lame will "go off its food," as the expression goes. It will hardly eat. Every stockyard worker knows that when day after day a cow or horse or hog or sheep eats much less food than normal, there is something wrong with the animal. It has *instinctively* reduced its food intake so that its body will have the energy to correct whatever is wrong. Pet owners know that when their dog or cat is sick or injured, the animal either refuses food altogether or hardly eats at all. Even when concerned owners try to entice their sick pets with the most tempting food, the animal will refuse. They find a secluded spot and rest until the body completes its healing work.

A similar reaction can be seen in children. When they are ill, they lose their appetite and won't eat. Parents frequently try to pressure them into eating by saying things like, "Eat this for Mommy," or, "The doctor says you won't get well if you don't eat." But having not been conditioned to believe that they have to eat when they're sick, they merely follow their instincts and refuse food. You have likely noticed a loss of appetite when you don't feel well. That loss of appetite is a natural tendency of the body to free up energy from digestion that is needed for other work. And although mono-dieting is a smart thing to do to speed recovery when you're not feeling well, the most intelligent use of periodic mono-dieting—indeed its prime use and benefit—is as a normal and natural part of your lifestyle, as a means of preventing illness in the first place. It is an approach that will help you shift the focus from illness to wellness!

Scheduling Your Mono-diet

I do not recommend that mono-dieting be used as an emergency measure (the same way you would use a drug) once the effect of continued neglect of the body has finally caught up to you. It should become a *regular part of your healthy lifestyle*, the same as anything else you do on a regular basis. Would you ever seriously consider not dusting and cleaning your house periodically? Would you ever dream of not periodically changing the old oil in your car? Then you mustn't consider not periodically mono-dieting to cleanse your inner body, because a clean inner body is easily as important—in fact, infinitely *more* important—than a clean house or car. Why? Because a clean inner body is what ensures your success in living a healthy life free of pain, ill health, and disease.

The type, length, and frequency of your mono-diets will vary according to your personal needs and wants. As you can see from the three options listed at the beginning of the chapter, some mono-diets comprise only juices, some comprise juices, raw vegetables, and salads. Some will last one day, some will last a week or ten days. You may do one every week, every month, or every three months. *There is no right or wrong involved in mono-dieting.* This point cannot be made too frequently.

How can you find the mono-dieting option that is best for you? The only way to make an intelligent, informed decision on how and when to mono-diet is to experience the benefits. Only then can you decide how and when to mono-diet on a regular basis. While any amount of mono-dieting is beneficial, only on mono-diets of three days and more do you really start to see the power behind this practice. But even a one-day mono-diet will get you started and give you some idea of what to expect from future mono-diets. With practice, it will become clear to you how to best incorporate mono-dieting into your lifestyle. Those whose lives are very orderly and regimented and who like knowing exactly when they are doing what will schedule their mono-diets the same way they schedule other important events in their lives. Those who are more spontaneous will wake up one morning and declare, "I'm doing fruit and juice for three days." One approach is not better than the other.

The following three mono-diets—one day on juice; three days on juice, whole fruit, and smoothies; one week on only uncooked food—are examples only, not dictums. Follow them precisely or modify them to your likes and dislikes.

One day on juice

For one day, intermittently throughout the day, take in only juice, either fruit or vegetable or both. I have found that fruit juices work best for the first part of the day, with vegetable juice in the second part, and more fruit juice in the evening. But any way you want to do it is fine. You can have only fruit juice, only vegetable juice, or have fruit, then vegetable, up and back throughout the day and evening. As long as it's only juice you're taking in, it doesn't matter which you have or when. Also, when having only juice, it's best to consume approximately 10 to 14 ounces about every two hours. Again, that is only a guideline; feel free to alter it to fit your particular needs and desires.

It is important that you consume only fresh juice for 24 hours. Many books on juicing will give you an amazingly wide array of different juice mixes, both fruit and vegetable. Experiment. These drinks are fun and they're delicious. One of my very favourites is apple-celery juice. "Ugh, apple-celery?" Right? Well, if you've never had it, you're in for a big surprise. Apple-celery juice is one of the most refreshing and delicious combinations I've ever had. There's something about that mixture that works. Just try it. You'll be hooked like so many other people I have turned on to it.

If you have read *Fit For Life*, you might be saying, "Hold on there, I thought it was a huge no-no to mix fruit with any other food." That is true, but like everything in life, there are exceptions to the rule. Since it is very high in water content and has no complex starches, proteins, or fats, celery causes no problem when eaten with fruit. But, remember, celery juice is very potent; when combining it with apple juice, make the mixture approximately three-quarters apple juice, one-quarter celery juice.

Three days, juice, whole fruit, and smoothies

On this mono-diet, in addition to fresh juices, fruit, and/or vegetable throughout the day, you also eat pieces of fresh fruit and fruit smoothies. Any fruit is O.K. as long as it is fresh. This includes dates, raisins, and other dry foods so long as they are dried naturally and do not contain sulphur dioxide. Dried fruit is very concentrated, so go light when having them.

Smoothies are extremely easy to make. Put either apple or orange juice (fresh, of course) in a blender, add a frozen banana and any other fruit you like, and presto, a fabulous smoothie. You can add frozen blueberries, strawberries, peaches, or other fruits to the juice and frozen banana. Have fun with these drinks. There are an infinite variety, and they taste incredible. (To freeze bananas, peel them first and put them in the freezer in an airtight plastic container.)

A week on only uncooked food

For a week eat nothing but raw, uncooked food—all fruits and vegetables, their juices, and salads. Have as much juice and whole fruit and vegetables as you like and have a good-sized mixed salad late in the day with a salad dressing of olive oil (which has been associated with a significant reduced risk of cancer),[204] lemon juice, and your favourite herbs and spices. You can have other types of dressing, preferably with a minimum of chemical additives. After you consume the salad, refrain from eating fruit or fruit juice for three hours.

Remember, the above three mono-diets are examples only. You could do any of them for any length of time. Number one could be done for several days or a week, as could number two. Or number three could be done for one day or three. Or you could do number one for a day, number two for a day, and number three for a day. Anything goes when mono-dieting in terms of duration as long as the fruits and vegetables eaten are uncooked.

Tips and Tidbits for Periodic Mono-Dieting

1) For the most effective results of mono-dieting, the juices you drink must be fresh, not pasteurized, canned, or made from concentrate. Drinking other than fresh, unheated juice almost entirely defeats the purpose of mono-dieting. These days, thanks to people like "The Juice Man," home juicers are readily available and are very reasonably priced. When measured against the benefits you will reap, the cost of a home juicer is insignificant. Owning your own juicer is a smart move. You probably have at least one television set in your house. Well, a juicer is a whole lot less expensive and has the added enticement of *helping you prevent disease*. Will your television set do that for you? If you don't own a juicer, buy fresh-squeezed juice. That will do fine.

2) When drinking juice, it is best not to gulp it down. Sip it instead. Drink it slowly so that all of it does not wind up in your stomach at once, which is hard on the body, can cause stomach-aches, and is counterproductive. Swallow one mouthful at a time after the juice has had a chance to mix with your saliva.

3) Fruit has a very interesting nature. Unlike other foods, fruit does not require a lot of time in the stomach for digestion. Most

foods stay in the stomach about three hours. Fruit leaves the stomach in about 20 to 30 minutes. Fruit juice leaves the stomach in less time than that. So, whether you are mono-dieting or not, you should not have fruit or fruit juice for about three hours after eating anything else.

4) If you have never eaten highly cleansing food exclusively for a few days, you may experience a side effect that is uncomfortable but quite valuable: diarrhea. Understand that a certain amount of waste will accumulate in the digestive tract over time. When all of a sudden nothing but juice and fruit, which are over 90 percent water, suddenly goes through your system for a few days, it is as though the digestive tract is being flushed and scrubbed. Diarrhea will rarely last more than 48 hours, and usually will last only 24 hours. Remember, every action of the body is the result of a cause. After consuming only high-water, cleansing foods, diarrhea is not at all surprising. Of course, if you experience diarrhea for longer than 48 hours, for any reason, check with your health care practitioner immediately. But to experience it because you're eating cleansing food is not something to be alarmed about.

5) Because their intake of food is so restricted while mono-dieting, some people think that they may not have enough energy to work or do other things they need to do. Interestingly, the opposite is true. Your energy levels will soar when you mono-diet. Remember that digestion requires huge amounts of energy. Since you are eating only uncooked food, you are eating the foods that require the least amount of energy to digest but that supply a great deal of energy. The one thing more people comment on when they mono-diet is the enormous increase in energy they experience.

6) People who are prone to hypoglycemia (low blood sugar) get a little nervous about eating only fruit or eating very lightly. First, let's examine what low blood sugar is. The brain constantly monitors the bloodstream to make sure there is sufficient sugar and nutrients in the blood. If there is an insufficient supply, the brain sets off an alarm in the form of edginess, discomfort, and sluggishness.

Fruit, whose sugar component of fructose turns to glucose, goes into the bloodstream faster than anything else. So if you have low blood sugar, eating fruit will stop the symptoms of hypoglycemia very quickly. There's nothing better for low blood sugar than fruit. But people with hypoglycemia have to eat quite frequently to stem the symptoms. No problem. When mono-dieting, if you have hypoglycemic tendencies you can eat as frequently as you feel you need to.

7) When mono-dieting on all raw, uncooked food, many people like to eat nuts. It's O.K. to eat raw nuts when mono-dieting; however, you have to be careful. Nuts are an *extremely* concentrated food that is exceedingly easy to overeat. They should be eaten very sparingly, and not more than once a day. Ten or twelve almonds, for example, are plenty. More than that makes your digestive tract work too hard, exactly what you want to avoid. If you can't eat only 10 or 12 nuts, leave them alone.

Also, whenever I eat nuts (I am partial to raw almonds and raw cashews), I always have either cucumber slices or celery with them. Not only does the combination taste great, but the high water content of the cucumbers and celery seems to assist in moving the nuts through the stomach more easily. You may question the suggestion of eating nuts at all because of their fat content. You should know that some fat in the diet is absolutely essential. Without some fat, you would die. In fact, vitamins A, D, E, and K cannot be broken down and used unless they are in the presence of fat. The issue is where the fat in your diet is coming from. The fat in animal products is the culprit, not the fat from raw nuts and seeds, or avocados.

8) If you mono-diet for a week or longer on all uncooked foods — salads, in addition to juices, fruit, smoothies, and vegetables—you may start to crave something cooked, but still want to con-tinue your mono-diet. The following approach, which is a slight exception to the rule of only uncooked food, allows you to continue to cleanse but also to eat a little heavier. Add steamed

vegetables to your salad. Choose whatever vegetables you like: broccoli, cauliflower, zucchini. Steam one, two, or three, put them in your salad, add dressing and voilá, an incredibly tasty and satisfying meal.

I suggest, however, that you don't add steamed vegetables on short mono-diets of only three or four days. But if you're going for a week, ten days, or two weeks, add steamed veggies for the last part of the mono-diet. In other words, on a one-week mono-diet, add steamed vegetables the last two days. On a ten-day mono-diet, add them the last three or four days. Also, make sure there is more salad than steamed vegetables, not the other way around. Remember, it is the regular eating of uncooked food that is the goal.

9) A beautiful side effect of periodic mono-dieting is that your overall diet tends to improve. After eating clean, healthy food for a while, you're not so anxious to put just any ol' thing in your body. Sometimes the change is obvious, sometimes it's subtle, but as time goes by and you are free of pain, you've lost weight, your energy is up, and you're feeling very good about yourself, you'll want to keep it that way. You'll find yourself making healthier menu choices in restaurants and eating those death-burgers and fries less frequently at the thousands of fast-food places that contribute so greatly to the level of ill health suffered by so many.

10) After a mono-diet of five days or longer, be particularly careful of what you eat the first one or two days. Eating a lot of very heavy foods too quickly can make you feel horrible. Your body accustoms itself to light, clean, uncooked food and you can catch it off guard by too quickly eating too heavily. Let's say you do a one-week mono-diet of juices, fruit, and salads. If on the eighth day you consume a big lunch of pizza or fried chicken or a burger and fries, and a dinner of steak and potatoes, bread, and apple pie, you're going to feel miserable the next day. It would be better to eat very lightly in the morning, only fruit and/or juice. Have a salad for lunch with a baked potato or piece of toast if you need more than salad, and perhaps a pasta-with-vegetable dish and a salad for dinner. This way you gradually reintroduce the

cooked food without jumping straight into consuming the heaviest foods possible. Wait until the second or third day after a mono-diet before having meat, chicken, or fish, and eat them sparingly (more on that in the next principle, Chapter 11).

11) This tip is of such importance that I considered making it the fourth principle. It has to do with what foods you eat in the morning hours. I know that North Americans have been raised to believe that a "big hearty breakfast" is the best way to start the day, but it ain't necessarily so.

To date, the *Fit For Life* books (*Fit For Life* and *Fit For Life II*) have sold about ten million copies worldwide. Nearly half a million people have written to share their thoughts, ask questions, and make comments on these books and the principles they impart. Without question, the comment made far and away more frequently than any other concerns what foods should be eaten in the early part of the day to ensure optimal health. I want very briefly to summarize that information for you here.

What we are trying to accomplish is a cleansing of your body— the elimination of waste—so that the lymph system will not be so overburdened that it has to store those toxic wastes in the lymph nodes, thereby opening the door for disease. Every physiological function of your body operates under cycles that are called circadian rhythms. The eight-hour period that the body's internal eliminative processes are most heightened is from 4:00 a.m. until 12 noon. That is when the lymph system is most active in picking up waste from the cells and taking them to the eliminative organs.

As discussed earlier, digestion takes enormous amounts of energy, so if you eat a heavy meal in the morning hours, some of the energy being used to cleanse and eliminate is diverted to the stomach for digestion. To get the absolute most from the three principles, eat as lightly as possible in the hours from the time you awaken in the morning until noon. If you can eat exclusively fruit and juice until noon, as much as you like, that is certainly the very best routine possible, because fruit and its juices require practically no energy at all to be digested. That way, the elimination cycle can operate at its fullest efficiency.

If you don't feel you can eat only fruit and juice until noon, try the following two suggestions:

- Eat only fruit and its juices until noon as often as you can. If that's only two days a week, so be it. If it's every other day, that's fantastic.
- At least make fruit and juice the first thing you put into your body, even if a half hour later you're having cereal or toast.

The goal should be to go as close to noon as you can on only fruit and juice. You'll only need one week to see the phenomenal difference that eating fruit until noon makes in your energy level and feeling of well-being. Millions have already learned about it, have made it a permanent part of their lives, and are enjoying the many benefits of the practice. The results will astound you. *In terms of experiencing your highest level of health, this tip is very important for your overall success, please do not minimize it.**

12) A question you are sure to ask is, "How often should I mono-diet and for how long?" Generally speaking, if you have never mono-dieted or fasted, or taken any other measures to cleanse or detoxify your system, and you are fairly certain your inner body could use a good cleansing, the more frequent and the longer the mono-diet, the better. In other words, at first, diligently mono-diet at regular intervals, more frequently than later, when you know your body is pretty clean. Later, your mono-diets will be more for maintenance, especially if you upgrade your diet by minimizing foods that would encumber your lymph system.

The best illustration I can give you is my own experience with mono-dieting. When I was introduced to Natural Hygiene and mono-dieting, I was highly motivated. I was sick, fat, tired, in pain, and living in fear because of the death of my father from cancer. The person who taught me the fundamentals of mono-dieting assured me that a series of mono-diets and simultaneous improvement in my dietary habits would quickly bring me to a level of health I had not enjoyed for a very long time.

---

*Refer to *Fit For Life* for an in-depth explanation of circadian rhythms and the value of consuming fruit until noon.

Let me tell you, he sounded totally sure of himself and I sorely wanted to believe. But for as long as I had been dealing with excruciating stomachaches, for as many weight-loss diets as I had been on, for as frustrated as I was over my continually declining health, I have to admit that I was more than a little skeptical that it would all be wiped away by what seemed to be hardly any effort. But there was something else. I was willing!

My mentor told me that the first thing I needed to do, since I was eating anything I desired at any time, was to have only fruit and vegetable juices and fresh fruit for five days. At that particular stage of my life, the idea of eating only fruit and juices for five days was like suggesting that I wet my finger and stick it in a light socket. But I did what my mentor advised because I desperately needed *something* to turn things around for me. The first day was the hardest. The first day is *always* the hardest. But on the *sixth* day, when I was supposed to start eating other foods, the most amazing, most unexpected thing happened: I felt so darned good, so energetic, so positive, so light and clean, that I decided to go for another five days! Me! The guy who would rather fall down a flight of concrete stairs than miss a meal.

I was riding my bicycle every day and reading books by Herbert M. Shelton, the acknowledged father of Natural Hygiene. At the end of ten days, my life was forever changed. I simply could not believe how good I felt. My stomach, which had hurt every day for more than 20 years, did not bother me at all, I had lost about 12 pounds, my energy level was through the roof, and I felt as if I owned the world.

My mentor, who had a rather quirky sense of humour, said to me, in a totally professional, serious tone, "Well, you have a decision to make now. You can either alter your dietetic lifestyle a bit and continue to cleanse your system, lose more weight, and feel euphoric, or you can go back to the way you were eating before your ten days and have your health go back to what it was. What's it going to be?" I didn't say anything, I just looked at him in a way that left no doubt what my decision was.

He told me that for the best results, the quickest results, I should cut out all meat at least at first. Then after I felt really good, I could reintroduce the meat into my diet, but not the way I was eating it before, which was not only every day, but every meal.

I decided to eliminate all meat, chicken, and fish from my diet at least until I lost 50 pounds. I basically ate whatever I wanted other than those foods, being sure not to overeat. Although I ate breads, cheese, pasta, and the like, fruits and vegetables dominated my diet. I mono-dieted two days a week, one day on juices only (fruit and vegetable) and another day (three days later) on juice and whole fruit, as much as I liked.

Astonishingly, I lost the 50 pounds in one month. Not only was my body ready to heal itself, I also helped it along by improving my diet, riding my bike every day, and flooding my consciousness with positive thoughts about how well I was doing and how successful I was going to be.

I made a commitment to do a ten-day mono-diet at least four times a year, one every three months. For the next two years, I did exactly that; every three months I did either ten days on juices and fruit or ten days on juice, fruit, and salads. In between, I ate very few animal products, exercised regularly, and did shorter mono-diets of one or two days in a row every week. After the first two years, with my weight loss maintained, no pain and an exuberance for life that I thought I'd never achieve, I knew I had found a lifestyle that would serve me forever. Now I do ten-day mono-diets two or sometimes three times a year, and I mono-diet one or two days a week.

I tried different kinds of mono-dieting routines. Once I ate only uncooked foods (fruit, vegetables, juice, and salads) every other day for three months. In between, I ate what I wanted. It was great! I felt absolutely incredible. When I was preparing for my first television tour to promote *Fit For Life*, I ate only fruit and juices for two weeks and only uncooked food for a month. Touring is unbelievably gruelling, but I sailed through three weeks of nonstop work with interviews from morning until night and a plane ride every day, with an abundance of energy and positive feelings. Over and over, television talk-show hosts would comment on how "up and energetic" I was for being in the middle of a tour.

So let's get back to your original question: "How often should I mono-diet and for how long? My advice is to start with a three- or five-day mono-diet of fruit and vegetable juices and whole fruit, just to see what it feels like. Mono-diet one or two days a week with longer ones (a week or ten days) every two to three months, depending on how much cleansing you feel your body needs and how motivated you are to get your lymph system cleaned out so that no lymph nodes become encumbered with waste. As I've said above, the duration and frequency of your mono-diet is up to you.

Having said that, I know some of you prefer to follow a more definitive program—something that removes the guesswork. Once again, a quick analogy: If you were in a canoe or a rowboat that had a lot of water in it because of a leak, you would have to bail aggressively to lower the water level and prevent capsizing. Once you reduced the level of water, you could relax and bail only periodically to keep the water level low. So it is with your body. To start, you should mono-diet more frequently and for longer durations, to lower the level of toxins in your body. Then you can mono-diet more infrequently as a means to keep the level of toxins low.

For the first year, mono-diet for at least ten days every three months. That's four ten-day mono-diets for the year. Two should comprise only juice (both fruit and vegetable) and fruit, and two should be all raw foods (fruits, vegetables, their juices and salads). In between the ten-day mono-diets, mono-diet at least two days a week, either two days in a row or twice within the week. After the first year, it would, of course, be ideal to continue the same pattern every year for the rest of your life, to be absolutely certain that your body's toxic level never gets out of control and your lymph nodes never become swollen, but as a maintenance program you can cut it in half. That would be two ten-day mono-diets a year and at least one day a week.

Understand this: *You cannot mono-diet too much!* The more you do it, the healthier you'll be and the likelihood of your ever developing cancer will diminish. You can, however, mono-diet too little. Therefore, you have to find out what your personal comfort level is and how motivated you are. As time goes by, you will know exactly how much you need to mono-diet for your particular lifestyle, especially when you experience the well-being that is the automatic result of regular periodic mono-dieting.

Benefits of the First Principle

When you are mono-dieting, you are allowing your body to be cleansed. You are cleaning and rejuvenating your lymph system. *You are preventing disease.* Please, please do not make the mistake of taking periodic mono-dieting lightly or minimizing the extent to which it can achieve that much-desired goal of helping you live your life without the fear of becoming a cancer statistic. Considering the havoc cancer has caused in so many people's lives and its apparent complicated and puzzling characteristics, I can understand an initial reaction being something like, "Yeah, right. Eating nothing but fruit and vegetables every so often is going to prevent something as pervasive and bewildering as cancer." Is there a problem with the solution being more simple and straightforward than you have been led to believe? If it was far more complicated, expensive and difficult to do, would you have more confidence in periodic mono-dieting then? In Chapter 1, I told you about the woman who called me from the hospital because she had a walnut-sized lump in her breast. *She got rid of the lump by mono-dieting!* As far as she was concerned, mono-dieting saved her life.

For most of you, periodic mono-dieting is an aspect of your life that you have yet to experience. If for no other reason than curiosity, try it just to see what, if anything, you've missed. Having done so, you will certainly know your body better. When you buy a car or a VCR or a camera, don't you read the owners' manual to learn all about the item's features so you can use it to your best advantage? It would be great if our bodies came with an owners' manual, but that isn't the case. Still, don't you want to learn all about its features so that you can use it to its fullest and not miss out? Here is something that holds such great promise and, until now, the knowledge of it has somehow escaped you. Now is your chance to discover a part of you that you haven't known before.

If you own a fax machine or a computer, you've probably marveled at the way such machines have revolutionized our lives. You often hear people say such things as, "I don't know how in the world my business ran before fax machines." Or, "How on earth would I ever get by without my computer?" These are common expressions of those who have learned to depend heavily on modern technological wonders. Imagine how they would feel if suddenly they had to give them up. They would feel sorely deprived. It would be one thing if they had never experienced them and were not aware of the ways in which they could dramatically improve their lives, but to have them and use them and then lose them would be unbearable. And that is exactly what periodic mono-dieting is like. If you don't know what you're missing, then you don't know, and that's it.

However, once you discover firsthand how periodic mono-dieting can transform your health and, therefore, your life, you will never want to give it up. You mustn't allow the fact that mono-dieting is simple, inexpensive, and totally in your control to discourage you from trying it.

Ill health will only be prevented if you live a lifestyle that does not cause it. Making period mono-dieting a *permanent* part of your lifestyle is that certain "something" people have been looking for to finally win the battle over cancer and the years of ill health that precede it. Mono-dieting is a gift, a blessing, and once experienced, you'll bless the day it became a part of your life.

A Personal Testimonial

I feel compelled to share a personal story with you here which should stand as a most impressive testimonial for periodic mono-dieting. In 1966, when I was 21 years old, I was in the United States Air Force and sent to Vietnam for a one-year tour of duty. While there, I was exposed to Agent Orange and now have a condition called peripheral neuropathy. All of the extensor muscles in both of my arms have atrophied. What that means is that I am unable to lift my arms unless my palms are facing upwards or unless I point my elbows out to the sides and then lift them up. I have a good grip in my hands but I am unable to open them back up on their own. I also have a slight limp in my right leg. It doesn't keep me from doing anything I want to do, but I have to use both of my hands for the most simple of movements that even a small child could accomplish with one hand.

Agent Orange, a derivative of dioxin, is one of the most deadly chemicals ever formulated, and works in a very odd way in that the deterioration of muscles that it inevitably causes starts approximately 20 years after exposure. I was exposed in 1966 and my muscles started to deteriorate in 1986.

Having been in touch with the Agent Orange Support Group in the United States, I've learned that thousands of individuals who were exposed while in Vietnam are dealing with the same thing as I. With one huge difference. It turns out that Agent Orange just continues spreading throughout the body, and five years after deterioration starts, individuals are either severely restricted in their movements, wheelchair-bound, or dead. But not so with me. It has been 12 years for me after deterioration started and it looks as if I've managed to stop it. How did I do that? I was exposed in 1966, and I learned all about the lymph system and the need to clean it out on a regular basis in 1970. Although I had no idea that I was exposed to Agent Orange until my arms started to wither in 1986, four years after my exposure I started to periodic mono-diet on a very regular basis for other health problems that I was aware of, and that practice, it turns out, saved my life!

The reason I'm telling you this should be glaringly obvious. If periodic mono-dieting can save me from something as deadly as Agent Orange coursing through my veins, do you see what an exceedingly powerful tool it can be in your life? I pray that you do. If I can make headway with one of the most deadly chemicals ever produced, imagine what you could do if you were to start using periodic mono-dieting *before* you have a crisis on your hands. And that, my friend, is truly the meaning of prevention: taking steps while you are well, to see to it that you stay that way.

As far as I am concerned, I am alive and able to share life-saving information like this with others, thanks to periodic mono-dieting. Whatever you do, *do not take lightly what you are learning here.* As regards your well-being and longevity, periodic mono-dieting may very well be the most important tool you ever learn about. It certainly has been for me!

The Second Principle
Part I: The Gradual Reduction
of Animal Products

In the previous chapter, you learned about the disease-preventing benefits of periodic mono-dieting. There are numerous other benefits associated with cleansing the inner body. As you become more familiar and more comfortable with the practice, these will become increasingly apparent. One of the more subtle side effects is the body's natural inclination to consume less of those foods that clog it with the most toxic waste and require the greatest amount of energy to digest.

As you might guess from what you've already read in this book, the food category that fits this description most accurately is *animal products*. Considering the fat, cholesterol, hormones, pesticides, antibiotics and other chemical pharmaceutical contaminants, uric acid and bacterial putrefaction and contamination they contain, it's hard to come up with a food more responsible for toxifying the body with harmful wastes than animal products. Moreover, animal products are also the most structurally complex and difficult foods to break down in the body, thereby requiring more energy to process than any other. Add to this that animal products are devoid of fibre and are associated with every major disease that afflicts the population, and you have more than ample reason to actively seek out ways of cutting down on them in your diet. However, although these days people generally know that animal products are no longer the "celebrity" foods they used to be, and although authorities the world over recommend diets that de-emphasize animal products, there is still that nagging voice at the back of your mind that may be telling you that protein is an important nutrient and protein means meat and other animal products.

The Big Protein Myth

So before presenting you with a simple, comfortable workable strategy for reducing the amount of animal products in your diet, I think it's important to give you at least a brief bit of background on some of the reasons you hold these not-so-healthy foods in such high regard.

Many of the health statistics in North America are the result of a deliberate campaign waged by the industries that would profit from our ignorance. For decades we've been pummelled with an avalanche of one-sided information pushing an animal-based point of view called the "Four Food Groups," half of which just happen to be animal products. This was done for profit, not health.

Interestingly, the idea that animals supply us with the finest source of protein can be traced back to studies on rodents that showed rats grew better on an animal-based diet than on a plant-based diet.[205] From these studies on *rats* researchers jumped to the conclusion that animal protein was superior to plant proteins—for *humans!* Now, that is a jump that can only be compared to leaping across the Grand Canyon in a single bound in a heavy thunder-storm with both legs in a cast, because physiologically and ana-tomically we are very different from rats.

The animal products industries, however, ran with the rat research and promoted it to the outer reaches of the universe. These studies were later shown to be inapplicable to humans, in fact, ludicrous, because rats require a much more concentrated source of protein, such as meat, and their amino acid needs are different from those of humans. It was too late. The myth had been born and the animal products industries were hardly going to let it die.

Dietary Models

In 1923, the United States Department of Agriculture (USDA) came up with the "Twelve Food Groups." Oddly, the Basic Twelve revolved around four diet plans that incorporated choices from each group and were structured to apply to different income brackets,[206] so protein could be obtained from the legumes (beans, lentils, split peas) and nuts category for lower-income individuals, or from the meat category for those who could afford higher-priced protein sources. Prestige was attached to animal products, because they were portrayed as preferred foods for the "upper" class. They were now "elitist foods." Long forgotten and extremely important to bear in mind is that it was never stated by the USDA that animal protein was *superior* to plant protein, only *more expensive!*

The Basic Twelve hung on until 1941, when the Food and Nutrition Board of the National Research Council, feeling that twelve were too cumbersome and difficult to remember, reduced the number to the "Seven Food Groups." Legumes and nuts were listed in the same category as meat, poultry, fish, and eggs. From the 1940s on, the National Egg Board, the National Dairy Council, and the National Livestock and Meat Board were running heavy campaigns praising the "ideal" protein in animal products.

By 1960, the now-famous (or infamous) "Four Food Groups" became the dominant dietary model in the country. Fruits and vegetables, which could rightly have been two groups, were lumped together, and animal products, which could rightly have been one group, were separated. Legumes and nuts were pushed out altogether as a named protein source! Animal products were now king of the mountain, representing 50 percent of our daily recommended dietary intake, thus appearing to be as important as everything else *combined*. The animal products industries, for reasons that hardly need explanation, were in nirvana.

The Case Against Animal Products Revisited

Ironically, at this same time, research funded by the National Dairy Council uncovered the link between increased blood cholesterol and dairy fat. Subsequent studies confirmed this link and verified the increased risk of heart disease when cholesterol levels were increased. At the same time that dairy products were being pushed by the animal products industries, research was busily destroying the myth.

During the 1950s, more conclusive evidence that linked heart disease to the consumption of animal products came to light from a most unexpected source. During the Korean War, both American and Korean soldiers killed were autopsied. In the young Americans, with their high animal product intake, 77 percent already had narrowed blood vessels due to atherosclerotic deposits. No such damage appeared in the arteries of the equally young Koreans, whose national diet included far fewer animal products, with a higher vegetable and grain intake.[207]

At the same time, studies on Japanese individuals who had a long line of healthy hearts showed that those Japanese who moved to the United States and adopted the western diet dominated by animal products, had enormously higher rates of heart disease than their counterparts who stayed in Japan and consumed diets low in fat and cholesterol. By the early 1960s it was becoming apparent that there were some significant problems with the basic Four Food Group approach to diet.

As research increasingly began to prove conclusively that the consumption of animal products was harmful to health, the meat and dairy industries *increased* their efforts to encourage meat and dairy consumption. As the seventies rolled around, it became more and more difficult for the industries to pull this off because the evidence against the health benefits of consuming animal products started to rapidly build. The Senate Select Committee on Nutrition and Human Needs brought together many of the nation's most respected researchers, and their resulting recommendations reflected the increasingly conspicuous relationship between the American diet and disease. Their "alternative diet" *de-emphasized* animal products and encouraged more selections from the plant kingdom. This was the first *official* statement that openly suggested a move away from a meat-based diet and made it clear that the result would be an improvement in health!

In 1977 a follow-up to the panel's findings was released in a report entitled Dietary Goals for the United States, which supported the need for a new national diet and once again de-emphasized animal products. The meat, dairy, and egg industries unleashed the pressure of the incredibly powerful cholesterol lobby and the original phrase in the report "eat *less* meat" was changed to "eat *lean* meat."[208] *The original text of the report actually advised Americans to eat less meat in the mid-1970s, but the animal products industries were successful in pressuring legislators to keep that from you!* How lovely.

The 1980s looked to be as progressive in terms of improving the American diet as the seventies, with further official recommendations instructing the public on the importance of minimizing their consumption of foods high in saturated fat and cholesterol (animal products). But right when everything was going along swimmingly, catastrophe struck. There was a political shift that very nearly sounded the death knell for nutritional reform.

The superpowerful animal food industries won out with the presidential election of 1984, after which efforts to continue educating the public were severely thwarted. In the words of Michael Jacobson, head of the Center for Science in the Public Interest, "When Ronald Reagan was elected President, the Department of Agriculture, the lead agency for nutritional education, was basically given over to the meat industry."[209]

Reagan's secretary of agriculture was a hog farmer. His deputy secretary had been president of the American Meat Institute for eight years. One of the assistant secretaries had been head of the National Cattlemen's Association, and the head of the Bureau of Land Management, the organization that decides how much public land would be given over to animal agriculture, was a Colorado cattleman. Not a moment was wasted in undoing advances that had been made in the effort to increase the public's knowledge about diet and health. Dissenting nutritionists were either silenced or fired.

Although the 1980s were not kind to nutritional education, they did end on a high note with the release of the Surgeon General's Report on Nutrition and Health, the report from the National

Academy of Sciences, the heart and cancer associations' positions and urgings from other health-related organizations (see Chapter 7). *All* were imploring Americans to reduce their consumption of foods high in fat and cholesterol, specifically animal products.

So, here we are in the 1990s, all primed to step into the 21st century. The year 2000 is but a cosmic breath away. Where do we stand with the Four Food Groups? To what extent is the government involved, either in terms of helping us or capitulating to the profit motive? These days there's hardly anyone who is not aware of the dangers of consuming meat. When was the last time you read an obituary column full of the names of people who died due to an insufficient amount of fat and cholesterol in their arteries?

The Eating Right Pyramid

This brings us to the most provocative story of the Four Food Group controversy to date. Thirty-five years of haggling and maneuvering to replace the Four Food Groups "wheel" with something more in line with our actual needs finally came to a resolution in 1991. "The Eating Right Pyramid" (see a representation on the next page) was unveiled by the USDA to replace the Four Food Group wheel. In this pyramid, although the actual recommended servings of each food group were not changed, the difference is in the *visual* presentation. The foods we are being encouraged to emphasize in our diets occupy the biggest space. Those foods that are harmful are no longer represented in 50 percent of the diagram. You see, the average number of servings of animal products recommended is five per day, the average number of servings recommended of fruits, vegetables, and grains is fifteen a day, *three times as many*. So you can see that the wheel, which gave the *visual* impression that animal products were to be consumed in equal amounts to everything else combined, was totally misleading. The pyramid ingeniously rectified this glaring inconsistency.

The Eating Right Pyramid

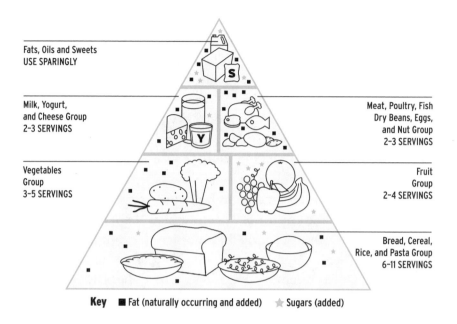

Fats, Oils and Sweets
USE SPARINGLY

Milk, Yogurt,
and Cheese Group
2-3 SERVINGS

Meat, Poultry, Fish
Dry Beans, Eggs,
and Nut Group
2-3 SERVINGS

Vegetables
Group
3-5 SERVINGS

Fruit
Group
2-4 SERVINGS

Bread, Cereal,
Rice, and Pasta Group
6-11 SERVINGS

Key ■ Fat (naturally occurring and added) ★ Sugars (added)

Those foods which we should eat the most—grains and legumes—are on the broad bottom. Then, in ascending order by number of recommended servings, are fruits and vegetables, then animal foods, then fats, which are represented by the tip of the pyramid, along with the admonition to use sparingly. Brilliant!

But only days before its release date, like a bolt of lightning out of the blue, Agriculture Secretary Edward R. Madigan withdrew it. "But why?" you must be asking. Just prior to the release of the Eating Right Pyramid, Mr. Madigan had a private meeting with board members of the National Cattlemen's Association. A few days later, he received a letter from the American Meat Institute, and then the National Milk Producers Federation complained that dairy products were too close to fat in the pyramid. The next thing we knew, the pyramid was out the window.[210] The Center for Science in the Public Interest released a statement that said, "The Department of Agriculture is just what the name says, The

Department of Agriculture. It consistently puts the interests of the meat, egg, and dairy industries ahead of the public's health."[211]

In what can only come under the category of rubbing hot sauce into an already open wound, Mr. Madigan's highly suspect reason for withdrawing the pyramid was "because it had not been tested on children."[212] This didn't come to him until only moments before the release date of the pyramid and after *three years of testing?* He would have had fewer eyes rolling skyward if he'd said that extraterrestrials came into his bedroom and warned that Earth would be destroyed if the Eating Right Pyramid was released!

But, fortunately, in a rare but welcome instance of victory for the beleaguered consumer, under tremendous pressure from an outraged health and nutrition community, the pyramid was reinstituted in 1992 and scheduled to supplant the antiquated food group wheel. The director of nutrition at the Center for Science in the Public Interest summed it up best when she said that the decision "shows that, at least sometimes, the public wins."[213] It's a funny thing with the truth, it doesn't go away. It can be stomped on, abused, distorted, corrupted, or buried, but like a balloon full of air that is pushed underwater, it keeps popping back up. And the truth here is indisputable and undeniable. Notwithstanding the self-serving, greed-motivated propaganda from the animal products industries, we *must* start to reduce our consumption of animal products—the second principle of the CARE program—for many reasons in addition to that of preventing cancer.

Guidelines to Reduce Animal Product Consumption

Undoubtedly, there are many people who know that they should minimize consumption of animal-based products in their diets, and genuinely want to eat less of these foods, but they don't know how to accomplish their goal in a way that allows them to enjoy the eating experience without creating turmoil in their lives. The second principle is *how*. It provides you with an intelligent approach to gradually change your "eating style," a workable formula that shows you a specific plan of action rather than just saying "cut back." It shows you *how* to cut back day by day, systematically, and in a way that will allow you to feel comfortable and not deprived.

The mistake most people make when confronted with the need to change their behavioural patterns—in this case, the excessive consumption of foods that are killing them—is that they take the all-or-nothing approach. They say, O.K., I'm not going to eat these things anymore, and then, when they find that their habits are too entrenched to abruptly break, they feel frustration, weakness, or a sense of failure. The second principle of the CARE program teaches you the key to successful detoxification through a *gradual* reduction of the animal products you are accustomed to eating. You will be able to eat reasonable amounts of the animal products you desire, in the healthiest way, offsetting their harmful effects through new behaviours you will be using, and at the same time you will be realizing your goal to CARE for your body by cleansing and rejuvenating it energetically.

Once again, please keep in mind that these new techniques you will be learning are *guidelines*, not edicts. I keep repeating this over and over whenever giving recommendations because people tend to view as failure *any digression* from the guidelines, which serves only to add undue pressure to realizing the goal at hand. Plus, I would rather overstress this idea than understress it. It simply is not realistic for me to try to address every possible variable, life circumstance, and personal choice of everyone in one book. So the guidelines serve as a pool of suggestions that can be drawn upon to satisfy each person's individual needs.

In the figure below, you will see that the area marked with an "A" is the largest, with "B" and "C" equal to each other but very much smaller. This is a way to illustrate the extent to which people practise certain habits. For example, if it were to show how often people exercise, the area marked "A" would represent the number of people who exercise at least sometimes. The area marked "B" would represent people who exercise every day, and the area marked "C" would represent those who never exercise.

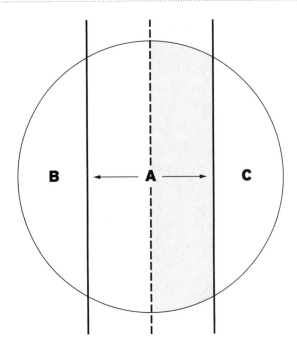

Here, it is used to illustrate to what extent people eat animal products. The large area "A" is the percentage of people who eat some form of animal product daily. Area "B" is the percentage of people who eat some animal products at every meal, and area "C" is the percentage of those who never eat animal products.

Areas "B" and "C" have no varying degrees. You either eat animal products at every meal or you don't eat them at all. Area "A," however, can have a wide and varying range of amounts of animal products eaten. Now, in terms of reducing animal products sufficiently to promote cleanliness of the inner body, keep your lymph nodes from swelling, keep energy levels high, and optimize health, while preventing ill health, you want your level of consumption of animal products to be in the shaded part of area "A" (to the right of the dotted line) that is closer to area "C." Somewhere in there should be your goal. Obviously, the closer to area "C," the less animal products you are eating. The closer to the dotted line, the more animal products you're eating.

To achieve the goal of being in the shaded area next to area "C," there are three simple, general guidelines to strive for. I emphasize again that they are *general guidelines*. I will refer to flesh foods when talking about meat, chicken, fish, and eggs, and dairy products to indicate any dairy product from milk to cheese to yogurt.

1) Try to avoid eating flesh foods and/or dairy products for breakfast.
2) Try to have flesh foods no more than once a day. Try to have dairy products no more than once a day. (On occasion, you will have both more than once a day, but again, I am talking about direction. The direction you're going in is to strive for no more than once a day.)
3) On some kind of regular basis, there should be some days where neither flesh foods nor dairy products are eaten at all. *This is exceedingly important.* The body needs a break from having to expend energy on processing animal products. I know people who only eat animal products every other day. They do not feel deprived in any way and they experience phenomenal good health. One small exception for nonanimal-product days is the use of a little butter on potatoes or vegetables or when cooking something that requires butter. This small digression will not hurt anything. And by all means, use butter not margarine, which is nothing but plastic fat and has been associated with a significant increase in the risk of breast cancer.[214] At least butter is real.

It is obvious that the more closely you adhere to and use these three guidelines, the more successful you will be in reducing your animal product consumption. One of the ways you can be more successful in implementing these tips is to understand as much as you can about *why* they are relevant. I have already given you ample reasons to cut back on animal products as you begin to CARE for your body. This is just one more understanding you will be able to incorporate into your lifestyle and use to your benefit for the rest of your life.

Benefits of the Second Principle

These tips may appear to be too simplistic to have any major impact on supporting the lymph system and preventing disease, but just the opposite is true. If you practise them diligently and incorporate them into your lifestyle, you will contribute greatly to your goal of vibrant health.

We have already seen that elimination in the body is an integral part of cleansing. It is the actual removal of waste matter through the bowels, the bladder, the lungs, and the skin, and because it cannot proceed without energy from the body, your dietary choices and your lifestyle will *dramatically* affect it. If most of the foods you eat are highly processed, full of chemicals, heavy, concentrated, high in fat and cholesterol, denatured, preserved or irradiated, you can expect that elimination will not be smooth. Too much energy will be required by the body merely to break down these foods and neutralize their negative elements, and unless you are like the lion who sleeps 20 hours a day, your body simply will not be able to thoroughly eliminate the waste products and toxins from the foods you are eating. Yes, it will eliminate somewhat, but not completely, and complete elimination is the key to a clean lymph system and the prevention of disease in general and cancer in particular.

The idea in upgrading your diet is to *gradually* remove from your diet those foods that have been proven to be harmful. All I can tell you is that the fresher the food, the closer to nature, the better. You want to minimize your consumption of highly processed, chemicalized, packaged foods, coffee, sodas, refined sugar, and so on. You know the stuff that's not good for you. It's what we're always being told to "have in moderation." Do the best you can in minimizing them. That's all. With periodic mono-dieting (First Principle—see Chapter Ten) and reducing animal products (Second Principle), you are way ahead of the game. You can get away with periodic indiscretions with no problem because your *overall* approach is so healthy.

World-renowned biochemist and researcher Dr. Paul Stitt has said: "The cure for cancer will not be found under the microscope, it's on the dinner plate."[215] The more foods that come from the plant kingdom, and the less that come from the animal kingdom, the less likely it is that cancer will ever be a part of your experience.

If you have decided that periodic mono-dieting and the gradual reduction of animal products make sense to you, and you are willing to apply the three CARE principles to your life, you will begin to make the health-supporting dietary choices so many others are making (and that you have perhaps been secretly yearning to know how to make), in a rational, systematic, and *very enjoyable* way. CARE gives you a comprehensive game plan for life, rather than a haphazard, hit-or-miss approach. You don't have to *hope* you will get results. From the moment you start, you will *know* you are getting them.

These principles will change forever the attitude you have toward your body, as you experience firsthand your own power to revitalize your physical body. You will be witnessing your ability to eliminate, by your own actions and behaviour, the underlying causes of ill health that you thought were beyond your control. The result will be a higher level of health and energy than perhaps you ever thought possible! And most important, you will live with the knowledge and confidence that you *can* go through this life in vibrant health.

Part II: The Fountain of Youth?

You are probably familiar with the expression "Big things come in small packages." If that saying is true, then this little section certainly falls into that category. In only a few short pages, you're going to learn about an astoundingly simple tool that, without exaggeration, *will* be one of the most profound and effective means by which you ensure for yourself that long, pain-free, and disease-free life that has been referred to throughout this book.

At public seminars I have given over the last 18 years or so, one question I always ask my audiences to respond to by raising their hands is, "How many people here love to eat?" Without fail, all in attendance throw their hands skyward as though they were reaching up to snatch hundred-dollar bills out of the air that have fallen from the ceiling. Many thrust both hands in the air with such enthusiasm you'd think I just asked them, "How many people here would like a brand-new car of their choice, for *free*?" When the audiences were large, a thousand people or more, the upraised arms looked like a flock of flamingos coming in for a landing on the Serengeti Plain. After the fluttering and laughter subsided, I would explain what I have spoken of earlier: that each and every one of us will consume some 70 tons of food in our lifetime. So it certainly makes sense that if we're going to spend the amount of time necessary to obtain and eat 70 tons of food, we might just as well enjoy ourselves while we're doing it. Don't you agree?

Freeing Up the Digestive System Revisited

I have already mentioned several times how much energy is required for the digestive process. The entire process of digestion and metabolism, the breaking down of the 70 tons, extraction and utilization of nutrients and elimination of the wastes, will require more energy in your lifetime than all other uses of energy *combined!* Reflect on that for a while and you are sure to be impressed.

The digestion of food takes a huge amount of your energy, more than for anything else you do. Ever notice how tired you are after a meal? And the bigger the meal, the more tired you are. Remember last Thanksgiving? What did you do right after eating? As I mentioned in Chapter 10, did you look for your running shoes, or a couch? All over the world people have what is referred to as the "afternoon siesta." People eat and get tired because the digestive process demands the expenditure of such a high amount of energy.

You know, from the time you are born until the time you leave this life, you have a certain amount of life energy available to you. When it's gone, life is over. Since it is an unassailable, physiological fact that more of that energy will be used up for the digestive process than all other uses combined, does it not seem prudent beyond measure for you to make use of any possible means by which to either streamline the digestive process or in some manner reduce its burden? To me the answer to that question is more obvious than the answer to the question "Is the sun hot?" Reducing the burden of the digestive process can have but one, long-term effect: It will improve the length and quality of your life. There's simply no doubt about that.

I have been studying and teaching a healthy lifestyle for over a quarter of a century now. All my books delineate methods you can use to decrease the work of the digestive process, to give it periodic rests; my ideas emphasize how important it is for you not to push the digestive process beyond its capabilities. I know many of you reading this right now have read *Fit For Life*, and that makes me extremely happy. And I know that there are those of you who have not read it. *Fit For Life* contains an entire section on proper food combining, an approach that has many benefits. Food combining is a way to optimize energy from the digestive tract by not mixing protein (such as meat) with starches (such as potatoes, rice). The number-one benefit of the practice is that it streamlines digestion. In this book, periodic mono-dieting shows you how to free up a significant amount of energy from the digestive process which is, in turn used by the body to thoroughly clean the lymph system; this ultimately prevents disease in the long term while dramatically improving all aspects of health in the short term.

In Chapter 10, I shared with you the work of Dr. Roy Walford, who *doubled* the lifespan and dramatically improved the health of mice he experimented with merely by totally resting their digestive systems for two days a week. I also made the observation that animals in the wild or kept as pets will stop eating when they're sick or injured in order to free up digestive energy for the healing process. And, of course, children and adults also lose their appetites when they are "under the weather," which is, once again, the body's protective mechanism trying to divert to the healing process the energy that would have been spent on digestion.

From what you have read so far, I'm certain that you see that anything you can do to reduce the work of your digestive system is an extremely wise thing to do. Only good can come from the practice. That being the case, I must say that I am astounded that one of the most simple, effective means by which anyone can immediately start to *dramatically* reduce the work of their digestive system, thereby ensuring a longer, healthier life, is largely unknown to the vast majority of the population. In fact, I wonder if there is anything, *anywhere*, that has the potential to do so much good that has been more overlooked and neglected. And what is this certain something I am referring to? *Enzymes!*

Life-saving Enzymes

To explain enzymes and what they do, I could launch into a convoluted, scientific dissertation about how amalase, which breaks down carbohydrates, splits starches into different disaccerides, or how pepsin, which works on proteins, split proteins into smaller peptide chains, all so food can be broken down and made small enough to pass through the villi, the small pores of the intestines, and into the bloodstream. And if my goal was to cause you to jump to the next chapter, I would do just that. Instead, I wish to give you an ultra-simplified, totally nontechnical explanation, to be absolutely certain that you fully grasp and recognize the immense, life-saving role enzymes play in your health. Anyone wishing a more detailed and scientific understanding of enzymes and their activity in the body can certainly read up on them.[216] But my primary goal here is to leave you with a newfound sense of the enormity of the role enzymes fulfil in our daily lives.

Enzymes are protein chemicals that carry an essential energy source needed for every chemical action and reaction that occurs in your body. We're talking about a number so immense you couldn't possibly comprehend it. Literally trillions upon trillions of chemical activities are taking place in your body right now. None would occur without enzymes. All life, *all*—that means plant or animal—requires enzymes to continue living. Enzymes mean life. Enzymes are life. Whenever you hear about or talk about your body doing something, *anything*, no matter what, that has anything whatsoever to do with the building, repairing, or maintaining of any part of your body, inside or out, enzymes are involved. And without them, nothing would get done. Life would cease to exist. The living body is under a great burden every day to produce the volume of enzymes necessary to run efficiently.

Metabolic Enzymes

There are three classes of enzymes you need to be aware of. First are metabolic enzymes, which are referred to as the body's labour force because virtually every activity of your body depends upon them. Without these power-packed little dynamos continually at work, you couldn't swallow, blink your eyes, circulate blood, breathe in and out, transform food into blood, muscle, and bone, walk, talk, or anything else. The activities of the lymph system and its role in keeping you well while preventing pain and disease is entirely dependent, as is every other function of the body, on metabolic enzymes!

We all know how exceedingly important it is to eat a good diet so that the full complement of nutrients, the vitamins, minerals, essential fatty acids, and amino acids, can be made available to the body to carry out all of its functions. But no matter how pure the diet, no matter how many high-quality nutrients are introduced into the body, it all means nothing without metabolic enzymes.

I'll use a simple analogy to explain why this is so. If you wished to build a house, you could bring to the site all the materials you need to build it: lumber, hammers, nails, cement, bricks, mortar, insulation, wiring, roofing material, everything. But just putting all the materials on the site won't create the house. Unless the construction workers show up to assemble all the materials, the house will not be built. No matter how plentiful the materials, no matter how high the quality of the materials, if there are no construction workers, there is no house. Metabolic enzymes are your body's "construction workers." Without them, nothing gets done, and I mean *nothing*.

Here is the single most important fact about metabolic enzymes that you *must* be aware of. *There is a finite number of metabolic enzymes that can be produced by your body.* I want to be absolutely certain you know exactly what I'm saying. Your body can produce a certain number of metabolic enzymes, and no more! *You can run out of them!* And there is a word to describe what takes place when you run out of them. It's called death. That's what dying means. There are no more metabolic enzymes to carry out the functions of life, so life ends. It would be as though when you were born, you were given a bank account that contained a certain amount of money for your entire lifetime from which you could remove, but not add, money. You can either be prudent with that money and make it last a long time, or you can squander it and let it run out sooner than you wish. So it is with metabolic enzymes. It's an extremely simple equation. The more metabolic enzymes you require and use up, the more unhealthy you will be and the shorter your life will be. The less metabolic enzymes you require and use up, the healthier you will be and the longer you will live. And of that, there is simply no doubt. Anything, and I mean *anything* you can do to use less of your metabolic enzymes is obviously one of the most intelligent and life-enhancing practices you can cultivate as regards your health and longevity.

Digestive Enzymes and Food Enzymes

The second type of enzyme are digestive enzymes. The function of these enzymes should be fairly obvious. That's right, they are involved in the specific job of digestion. Food in the stomach is a number-one priority for the human body and digestive enzymes are required to perform the process of digestion of food in the stomach. Pretty simple stuff.

Now, right here I would like to jump to food enzymes, which are the third type of enzyme, as a discussion will clarify the role of digestive enzymes. All food that has grown out of the ground, as part of God's grand scheme of things, has contained in them all the necessary enzymes to break it down in the body for digestion. Before going into the immense importance of food enzymes, I need to give you some corollary information that will help you more fully appreciate the importance and significance of not only food enzymes but also digestive and metabolic enzymes.

There are many elements that set humans apart from all other animal species on the planet. One of the more impressive differences is our more highly developed brain and our ability to think and reason. It is what allows us to accomplish so much of what is not even in the realm of possibility for all the other so-called lower animals. Ironically, it also is what gets us into trouble as regards our health and well-being. Trouble that the lower animals don't have to contend with. Trouble that is associated with diet, nutrition, and health. For example, do you realize that we humans are the only species on earth to cook our foods before we eat them? The only one. We are also, coincidentally, the only species to suffer from the diseases of affluence discussed earlier. Remember, the diseases of affluence are heart disease, cancer, diabetes, osteoporosis, and obesity. Am I making a correlation between cooking food and disease? You bet your sweet life I am. Food keeps us alive, that is a simple, self-evident fact. Stop eating and you die. It is the food we eat that becomes the building blocks for our living cells. Way back in our history, we started cooking the life out of our foods before eating them and we have been paying the price with ill health and premature death ever since.

Animals in nature do not ever eat cooked food and they do not suffer from the diseases of affluence. There are, of course, exceptions to this, but those exceptions only come into play as other animal species come into close contact with humans. And the closer the contact, the more disease occurs. For example, animals in zoos or animals we take as pets, or animals that are in some way forced to interact with humans suffer from the same diseases of affluence that afflict humans. Because we feed them our cooked food! Could anything on earth be more obvious?

I must share with you one phenomenally impressive study that is recognized the world over as one of the most convincing scientific studies on this subject ever conducted. I lived in Los Angeles for 35 years, so I did the bulk of my research at the UCLA medical library, one of the best in the country. I spent hundreds of hours there poring over studies to substantiate much of my work. Finding this amazing study, which I wrote about in *Fit For Life II*, was like winning the lottery. The study has come to be known as Pottenger's Cats.[217]

Dr. Francis M. Pottenger carried out a meticulous, thorough, ten-year experiment using 900 cats placed on controlled diets. Only two items of food were used and were given either in their raw or cooked state. The results were so overwhelmingly conclusive and convincing that there can be no doubt whatsoever of living, uncooked food's superiority over cooked food. The cats fed only the living, raw food produced healthy kittens year after year. There was no ill health, no disease, and no premature death. Death came to those cats only as the natural consequence of old age. However, the cats fed on the same food, cooked, developed every one of humanity's modern ailments—heart disease, cancer, kidney and thyroid disease, pneumonia, paralysis, loss of teeth, arthritis, difficulty in labour, diminished sexual interest, diarrhea, irritability so intense that the cats were dangerous to handle, liver impairment, and osteoporosis. The excrement from these cats was so toxic that weeds refused to grow in the soil fertilized with it, whereas weeds proliferated in the stools from the cats fed the living, uncooked food. Here is the clincher: the first generation of kittens born to the group of cats who were fed only cooked food were sick and abnormal. The second generation were often born diseased or dead. By the third generation, the mothers were sterile. Dr. Pottenger conducted similar tests on white mice and the results coincided exactly with those of the tests run on the cats.

So what do Pottenger's Cats and cooked foods have to do with my discussion of enzymes? Just this: Far less heat than is required to cook food *entirely obliterates* all food enzymes. I want to be certain that you are clear on what I am saying. *When you cook your food, the enzymes necessary to break down that food in your body are destroyed.* Not some of them. *All of them.* And they're not merely degraded or made to be less effective. They are, every last one, completely and totally wiped out. This sets up quite a predicament for your body. One that has some very negative results. You see, food in the stomach, as I said, is a number-one priority for your body. Food can't simply sit around in your stomach, it has to be dealt with immediately. But if the food has been cooked, the enzymes that would have done that job are gone. At this crucial moment, the wisdom and intelligence of the body snaps into action and calls upon the mechanism in the body that produces metabolic enzymes and forces it to produce the digestive enzymes necessary to digest the food. Now remember, this mechanism that produces metabolic enzymes is the very same one that determines the length and quality of your life. We know that this mechanism can only produce a certain number of enzymes, and then life ends. So every time you eat something that is cooked, you are literally inviting ill health and shortening your life.

The reason this is so is that when you suddenly force the metabolic enzyme mechanism to produce digestive enzymes, the work that the metabolic enzymes would have been doing to keep everything working efficiently and effectively, thereby keeping you well and healthy, is compromised and thwarted. The very mechanism in the body designed to keep you healthy and energetic is kept from doing its job. If your lymph system is overburdened, that means your body is working to decrease the amount of waste that has accumulated, which can ultimately make you sick. Every time you eat cooked food, you not only lessen the effectiveness of your body's labour force (metabolic enzymes) that is trying to cleanse and strengthen your body, but you also rob unnecessarily from the very mechanism that determines how long and how well you will live. And that has to be the last thing on earth you would ever want to intentionally do.

Live Plant Enzymes

Right about now you might be thinking that I'm getting around to convincing you to become a total raw fooder, eating only uncooked food. Nope! That is not my intention. Hey, I like cooked food and I'm not about to give it up. So I'm sure as heaven not going to suggest that you do. Now, without question, the amount of uncooked food I eat does far outweigh the cooked food I consume, but no, I'm not going to suggest that we stop eating all cooked food. But here is what I *am* going to suggest, and it is the very purpose of these few pages.

Thanks to technological advances that did not exist 12 years ago when I wrote *Fit For Life*, there are now available to one and all what are called live plant enzymes, which can be taken just prior to eating anything cooked, that do the job that the cooked-away enzymes were supposed to do. They come in very small capsules, they are totally non-toxic, have no side effects other than increased health and longevity, and they prevent the unnecessary squandering of your precious metabolic-enzyme capacity. These pharmaceutical-grade, live plant enzymes are grown and harvested in a laboratory setting without compromising them with heat. In my opinion, the ability to make these live plant enzymes available to us is one of the most significant and beneficial advances of the 20th century. If there is a substance that could rightly be called the fountain of youth, this is surely it.

From the day I found out these live plant enzymes were available, until now, I have been taking them whenever I eat *anything* cooked. No matter where I am, no matter who I'm with, no matter what I'm doing, I always carry them with me and take them before eating any cooked food. At this point in my life, I would just as soon pass on eating than to eat something cooked without my enzymes. I'm serious. I simply don't eat anything cooked if I don't have my enzymes with me, and as much as I love to eat, you can be sure that if you run into me somewhere, I'll have the capsules with me. If I don't, then you can be just as sure that I'm not on my way to a restaurant, unless, of course, I plan on eating a salad or something else that has not been cooked.

I paid people to find out for me which enzymes were the absolute finest, purest, most high-quality live plant enzymes available anywhere in the world, and those are the only ones I take. Consider the words of Dr. Edward Howell, the man considered to be the father of enzyme nutrition:

> I like to think of life as an integration of enzyme reactions. Life ends when the worn out metabolic enzyme activity of the body machine drops to such a low point that it is unable to carry on vital enzyme reactions. This is the true trademark of old age. Old age and debilitated metabolic enzyme activity are synonymous. If we postpone the debilitation of metabolic enzyme activity, what we now call old age could become the glorious prime of life.[218]

Allow me to ask you a question. Would there be any possibility at all, *any*, of you going to the bank on a regular basis, taking out your hard-earned cash and then using it as toilet paper? Any chance at all? Can you even think of anything that would be more absurd and ridiculous? No? Well, I can. I can think of one thing more preposterous than using your cash as toilet paper and that would be using up the metabolic enzymes in your body that keep you healthy and alive, in order to digest cooked food that you could have taken live plant enzymes for. If a long life free of pain, ill health, and disease is one of the goals you have for yourself and your loved ones, then start using live plant enzymes *NOW!* Do this for yourself: you're worth it.

For information about live plant enzymes, call Natural EFX (pronounced effects) at (888) 966-5777. You will be sent information about live plant enzymes and you will find out how to obtain the very same high-quality enzymes that I take.

Ten years from now the need to take live plant enzymes with cooked food will be as well established as today's dictum that to acquire and maintain a high level of health we must exercise and eat right. Don't wait! Take advantage of this information now and get a jump on it. You will be glad for the rest of your *long and healthy* life.

12

The Third Principle: The Mind Matters

If we are to be well and happy, not only the body, but the mind also must be peaceful and harmonious.
Ernest Holmes
The Science of Mind

It is well documented that in a climate of negativity, the ability to heal is greatly reduced—depressed people not only lower their immune response, for example, but even weaken their DNA's ability to repair itself.
Deepak Chopra, M.D.
Quantum Healing

Many of (the mind's) effects are achieved directly on the body's tissues without any awareness on our part. The body responds to the mind's messages whether conscious or unconscious.
Bernie S. Siegel, M.D.
Love, Medicine and Miracles

Your thoughts create your experience of your health, wealth and every detail of your world.
Wayne Dyer, M.D.
Real Magic

If you would perfect your body, guard your mind.
James Allen
As A Man Thinketh

*What things soever you desire, when you pray, believe that you receive them,
and you shall have them.*
Jesus

All that we are is the result of what we have thought.
Buddha

The temptation was there to continue the list of quotes above and let 70 or 80 of them comprise this chapter, so great is the amount of material that has been written over the years on the inextricable relationship between the mind and the body. The two parts of the mind that can be discussed are: that part which we know something about; and that part about which nothing is known. Studying the mind is like studying the cosmos itself.

What is actually known about the mind can be likened to a single grain of sand on a vast stretch of beach. Nevertheless, the tiny bit that we do know about is extraordinary and supercharged with power. *And it is a power we can use!* It is what Norman Cousins is referring to when he says, "The growth of the human mind is still high adventure, in many ways the highest adventure on earth."[219]

Have you ever heard statements like "Attitude is everything," or "You are what you think you are," or "Your mind can make a heaven of hell or a hell of heaven"? Have you heard athletes refer to their "mental game" and the role it played in a win or loss? Indeed, one of the most renowned tennis instructors in the world told me that the game of tennis is 10 percent talent, 90 percent mental. In fact, you'll hear tennis players frequently say before a match, "If my mental game is there, I'll win." And after a loss, "My mental game just wasn't there."

You know the story of the little red engine going up a steep hill, don't you? "I think I can, I think I can, I think I can." And, of course, the Master Teacher, Jesus, tried to teach us all this lesson when he said, over and over again in many different ways, "It is done unto you as you believe." What other possible meaning could this statement have but that the power of the mind, through right thinking, can bring into our experience absolutely anything we desire.

Volumes have been written on the power of the mind and its ability to strengthen us or weaken us, uplift us or bring us down, heal us or make us sick. And yet, although there is more than ample evidence that the mind, properly channelled, can be one of the most potent tools in the health and healing of the body, no other area of health care has been more minimized and neglected. It seems that when we cross from the seen to the unseen, all manner of biases come into play. As long as we're dealing with the physical world, the world that we can hear, see or touch, we're comfortable. As soon as we move to that part of our existence that has no presence that we can relate to with our senses, the terra firma gets mighty shaky. There's an air of hocus-pocus, or cultism, or some other such nonsense attributed to the idea of the power of the mind to heal that results in scepticism.

All you have to do to see that this is an area well worth your consideration is to read any of the books by Dr. Deepak Chopra, Dr. Wayne Dyer, Louise Hay, Dr. Bernie Siegel, or Ernest Holmes; you will learn about the many remarkable instances of people using their minds to send positive messages of love and healing to their bodies to overcome even catastrophic cases of cancer.

The Mind-Body Connection

In the physical world, it is well understood that there are natural laws that are simple and undeviating. If one plants the seed for a peach tree, a peach tree will grow. On the other hand, if the seed for a thistle bush is planted, there will be no peaches, only thistles. This fact is so utterly simple and obvious that some may say, "Gee, you don't say." But few understand that in the mental world, the law still holds true and is just as unyielding.

Your thoughts are like seeds in that thoughts become things, the same way seeds become plants. Good thoughts produce good things and negative thoughts produce negative things. Good thoughts will never produce negative results, and negative thoughts will never produce good results.

Although far too many medical scientists are quick to discount the role the mind plays in healing, favouring drugs instead, there is a wealth of scientific evidence that proves the astounding power of the mind to heal. In the area of psychiatry and psychology, there has been an explosion in mind-body research over the last decade. Dr. Martin Seligman, a professor at the University of Pennsylvania and author of *Learned Optimism*, has done research showing that pessimistic people have weaker "immune systems," are more prone to colds and flu, and have more major health problems after age 50. Their bodies are less likely to fight off killer diseases such as cancer.[220]

A colleague of Dr. Seligman's, Dr. Gregory Buchanon, also a researcher at the University of Pennsylvania, conducted tests on a group of subjects to determine if they were essentially pessimists or optimists. According to Dr. Buchanon, more of those who were identified as pessimists died within ten years. Those who ranked within the top 25 percent as the most negative had the highest death rate: 26 of 31 subjects died. By contrast, only 10 of the 31 who ranked as the most optimistic had died.[221]

The Placebo Effect

Some of the most impressive and convincing evidence of the power of the mind to heal the body comes from what is referred to as the "placebo effect." In studies to determine the effectiveness of a drug, a group afflicted with a certain malady is divided into two groups. One group receives the drug to be tested, the other group receives a dummy pill or placebo, usually a coated sugar pill. Neither group knows which it is receiving, the real drug or the placebo. If the group receiving the real drug shows a marked improvement over the placebo group, the drug is deemed effective. But what has happened over and over again is that in many instances the placebo turned out to be as effective as the drug. Not everyone responds this way, but generally 30 to 60 percent report relief of pain, even stabbing pain, from the placebo, thus the placebo effect.[222]

Stated differently, being convinced of the potential effectiveness of a particular medicine or surgical procedure actually assists in making one well and improves chances of recovery. Conversely, feelings of scepticism and doubt in the same situation will bring about the exact opposite, less of a chance of recovery.[223] This phenomenon has been noted for *centuries!*[224] At the beginning of the 20th century Dr. William Osler enjoyed enormous notoriety as a foremost physician and healer. He regularly taught his students that frequently many of his patients were healed because of their faith in the treatment they received, *not* the treatment itself.[225]

One of the most celebrated cases in history of the mind as healer of the body occurred early in the 1800s and involved Dr. Isaac Jennings. After 20 years of practising medicine, Dr. Jennings became so disillusioned with drugging and bleeding his patients that he discontinued the treatments. To meet the demands of his patients for "medicines," he gave them an assortment of bread pills, a variety of powders made of wheat flower variously scented and coloured, and vials of pure water of various hues. Much to his surprise, his patients made recoveries far in excess of what he saw when he administered drugs.

It was not long before Dr. Jenning's fame spread far and wide and his practice extended over a large territory, putting drugging doctors out of business. He continued substituting his innocent placebos for 15 to 20 years before he revealed to his medical colleagues and to the community what he had been doing. Some of his colleagues were intrigued. Others were angry at him. Some of his patients said they didn't care what he gave them, whatever it was it had healed them. Some were angry and called him an impostor and refused to continue seeing him. The fact that the duration of their illnesses had been greatly shortened did not weigh in Dr. Jennings's favour. They paid for drugs and they wanted drugs. In spite of the puzzling, mixed reactions of his patients, Yale University conferred an honorary degree upon Dr. Jennings in recognition of his success.[226]

The reason placebos work is that the people taking them are convinced that they will help. In their minds, they think the treatment will make them well, so it does! Placebos support the fact that positive beliefs enhance healing. Many present-day "authorities" doubt the scientific validity of the ability of the mind to heal the body, in spite of the fact that there exists a large body of scientific studies that support the argument that the mind has the power to heal the body. There are examples galore, all documented, of people healing themselves—sometimes of some very serious problems—all with their minds, their thoughts. They so strongly believed they were going to get well that they did! Take a look at Dr. Larry Dossey's *Healing Words*. A most fascinating and informative book (by a medical doctor!) on the subject of the power of prayer to heal. Very interesting stuff.

This awesome power resides in you right now. Nothing prevents you from using it on your own behalf other than your own thoughts. Whatever you want to call it, be it a positive mental attitude or the power of prayer, that power *will* respond to your thoughts, words, and beliefs. If you wish to make the determination with absolute certainty that you have tremendous influence over your health and well-being and *know* that it is so, you can! Indeed, you can just as easily think you are in charge as not.

Before giving you the tools to help you start to redirect your mind to think in a more positive light about the power you have over your own health, let's look at just a few of the more impressive examples of the placebo effect. Placebos have provided relief in cases of angina, arthritis, pain, hay fever, headaches, coughs, ulcers, hypertension, cancer, and heart disease.[227] Numerous studies of certain religious practices have shown a direct correlation between deeply held beliefs and the lessening of health problems.[228] One ten-year study on elderly people showed that those who actually thought of themselves and labelled themselves as old or elderly had significantly higher death rates over the course of the study than those who thought of themselves as middle-aged.[229]

The number of documented cases that prove the power of the mind to heal the body would easily fill this entire book. I will share two particularly striking illustrations, one each pertaining to the two biggest killers in North America—heart disease and cancer.

In the late 1950s and early 1960s, a new operation for the relief of angina became quite successful and popular. Angina is the medical term for pain, and it causes sudden and severe discomfort of the lower chest accompanied by a feeling of suffocation. If it is not dealt with, it is often a precursor of a more serious heart condition because it is a warning that blood flow to the heart is being restricted. Anyone who has experienced this excruciating pain does not cherish the idea of a repeat performance.

The operation, which has been largely replaced by what is referred to as a coronary bypass, involved opening the chest and ligating or tying off a certain artery in order to force more blood through other branches that were being obstructed. The operation brought a marked relief of pain in 70 percent of patients. In a controlled study, randomly selected patients who were to receive this operation were anaesthetized and an incision in the chest was made in the appropriate area, and that was all that was done. There was no tying off of arteries or anything else. The incision was closed back up and the patients were told it was a successful operation. These individuals, *believing* they'd had the operation, experienced a 70 percent improvement in relief of their pain. *Precisely the same degree of relief as those who actually had their arteries tied off!*[230] Now, that's impressive stuff.

The second illustration of the power of the mind to heal the body is as startling as anything I have ever come across. This case pertains to a profoundly sick gentleman who, amongst other attendant problems, had large cancerous tumours all over his body. All standard treatment had been tried and abandoned and he was close to the end with a prognosis that he would not survive another month. At the time, there was a widely touted cancer "cure" called Krebiozen. The man heard about it and felt it would help him and begged for it to be administered to him. His condition was so bad that he must have thought there would be no harm by trying it; after all, he was already so close to death.

Two days after the first injection, the man's tumours had shrunk to one-half their original size. He was given injections three times a week and was discharged from the hospital in ten days. He enjoyed two months of practically perfect health, but as fate would have it, he received some conflicting reports on Krebiozen. He immediately relapsed to his preterminal state. The tumours returned. His physicians told him to disregard what he'd read because the Krebiozen had deteriorated from standing too long and they were going to give him a new "double strength, super refined batch." He perked up with a very strong anticipation of cure, but this time he was injected with *distilled water*. Nevertheless, the tumours once again melted and he was again symptom-free for two more months! He then had occasion to read the final American Medical Association report that Krebiozen had been shown to be worthless. He died two days later.[231]

So powerful is the mind in creating whatever reality it is convinced of that up to 50 percent of subjects in some studies actually exhibit side effects from the placebos.[232] In one astonishing case involving the testing of an antihistamine, the subjects receiving the placebos experienced more side effects than those who received the medication![233] Results of recent studies show the placebo effect to be twice as powerful as previously thought,[234] and most powerful when a trusted physician enthusiastically offers a patient a new therapy.[235]

Knowing that there are those who accept suggestion from authority figures so strongly that they view the suggestion as reality and actually cause the expected result to occur, it should be a punishable crime for anyone in a position of authority to tell a patient that he or she is going to die or has but a short time left before dying. Even if there is a minuscule chance that a person would survive if not told death was inevitable, it is ignorance and arrogance of the highest order for anyone to tell another person when he or she is going to die. That's God's decision. And only God knows how many people have been ushered to an early grave because they had the idea planted in their minds that their time was up. I wonder if there is anyone who hasn't heard of someone living far beyond the time they were told they would die.

Medical doctors have notoriously discounted the idea that the mind can heal the body. The American Medical Association queried their members in 1990 and found that only 10 percent believed in the mind-body connection.[236] Nevertheless, wouldn't the decent thing be to tell a patient about those instances where other patients conquered the disease and survived or beat the odds? I cannot think of even one woman who had a mastectomy that I know who was not told it was either a mastectomy or death.

It's just not right. The death-sentence approach in our health care system is one that sorely needs to be changed.

Guidelines to Positive Thinking

After what you've read, you could easily be thinking that the mind might be the most powerful tool of all in your quest to achieve vibrant health. And who's to say you would not be right? The task for many of us, however, is to figure out how to retrain ourselves to think in such a way as to take full advantage of the potential that resides in the mind, the same way a mighty oak tree resides in a single acorn. Under the right circumstances, that acorn will become the oak tree. And under the right circumstances, the extraordinary and dynamic source of power that is the mind will unleash its gifts. It waits patiently for your direction.

If your commitment to health is such that you will be periodically mono-dieting (First Principle, Chapter 10) and gradually reducing your consumption of animal products (Second Principle, Chapter 11), the addition of your knowing, *really knowing*, that your efforts will prevent you from ever becoming sick, then you have a winning combination that vastly improves your chances of success. But trying to turn around a lifetime of negative thinking, or thinking that is not supportive to your goals, can be a challenge. Like other habits that have become fixed or routine, the way to change them is to crowd them out with other more favourable ones.

There is no question that you can accomplish this. You are in charge of how you think, and at any moment you have the choice to change your thoughts in any direction you wish. The mind is enormously receptive to your directives. It doesn't matter how long you have been thinking negatively. You can instantly turn it around by positive thoughts that will override negative ones right away. It's like turning on a light in a dark room. No matter how long the room has been dark, the moment you switch on the light, the darkness is removed.

In all likelihood there are hundreds of tools or guidelines you could use to assist you in training the mind to think about your daily life in a more positive way. Consider the following three that I and thousands of others have used with enormous success, and that you can use specifically to help in your quest to live a pain-free, disease-free life:

1) Ask better questions.
2) State your best case to the universe.
3) Acknowledge and accept your many "I's."

Ask Better Questions

This is a tool that can bring about remarkable, almost miraculous results, is as easy as anything could ever be, and is interesting and fun to use. I first learned about the power of questions from Anthony Robbins, author of the best-sellers *Unlimited Power* and *Awaken The Giant Within*. I have been friends with Tony for more than 18 years and he is one of the most consistently positive people I have ever known.

You may not even be aware of it, but you are constantly asking yourself questions either silently or out loud, and your brain is constantly supplying answers. "Ask and you shall receive." Most everyone has heard this phrase from the Bible. When you ask for something from the brain, it snaps right to and answers. It's just like a computer that contains thousands or millions of pieces of information. You punch in a question and up pops the answer on the screen. Whatever you ask of yourself, *good* or *bad*, receives an answer. So if you ask, "Why can't I ever lose weight?" your brain tells you why you can't. "Well, you eat too much, you don't try hard enough, you're not real serious, you don't exercise enough, you were born that way." Your brain *will* come up with an answer. So questions have the power to create positiveness or negativeness in your life. But what if you asked instead, "How can I lose weight and enjoy myself while I'm doing it?" Wouldn't you rather have an answer to *that* question?

Have you ever heard some of these?

"Why can't I ever get ahead?"

"Why does this always happen to me?"

"Why does so and so always treat me so badly?"

"Why am I so fat?"

"Why am I always suffering from one thing or another?"

If you ask why you *can't* do something, your brain will tell you why and you compound your unwanted situation. The secret of turning this around is to *ask better questions!* You can make a major positive change in your life starting right now with the right questions. It has a lot to do with what you choose to focus on. You see, *whatever you focus on, you get!* And the decision is yours and no one else's. You can focus on what's good in your life or what's not. It's totally up to you.

If you watch the news on television and hear a story about some heinous crime, and later hear a story about a group that takes children with balloons to visit a retirement home just to bring some joy and light into the lives of the folks who live there, on which story would you focus? There are people who focus on all the pain and suffering in the world, and there are those who choose to see the beauty and goodness that exists in the world. You always have a choice to focus on either the positive or the negative in your life.

If you focus on how things just don't seem to work out, they won't! But, hey, guess what? The opposite is also true. Focus on how things *will* work out and they will. Remember: "It is done unto you as you believe."

The only difference between you and people you admire greatly for what they have achieved and the positive feelings they always seem to project is what you have chosen to focus on and what questions you ask of yourself. You can be sure that people like Anthony Robbins, and the people you admire most, are not asking themselves negative, disempowering questions. They're the ones asking questions like, "How can I turn this around and benefit from it?" instead of, "Why does this always happen to me?" They are asking the kind of questions that constantly spur them on to more and more achievements.

If you want things to work out in terms of your health goals, you must decide on what you're going to focus and what questions you're going to ask yourself. The right question can change your focus and that can change your life. Ever hear the story of the man who constantly lamented his situation of not having any shoes until he met another man without any feet? His focus changed in a hurry.

This all may sound so simple, even silly, but it makes such a massive difference, it would be a tragedy to have this powerful tool right in front of you and not take advantage of it.

As you pursue your goal to live happily, healthfully, and disease-free, always be asking yourself positive, uplifting questions:

"How can I support myself today to be healthier?"

"What can I do to specifically assist my lymph system's effort to remove toxins and waste from my body?"

"What can I do to make exercise more interesting and enjoyable?"

"What will I do with all of the newfound energy I'm going to have?"

"What did I do to be so blessed to find this information?"

Regularly ask yourself positive questions; this will create a positive atmosphere around you, and good things will happen as a result. And before you ask a question like, "Gee, do you think this can really work?" ask instead, "How can I *make* this work?"

Here's something you can start doing tomorrow morning that will progressively make you stronger and stronger, and more positive-feeling about CAREing for your body. Just take a few moments each morning to start the day off with a burst of positive energy.

Have you ever awakened in the morning with the question on your lips, "Why do I have to go to work today?" or some other negative-based question? Not a very good way to start the day.

What if you woke up and said, "What can I do today to make it a more joyous day?"

Further, if you will think of a general group of positive questions to ask yourself every morning, you will energize your entire life. Here's a sampling, but you can think of your own also:

"What am I happiest about in my life?"

"What are the things I have to be grateful for?"

"Who are my friends?"

"Who loves me?"

"What have I accomplished that I am deeply proud of?"

Before leaping out of bed and tackling the tasks of the day and becoming all involved in everything you have to do, lie there and ask yourself positive questions and briefly answer them to yourself. It will take three to five minutes to ask and answer these questions.

What if you started every day like that? You might begin to buzz with positive energy! If this became a habit in your life every morning, just like brushing your teeth, over time, merely waking up would automatically put you into a positive state. This is how the mind can be retrained to think in a way that is more supportive of the healthy lifestyle you desire. One last question to ponder: "Isn't it great that you are so open to making these positive changes to improve your life, and these tools are now available to help you?"

State Your Best Case to the Universe

Have you ever been in someone's home or office and seen either on the wall, desk, or table a plaque with some kind of inspirational or uplifting quote or saying? Why do you think they are displayed in such prominent places? Do you have these kinds of inspirational messages around your home or office? If so, why? The answer couldn't be more obvious. They are reminders designed to inspire the reader, to remind the reader of all the good and positive things that can exist. When you read a message on love or happiness or success or some other positive aspect of life, for those few moments while you are reading it, don't you feel good? If it's particularly applicable to something that is happening to you at the time, don't you kind of purse your lips a little, nod in recognition, and think, "Of course, of course"? It's as though the message was written just for you.

The written word can be, and is, enormously powerful. "The pen is mightier than the sword" is a wise saying that illustrates the point. Words written on a page can make you weep or make you laugh, make you sad or make you happy, make you feel anger or make you feel compassion. When you read something, it is imprinted in your mind's eye. Have you ever heard the name of a person or place or object of some kind and not been able to pronounce it properly until you saw it written?

The power inherent in writing something down is the very reason so many people write affirmations on a regular basis. Say, for example, someone is desperately trying to change jobs for something that is more rewarding both financially and professionally. He or she may write the affirmation "I know that the position I am looking for that is perfect for me will present itself soon." It may be written one time, ten times, fifty times or a hundred times every day. The affirmation becomes a permanent part of the person's consciousness, a way of thinking that leaves no room for anything but what is desired. It is also felt that by writing down the affirmation the desired goal is actually created and it's just a matter of time before it appears. That is why so many people believe in writing goals down on paper. Seminars are held all over the country on goal setting to show people exactly how to use it to attract what they desire. Invariably these seminars involve the writing down on paper of what you wish to come into your life.

Other people will write a word on a piece of paper every morning with the idea of concentrating on that one word all day. Words such as "health," "love," "peace," "compassion," "forgiveness," "success," "joy," "concentration" or any number of different possibilities. The next day another word is written down, and it is the focus of attention for the day.

There are many tools such as these that people devise to use the written word not only to attract what they want, but also to train their minds to focus in a positive rather than negative way. One approach I have used for years that I would like to suggest works well with the first tool of asking better questions (see above) by *stating something as fact rather than asking about it*. This can be done with one, two, three, four or however many statements you wish. You write neatly on a piece of paper statements of fact as you *wish them to be*. For example:

- My body is becoming cleaner, stronger, and healthier every day.
- My lymph system is working at optimum efficiency, preventing cancer from ever developing.
- My lymph nodes are clean and they are going to stay that way.
- I am open and receptive to the vast number of possibilities available to me.
- I enjoy the work I have chosen to perform and it is important.
- Outer circumstances cannot disturb my sense of well-being. I am in charge of my happiness.
- My life is supercharged with all the energy I need to be happy and well.

I have many of these statements posted all around my home. I would like to share with you one that I saw many years ago and I have been reading to myself every day, sometimes several times a day, ever since. It sits on my desk where I write and I always read it before I begin my writing day:

> I go forth as an empowered and an empowering person. I come from strength, and I bring strength into all that I do. I call upon inner wisdom and love to guide me in the right use of my time and talents, all to bring a greater good to life.

Remember, there can be as many or as few of these statements as you like on any subject whatsoever. You then put the piece of paper with the most empowering statements you can think of in some *conspicuous* place where you will be sure to see it during the day. On your desk, on the refrigerator, on the dashboard of your car, anywhere. You then make a commitment to read these insights at least once a day. This can be at any time during the day that you feel is most convenient, upon awakening in the morning, before going to sleep at night, at lunchtime. I'm not talking about a huge expenditure of time. It takes less time to read these statements than to see what's on television tonight. When you read the statements, don't just read them mechanically, say them to yourself with feeling and conviction. *Mean it!*

Now, you may be asking, if it's being suggested to read them just once a day, why do they have to be in a conspicuous place? If you *are* asking that question, then you are really paying attention, so thank you. This is the reason I keep these statements conspicuously placed: Being a writer, I spend considerable time at my desk. My statements are within easy grasp. As it happens, as I pause to ponder something pertaining to my work, I can see the statements sitting there. This has two benefits. First, it's so easy to read one or two of the statements, which immediately refocuses my thoughts and gives me a real charge, an energy boost, making sure my thoughts remain positive and high-minded. Second, after you have made the daily reading of your statements a habit and you have been doing it for several weeks or months, just seeing the piece of paper with the statements on it instantly has the same effect as reading one or more of them.

You *know* what's on the list. So every time you look at it, you are, in effect, keeping your mind on track. The positive track. You can add or delete statements at any time, and to be sure, feel free to read them as many times a day as you wish. The minimum is one time, but you *can't* read them too often. Please don't underestimate this approach. It is a powerful tool as you will quickly find out.

Acknowledge and Accept Your Many "I's"

Have you ever made comments similar to these:

"I don't know what came over me. That's just not like me at all."

Or,

"I had a real battle with myself."

Or,

"I can't make up my mind. I keep going up and back."

Or,

"If I did that, I'd never forgive myself."

Or,

"One moment I want to do one thing, the next moment I want to do the opposite."

Do these statements sound at all familiar? It is probably a safe bet to say that at one time or another we have all had thoughts like these. It's as though there is more than one person living in our bodies, all with their own likes and dislikes, wants and needs, and all vying to be heard and be in charge. The idea may sound a bit odd to you, but it is a point of view held by quite a few people around the world and one which was written about extensively by one of the world's most intriguing philosophers, George Gurdjieff. His writings and works, and writings about him, have been the object of study and discussion by huge numbers of people all around the world.

One of the central themes of Gurdjieff's philosophy was that we all have many "I's" but that we don't realize it. Because we have one body and one name, we think we are one. But we are many. We may have dozens, perhaps hundreds, of lesser "I's" all wanting to be heard.

What exactly do I mean when I say "I's"? The "I's" refer to the different parts of you that want different things at different times. For example, "I want to buckle down and get on a good diet and lose some weight." Now when these words are spoken, they're meant! But at another time of day, that particular "I's" resolve is weakened and a different "I" says, "I want to enjoy myself and eat whatever I like." These two "I's" are each trying to get an upper hand over the other. "That does it. I'm going to start exercising a half hour a day at least four times a week. I'm going to get in shape."

You say it with absolute conviction. Then,

"I have so much to think about, I'm going to start exercising first thing next month."

"I want to clean out the garage."

"I want to kick back, read a novel, and have some chocolate."

"I'm going to put in some extra hours at work and really solidify my position there."

"I can't wait to get home and just forget about work."

"I want to read a good book."

"I want to go to the movies."

"I'm going to have a really healthy lunch today."

"I want a burger and fries."

"I want to do more with the children on the weekend."

"I just want to take it easy and do nothing this weekend."

"I want to go out tonight."

"I want to stay home."

And on and on and on for practically every situation in life. The fact is, each and every one of these statements is real! When they are spoken, the "I" that is in charge is speaking for the whole, even though many other "I's" may disagree but do not have the floor at that moment. Think of fictional Jane Doe going through a day. Each of her separate "I's" is able to call itself Jane, is able to act in her name, agree or disagree in her name, make decisions or promises in her name with which another "I" in Jane will have to deal. This explains why people so often make decisions that are frequently not carried out. One "I" makes the decision, another "I" ignores it. It's as though someone writes a cheque in your name and then you have to make good on it.

Understanding this aspect of your life can be very freeing. You can start to recognize certain "I's" and become familiar with them. Once you know which ones are there and how they operate, you can start to bring them in line with the "I's" that are more aligned with your quest for vibrant health. You *know* that there are "I's" in you that absolutely want to eat properly and exercise regularly. And there are other "I's" in you that don't. Just having that understanding is a breakthrough.

Each "I," whether a strong, positive one or a weak, negative one, wants to have its way whenever it can. It wants to do what it is accustomed to doing and does not want to change or allow any other "I" to take precedence.

This creates a lot of turmoil in people who are not aware of the many "I's" and don't know what's causing them so much indecision and anguish. But when you know what's going on, you can observe the different "I's" and even say out loud to the ones you know don't care about your optimum well-being, "So, you're back. Here to try and influence me to disregard my health, are you?" Of course, this confrontation with the "I" is done in private. If you do it in front of people, they may start to chase you with a big butterfly net. Standing around waving your finger at yourself, admonishing yourself to go away and leave yourself alone could attract the wrong kind of attention. But observing the different "I's" that come up in a day and confronting them can be very interesting. And only when you recognize that they're there can you begin to take charge of them and create some order.

Knowing this theory of the many "I's," the next time you say something like, "I can't believe I ate those doughnuts. I don't know what I was thinking. I'm trying to cleanse and rejuvenate my body!" you will know that there are two different "I's" at work. One wanting to CARE for itself, the other hell-bent on self-destruction. The more you observe this phenomenon, the more familiar you will become with your own diverse makeup, and the more likely you will be able to give dominance to the "I's" that support your health goals and maintain a positive direction in your life.

You can also stop browbeating yourself or feeling guilty about one thing or another you did or wish you didn't do, or didn't do and wish you did. Just know that at some time different "I's" are stronger than at other times and forgive yourself your human frailty. Better to work at strengthening your positive "I's" than bemoaning the action of your negative ones.

The idea of many "I's" all vying for control can be likened to a house being built by a group of workers with no supervisor in charge. The workers have not been instructed as to their specific duties, so each, feeling he knows best what to do, takes a hand at being in charge. But others feel they could handle the situation better and disagreements erupt.

The building of the house is not progressing in an orderly fashion. Instead, there is chaos. The only chance is for the supervisor to show up and organize everyone and assign the right job to the right person so the entire crew is working as a team. When it comes to your many "I's," the "supervisor" in this case would be your strong, positive, health-seeking "I." The one that is committed to keeping you on track and seeking out the most supportive conditions in your life. The only way to make this "I" stronger and more capable of governing the other "I's" is to habitually perform certain practices that will strengthen it and give it power and confidence. There *is* an "I" in you that wants to believe, that *does* believe, that you have the information, the tools, and the ability to live a vibrantly healthy life free of disease.

There is also the "I" that doesn't, so anything you can do to strengthen the positive "I" and silence the negative "I" is going to weigh heavily in your success. By recognizing that you have these different "I's," and consciously asking better questions so your strong "I's" will answer, and stating your intentions to the universe, you are taking a huge step in strengthening the strong, positive, health-seeking "I" that *knows* you will never become sick, so that it is the one that predominates in your life.

Emotions and Self-Healing

There is one last issue I must address as regards cancer—either preventing it or beating it. Although this is an area of immense importance, it somehow has received scant attention. As indicated earlier, there are many variables that contribute to the development of cancer. I have focused primarily on the effects of diet on health both because I am certain that it is *the* main risk factor, and because diet happens to be my area of expertise.

Scholars and researchers have shown that repressed, unvented anger, coupled with a lack of self-love, has been a major contributor in many cases of all kinds of cancer. Although this is not my area of expertise, it would be remiss of me if I did not bring it to your attention and encourage you to take a close, hard look at this area of your life. To help you do so, I would like to introduce you to the work of a most remarkable woman.

Louise L. Hay is an internationally respected author and lecturer. I have the very good fortune of having a personal relationship with Ms. Hay and I can tell you without hesitation that she is one of the most genuinely loving, compassionate, and concerned people I have ever met. Merely being in the same room with her lifts your spirits and fills you with good feelings.

Ms. Hay was diagnosed with incurable, terminal cancer. Even if she were to submit to incredibly extensive surgery, her chance of survival, she was told, was nil. She rejected the medical approach entirely and instead decided to focus on why she had such negative feelings about herself. She scrutinized the abuses she had endured both as a child and as an adult and realized the full extent to which these unresolved issues had been fermenting within her, culminating in cancer. She simultaneously detoxified her body with a cleansing diet.

In one of the most remarkable instances of self-healing I have ever heard of, Louise Hay *totally healed herself!* Only six months after her diagnosis, her doctors told her there was not even a trace of cancer. This was many years ago and she is still cancer-free.

Ms. Hay's many books and tapes are available to you. I suggest that you take a look at *You Can Heal Your Life*, which made the *New York Times* best-seller list and has been read by millions worldwide. I know people whose lives have been changed merely by *reading* this book. You can be one of them.

The Benefits of the Three CARE Principles

The stronger you become, the more you will want to use the three principles of CARE I have laid out in Chapters 10, 11, and 12. The frequency with which you use them depends entirely on your level of motivation. How quickly do you want to start to cleanse and strengthen your lymph system, which in turn protects you against becoming sick? How truly committed are you to experiencing a long life predominated by high spirits, vitality, and health, rather than aches, pains, and illness?

These are the kinds of questions we are all grappling with. At night when you lay your head on your pillow and you are alone with your thoughts in the dark, these are issues that can loom large. By using the three CARE principles, with an attitude of knowing that they will work and that ill health will never be a part of your life, you will be able to live out your life in health, confident that you are the one in charge and in control of your destiny.

13

You Have a Choice

In an article in the *New York Times*, Dr. Yitzhak Koch states that, "The breast is a unique gland, an underestimated gland. Its activity is much more complex than people had thought."[237] And I would like to add to that, that a woman's breasts are exactly where they belong. So is a man's prostate gland, and every other part of the body that God put there. They do not have to be removed and they do not have to be mutilated. You can prevent cancer, there is no doubt whatsoever about that. It is a daunting challenge, I know, especially in light of the "experts," who are supposed to know how, declaring that they don't.

What I have offered in this book is one way to prevent cancer and the years of pain, ill health, and anguish that precede it. There may be other ways, to be sure, and if there are, I am hopeful that they will be discovered and offered to people everywhere so that the suffering can end. Preventing cancer is not something that is accomplished by taking a onetime action that achieves the goal. It certainly would be lovely if there were a pill or a shot or some other "magic bullet" that would do the job and remove the need for ongoing diligence, but there isn't, and that's that.

If you have a doorway in your home that is too low and you smash your forehead into it every time you go through it, all you have to do to prevent that from happening is to have the doorway raised and that's the end of the problem. You don't have to think about it anymore. When it comes to the prevention of cancer it's not that simple. It's not one action that you perform. *It's the way you choose to live your life!* You can either live in a manner that opens the way for cancer to develop· or you can live in a manner that produces vibrant health. To prevent cancer, to really, truly prevent it, an ongoing effort is called for.

I may be accused of being naive in thinking that by cleansing the lymph system, cutting back on animal products, and maintaining a positive attitude, something as *seemingly* complex and baffling as cancer can be prevented when medicine's greatest minds have not yet been able to get a handle on it. But my questions to you are: What if I'm right? What if the approach suggested in this book will do the job? If it works, does it matter one way or the other that I'm not a medical doctor and that the approach is straightforward, uncomplicated, and not dependent upon expensive diagnostic procedures and invasive treatment?

I'm not saying that this book will end cancer, but I can tell you it will definitely prevent it for a lot of people and perhaps you are one of them. The thing is, what do you have to lose by trying what I'm suggesting? Even if I'm wrong, what possible harm could there be in cleaning your inner body so it operates more efficiently, reducing your intake of the foods that every health professional recommends you should eat less of, exercising regularly, and keeping a positive mental attitude? You sure as the dickens will never see any of those things on a death certificate.

What else are you being offered? Remember, the experts don't know how to prevent cancer and only 5 percent of research money goes toward prevention. If you sit around and wait for some magic bullet, you might find yourself under the knife. That *must* be avoided. To do that, you must think prevention, prevention, prevention. If someone offers you something to prevent becoming sick that makes more sense to you than what you have read here, then *do it!* By all means. *But don't do nothing!*

You wait for early detection as it is being suggested to you and you *have* the disease. I guarantee, if you were to hear the words "I'm sorry, you have cancer," you would try anything to avoid losing a breast or your prostate gland and undergoing chemotherapy. *Don't wait!* The time is now and prevention is the key.

Devra Lee Davis is a specialist in public health policy and a scholar in residence at the National Research Council of the National Academy of Sciences, a prestigious position she has held since 1989. She has compiled one of the few systematic comparisons of current changes in deaths from cancer. With one out of three people a cancer victim in this country, we are all pained by the abysmal failure of the highly publicized and costly "war on cancer." Ms. Davis is fully aware of this situation as well, and when it comes to demanding change, she's not shy!

She rightly points out that the National Cancer Institute's 1982 goal of reducing cancer deaths by 50 percent by the end of the 20th century looks ludicrous today. The mortality rate is actually *higher* than it was when the "war on cancer" began more than 20 years ago. Referring to the need to investigate further lifestyle changes such as diet and exercise and environmental causes, she states that, "The United States is not putting enough money into research on cancer prevention!"[238] She offers a plausible reason, too: "When you treat cancer, profits are made through drugs and surgery. But when cancer is prevented, nobody makes any money."[239]

As you might well imagine, her public position has not exactly endeared her to the old boy network of the cancer establishment. Fortunately, standing outside the old boy network are progressive and enlightened physicians like Dr. Edmund Sonnenblick, chairman of cardiology at the Albert Einstein College of Medicine in New York. In Dr. Sonnenblick's words: "The public wants drama, but prevention is more important. The major thrust has to be prevention."[240]

At the end of an article on Ms. Davis in the *New York Times*, she ponders where the constituency for prevention is. The article ends with, "Perhaps Davis knows better than anyone how hard building that constituency will be." It may be idealistic of me, or perhaps it's just positive thinking with a dash of wishful thinking thrown in, but in my opinion it's *you* who are that constituency. In taking this step to eliminate the causes of cancer by CAREing for your body, you thereby distance yourself from the disease establishment and those who "don't know." You become a vital part of the real "health care" system—that network of health-conscious people who have taken charge of their lives and their health and are living the vibrant and vital life that our creator intended us to live.

Congratulations, and may God bless your every breath and step.

Appendix:
A Product For the 21st Century

Over the years, especially since the success of *Fit For Life*, I have been introduced to numerous products. On occasion, some are so intriguing, so innovative, and so ahead of their time that the immensity of their potential benefit simply cannot be ignored. It gives me a great deal of pleasure to be able to introduce you to such a product: greens+®.

greens+® is a relatively new product on the market that I learned about in late 1993 and have been using every day since. I am 100 percent convinced that it is the finest product of its kind available anywhere. I have met the people who manufacture and distribute it and if there were more people like them in the world, it would be a much nicer place to live. You know, sometimes you read about people who set themselves up selling a product that is purported to be the best there is and the whole thing is a scam to make as much money as quickly as possible.

At the other end of the spectrum are those people who are impeccably honest and of the highest integrity, whose greatest desire is to do something of inestimable value for humankind. The people who have brought greens+® to the marketplace are the epitome of this type. Their commitment to excellence and the health of all people everywhere is truly inspiring. The brainchild behind greens+® is Mr. Sam Graci, a chemist and psychologist by profession and a joy of a person to know.

I am not a chemist, so rather than try to explain the product to you, Mr. Graci, author of the number-one best-selling *The Power of Superfoods: 30 days that will change your life,* has graciously agreed to describe it to you.

The Story of greens+®

In the 1970s, I had the privilege of working with a group of Down's syndrome teens. My main objective was to help them develop better social interaction skills and determine why they missed so much school due to flu, constant colds, and low energy. While working closely with Dr. Zoltan Rona, an orthomolecular physician in Toronto, we discovered that each of the teens had severe vitamin, mineral, and enzyme deficiencies. Then I consulted with Dr. Abram Hoffer, a psychiatrist practising in Saskatchewan who suspected that many of his patients were also suffering from nutritional imbalances. Remember, this was in the 1970s. Clearly, we noticed that the standard American diet was based on overly cooked or processed foods, which are low in fibre, enzymes, vitamins, organic minerals, and quality water, but high in fat.

Next, we adjusted the Down's syndrome teenagers' diets to the "mono-diet" (see Chapter 10) consisting of fresh, organically grown foods and 8 to 10 glasses of quality (pure) water a day. We included proper exercise and sufficient rest in their daily program. After six months, we documented the dramatic increase in the teens' health, energy, and outlook on life. At that time, we all realized that foods, everyday foods, can either put us in a coffin and nail it shut or stimulate and sustain us with vibrant good health and well-being. The choice was clear.

I continued my research and was most fortunate to be tutored in various degrees by Dr. Linus Pauling (vitamin C pioneer), Dr. E. Shute (vitamin E pioneer) and many other humanitarian nutritional researchers. These physicians and Dr. Rona encouraged me to develop high-quality vitamin and mineral formulas for professional use. This I did. In early 1988, I realized that vitamins and minerals, selectively taken from foods and put into capsules or tablets, were actually missing many of the other complex nutrients found in the original foods. Simply put, it is better to eat the whole food, raw if possible, and organically grown preferably, for superior good health. Later in 1988, I began researching the most nutritious, easily digested foods we have on earth. I stopped producing vitamins and minerals.

By 1992, my research was complete and the outcome was the development of a synergistic blend, nutrient-rich, enzyme-live, alkaline-forming whole food we call greens+®. It is a combination of *every nutrient required by the human body.* Four years of conscientious and intense investigation showed my research group how to properly combine 22 foods derived from the ocean and those grown in naturally fertilized soils, in very select places around the world.

For example, we have chosen to use a blue-green algae called *spirulina*, grown on the pristine Kona Coast of Hawaii (spirulina is 65 percent biologically complete protein, nature's richest source of vitamin B_{12}, and the most easily absorbed form of iron for red blood cell development); organically grown *wheat grass* and *beets* (both rich in chlorophyll, and a potent source of all necessary vitamins and minerals); *acerola berries* grown without herbicides in Brazil (these berries are the richest natural source of vitamin C and bioflavonoids, which enhance immunity and protect us from infection); organically, as well as hydroponically grown *soy sprouts* (these sprouts contain no allergy-causing gluten and are nature's richest source of antioxidants, enzymes, and phytochemicals).

greens+® was designed and is today an alkaline whole food, concentrated as a powder that you simply mix with quality water, fresh vegetables, or fruit juice, or that you take in convenient capsule form. It tastes remarkably good! It is ideal for a mono-diet or to support superior well-being in any diet. greens+® is economical, convenient and naturally good-tasting without the added use of any sugars, salt, dairy products, animal products, fats, gluten, preservatives, MSG, yeast, or eggs. It is a powder you mix with 4 to 8 ounces of liquid and sip.

It is best to drink greens+® on an empty stomach so it is thoroughly absorbed and digested. It will be emptied from your stomach in 15 minutes, then you may consume other food. For optimum results, first drink one or more glasses of room-temperature pure water through a straw, upon rising. Then drink your greens+® 15 minutes later. You may consume food 15 minutes after drinking greens+®. On days of extra stress, take your greens+® at about 3:30 p.m. This will give you added energy, mental acuity, a continued sense of well-being, and will accelerate your body's optimum healing.

You cannot overuse greens+® as it is a food. Because I travel so frequently and have many demands placed upon myself, I use it three to four times a day with great results. Sip it rather than gulp it down and greens+® will begin to be digested and absorbed immediately while in your mouth. The live enzymes it contains will help you digest and absorb it easily.

The USDA's new food pyramid (see Chapter 11) recommends we consume at least 3 servings of fresh vegetables daily and 2 to 4 servings of fresh fruit. Sounds easy, right? But only 9 percent of the population consumes 3 servings of fresh vegetables daily. In today's busy world, it is sometimes difficult to find the time and opportunity to prepare and eat all of the needed vegetables. greens+® is a convenient way to increase one's daily intake of organic vegetables. You may be surprised to learn that children really enjoy taking greens+®. Children should take one teaspoon a day up to the age of six, two teaspoons up to the age of eight, and three teaspoons daily through adulthood.

The commitment of my dedicated research team to premium quality created two challenges. First, where would I make the product—in a big urban area setting where almost all manufacturers are located? The solution became obvious. We chose to make it in the pristine Rocky Mountains. There we have a pure air and water environment. The second challenge I faced was how to take a lot of nutritious vegetables in their original form and reduce them to a blendable powder without altering the delicate enzymatically alive nutrients of each whole food.

We discovered a patented process that reduced vegetables to a fine powder without the application of heat, thereby maintaining their molecular makeup and retaining their living enzymes. The process works perfectly. After gently washing and juicing these vegetables, we spray-dry them with absolutely no heat, to preserve each delicate nutrient. Spray drying is like putting your garden hose on an extremely fine mist. The small mist-sized particles dry immediately with no heat. To keep these foods alive and fresh inside the bottles, we nitrogen flush each one, pushing out all the oxygen. We also put both an oxygen and moisture absorber in each bottle, and the product is shipped in 100 percent recycled cardboard boxes.

What Will greens+® Do For You?

1) Gently sweep your intestines clean with its 17.2 percent soluble and insoluble fibres.

2) Expel toxins and poisons from the body. As an alkaline food, it neutralizes acidity.

3) Set the right PH in your intestines.

4) Replenish "friendly bacteria" (see below) in your intestines so you can digest foods better. There are 2.5 billion bacteria per serving of greens+®.

5) Support the superior performance of the "immune," adrenal, and lymphatic systems.

6) Help women who are going through perimenopause, meno-pause, and premenstrual syndrome (PMS).

7) Increase mental acuity and support good brain functioning.

8) Support hair and nail growth and provide the nutrients necessary for skin tone.

9) Allow more extended energy throughout the day without any stimulants.

10) Provide 18 various food pigments—orange, yellow, red, green, blue, etc—full of phytochemicals.

Did you know that the National Cancer Institute has just initiated a five-year, $6-million research program into the disease-preventing "secret ingredients" contained in vegetables? These "secret ingredients" in vegetables are phytochemicals. greens+® is a synergistic blend of such vegetables. It was especially designed to provide maximum health protection through these phytochemicals.

Kudos for greens+®

greens+® is a powerful food that is easily digested, readily absorbed, and contributes every nutrient needed for superior health. In 1996–97, greens+® was voted the Natural Nutritional Foods Association's People's Choice gold winner as Product of the Year in the United States in the category of nutritional drinks, beverages, and waters. In Canada, greens+® was awarded the 1996 Beverage of the Year gold medal as well as the Food Supplement of the Year gold medal. Also in 1996, greens+® won the prestigious International Hall of Fame award as Nutritional Product of the Year. greens+® won two more awards in 1997 for Best Beverage and Best Food Supplement in Canada, making greens+® *the most awarded health product in North America.* To me, however, the best awards are the countless individuals who approach me daily, excited about their health restoration and the part greens+® has played in their personal wellness program. My one hope is that greens+® will encourage you to renew your commitment to supporting the healing power of your body, give you vigour and zest to live your life fully, and allow you to contribute to the development of all humanity.

> Wishing you abundant good health,
> Sam Graci

My Experience With greens+®

Since I have been using greens+®, my appetite is kept more in check, I don't need to eat as frequently or as much as I used to, I am more alert, I sleep more soundly, my energy level is high and constant, and I feel great all the time. I like to have it with apple juice because the combination of the juice and greens+® is so delicious I can hardly believe it's legal. It is also a perfect food to consume while mono-dieting. I have found that it makes mono-dieting much easier and more effective. In fact, because it contains all the nutrients required by the body, greens+® makes you feel satisfied, and you find that you do not crave food as much when mono-dieting. It is as though this product was made for mono-dieting. It helps make it such a breeze. For further information about greens+®, call 1-800-258-0444 (Canada). Or you can visit their Web site at www.greenspluscanada.com.

For Your Information

FIT FOR LIFE
Health Resort and Spa
1460 S. Ocean Boulevard
Pompano Beach, FL 33062
800/583-3500

American Natural Hygiene Society
P.O. Box 30630
Tampa, FL 33630
813/855-6608

greens+® (Canada)
EHN Distribution
689 Queen Street West, Suite 94
Toronto, Ont.
M6J 1E6
800/258-0444
416/977-3505
www.greenspluscanada.com

National Institute of Fitness
202 N. Snow Canyon Road
Box #380938
Ivins, UT 84738
801/673-4905

Natural EFX Company Store Canada
Box 34030
17790 #10 Hwy
Surrey, B.C.
V3S 8C4
888/966-5777

I would dearly love to hear of your experiences with the CARE
principles. To share them, please write to me:

Harvey Diamond
5221 Ocean Blvd., Suite 271
Sarasota, FL 34242

Glossary

AMINO ACIDS	any of 22 nitrogen-containing organic acids from which proteins are made
ANGINA	severe, constricting pain in the chest, often radiating to the left shoulder and down the arm
ANIMAL-BASED DIET	a diet that is predominated by animal products
ANTIOXIDANTS	a chemical compound that neutralizes the cell-damaging free radicals that are created when oxygen is used inside the body's cells
ATHEROSCLEROSIS	a build-up of cholesterol and fats in the arteries and blood vessels of the body; hardening of the arteries
BIOFLAVONOIDS	potent antioxidant compounds that have anti-inflammatory effects; also necessary for the stability and absorption of vitamin C
CARCINOMA	a malignant cancerous tumour
CARDIOVASCULAR DISEASE	any disease pertaining to the heart, arteries, and blood vessels of the body
CAROTENES	an orange to yellow colour in produce that is converted into vitamin A in the body
CAT SCAN	a computerized "picture" of the inside of the body used to determine if there are areas exhibiting pathology
CHEMOTHERAPY	a treatment of drugging that consists of several drugs simultaneously given to a cancer patient when the patient's condition is thought to have progressed beyond surgical intervention
CHOLESTEROL	a type of fat found in all animals; synthesized in the liver and is involved in practically every activity of the body

CIRCADIAN RHYTHMS	the rhythmic occurrences at certain times during a 24-hour period
COMPLEX CARBOHYDRATES	sugar molecules linked together that make other digestible molecules
CORONARY BYPASS	when flow of blood to or from the heart is blocked, a blood vessel is taken from the leg and attached to the affected artery to bypass the obstruction
DIGESTIVE ENZYMES	enzymes produced by the body that are involved in the digestion of food
DISEASES OF AFFLUENCE	heart disease, cancer, osteoporosis, diabetes, and obesity
ENZYMES	a protein produced by the body that serves as a catalyst for all chemical reactions in the body (*See also* digestive enzymes; food enzymes; live plant enzymes; metabolic enzymes)
FAT	composed essentially of fatty acids and glycerol; the least essential element in food because it can be manufactured by the body out of other food substances (*See also* saturated fat)
FATTY ACIDS	one of the building blocks of triglycerides which comprise 95 percent of the fats in the human body
FIBRE	plant fibre includes that structural portion of the plant that is indigestible tissue made up largely of cellulose
FLAVONOIDS	any of a large group of compounds found in foods that assist with vitamin C absorption and are powerful antioxidants
FOOD COMBINING	a way to optimize energy from the digestive tract by not mixing protein (such as meat) with starches (such as potatoes, rice)
FOOD ENZYMES	enzymes that are found in every food; they digest the food in the body, provided the food has not been cooked, which destroys all food enzymes
FREE RADICALS	an atom or group of atoms that is highly chemically reactive because it has a single unpaired electron which, wanting to be paired, steals electrons from other pairs; considered to be a factor in a wide range of disorders including heart disease and cancer
FRUCTOSE	a monosaccharide; a simple sugar sweeter than sucrose that is plentiful in sweet fruits
GLUCOSE	a simple sugar that is the principal source of energy for the body's cells

GREEN DRINK — natural food formulas made from organic, nutrient-rich land and sea vegetables that are superior detoxifiers and blood cleansers; GREENS+ is an example (See Appendix)

HOMEOSTATIS — a term meaning unchanging status; refers to the uniform balance the body maintains within

HYPOGLYCEMIA — a lower than normal level of glucose (sugar) in the blood

IRON DEFICIENCY ANEMIA — a condition that results from deficient intake or absorption of iron or from excessive iron loss, which results in a deficiency of haemoglobin

LESION — any pathological or traumatic discontinuity of tissue (i.e., an open sore)

LIVE PLANT ENZYMES — pharmaceutical enzymes used for digestion that are obtained from living plants in a laboratory setting

LYMPH NODES — the rounded masses of lymphoid tissue that are surrounded by a capsule of connective tissue that removes foreign particles from the lymph fluid

LYMPH SYSTEM — the body's "garbage collector"; collects, degrades, and removes waste from the body

LYMPHOCYTES — a colourless blood cell produced in the lymphatic system as an antibody to keep the tissues of the body clean and protected

METABOLIC ENZYMES — these enzymes run the body; every organ and tissue, every activity of the body depends upon them

NATURAL HYGIENE — a 160-year-old approach to health that believes the body is self-repairing, self-healing, and self-maintaining

OSTEOPOROSIS — a loss of calcium from the bones to the degree that the bones become porous and brittle, and can easily fracture as a result

PERIODIC MONO-DIETING — the consumption of only uncooked food for various lengths of time periodically throughout the year

PHAGOCYTIC CELL — a cell that engulfs or consumes debris and foreign material in the body

PHYTOCHEMICALS — powerful cell-protecting chemicals found in all plants to protect the body from disease

PLACEBO EFFECT — an effect produced by a test where a harmless substance is given for its suggestive effect

PLANT-BASED DIET — a diet gleaned exclusively from the plant kingdom

PLAQUE — a build-up of fat and cholesterol in the arteries that is an indication of impending cardiovascular disease

PROTEIN	the primary substance of life; the building materials of organisms; composed of amino acids in an endless variety of linkages
RADIATION	the treatment of disease with any type of radioactive material such as X-rays, beta rays, and gamma rays
SATURATED FAT	a fat so constituted chemically that it cannot absorb any more hydrogen; usually the solid fats of animal origin such as those in milk, butter, and meat
STROKE	a sudden loss of consciousness, motion, or feeling caused by rupture or obstruction (eg. a clot) of an artery of the brain
SULPHORAPHANE	a phytochemical found in cruciferous vegetables (broccoli, cabbage, cauliflower, Brussels sprouts) that amplifies the body's defences against carcinogenic chemicals
TOXICOSIS	a saturation of the body with toxins
TRIGLYCERIDES	fats found in the bloodstream
TUMOUR	a hardened area of tissue formed to wall off a highly toxic area
VEGANS	those who eat absolutely nothing that comes from an animal (no meat, fish, poultry, eggs, milk, or dairy products); eat exclusively foods from the plant kingdom
VEGETARIAN	a person who eats no meat, chicken, or fish

References

1. CNN Health Week, March 14, 1992; "No Breast, No Cancer," the Maury Povich Show, June 18, 1992; "Preventive Mastectomy, Part I & Part II," Health talk, March 10 & 11, 1993; "Siblings Opt for Preventive Mastectomies," All Things Considered (National Public Radio), Aug. 8, 1993; Angier, Natalie, "Vexing Pursuit of Breast Cancer Gene," *New York Times*, July 12, 1994.

2. "Surviving Breast Cancer," Health Works, CNN News, March 12, 1994.

3. Raloff, Janet, "EcoCancers," *Science News*, Vol. 144, #1, July 3, 1993.

4. "The Breast Care Test," PBS-TV, Oct. 18, 1993.

5. Ibid.

6. Quillin, Patrick, Dr., *Beating Cancer With Nutrition*, NTP Press, Tulsa, OK, 1994.

7. Ellerbee, Linda, "The Other Epidemic—What Every Woman Needs to Know About Breast Cancer," ABC-TV, Sept. 14, 1993.

8. Stephen, Beverly, "Her Most Serious Medical Problem," *Los Angeles Times*, Dec. 5, 1982.

9. Ibid.

10. Op. cit. note #7

11. Op. cit. note #7. "Fighting Cancer—Are We Doing Enough?" CNN-Newsmaker, Sunday, July 7, 1991.

12. "Conflicting Advice in Breast Cancer," ABC-Nightline, March 19, 1993.

13. *New England Journal of Medicine*, Oct. 24, 1985.

14. "Funds Urged for Breast Cancer Study," The Associated Press (*Sarasota Herald-Tribune*), Oct. 28, 1993.

15. Op. cit. note #7.

16. "Breast Cancer—Speaking Out," PBS, Oct. 13, 1993.

17. Op. cit. note #4.

18. Kolata, Gina, "Weighing Spending On Breast Cancer Research," *New York Times*, Oct. 20, 1993.

19. Op. cit. note #12.

20. Op. cit. note #3.

21. Op. cit. note #12.

22. Op. cit. note #4.

23. Kolata, Gina, "Mammograms Before 50? A Hung Jury," *New York Times*, Nov. 24, 1993.

24. Op. cit. note #11.

25. Kolata, Gina, "Avoiding Mammogram Guidelines," *New York Times*, Dec. 5, 1993.

26. NBC Nightly News, Oct. 3, 1994.

27. Ibid.

28. Op. cit. note #4.

29. "It Could Happen to You," ABC News—20/20, Aug. 27, 1993.

30. Op. cit. note #1.

31. Angier, Natalie, "Move Abroad Can Change Breast Cancer Risk," *New York Times*, Aug. 2, 1995.

32. McDougall, John, M.D., *McDougall's Medicine: A Challenging Second Opinion*, New Century, Piscataway, N.J., 1985.

33. Angier, Natalie, "Chemists Learn Why Vegetables Are Good For You," *New York Times*, April 13, 1993.

34. Elizabeth Berg, author of *Talk Before Sleep*, on the Oprah Winfrey Show, Aug. 1, 1994.

35. Op. cit. note #11, CNN Newsmaker.

36. "Breast Cancer Defenses Sought," The Associated Press (*Sarasota Herald-Tribune*), Dec. 15, 1993.

37. Op. cit. note #12.

38. Op. cit. note #4.

39. Op. cit. note #23.

40. Op. cit. note #25.

41. Op. cit. note #23.

42. Kolata, Gina, "Value of Mammograms Before 50 Debated Anew," *New York Times*, Dec. 16, 1992.

43. Ibid.

44. Ibid.

45. Ibid.

46. "Ten Facts About Breast Cancer That May Surprise You," The Breast Cancer Fund, San Francisco, Calif.

47. Ibid.

48. "Mammography: Investigation," ABC News Primetime Live, Feb. 27, 1992.

49. "Medical Malpractice Law," Good Morning America, Aug. 29, 1991.

50. "Woman Wins $2.7 Million for Mistaken Mastectomy," The Associated Press (*Sarasota Herald-Tribune*), April 20, 1994.

51. Op. cit. note #48.

52. Op. cit. note #32.

53. Ibid.

54. "Mammogram Interpretations are Questioned in a Report," *New York Times*, Dec. 2, 1994.

55. Taylor, Paul, "Mammogram Study Sparks Controversy," *Globe and Mail*, Nov. 14, 1992.

56. Op. cit. note #32.

57. McDougall, John, M.D., and McDougall, Mary, *The McDougall Plan*, New Century, Piscataway, N.J., 1983.

58. Kolata, Gina, "New Ability to Find Earliest Cancers: A Mixed Blessing?" *New York Times*, Nov. 8. 1994.

59. The Oprah Winfrey Show, Aug. 1, 1994.

60. Op. cit. note #18.

61. Op. cit. note #4.

62. Op. cit. note #29.

63. Passwater, Richard A., Ph.D., *Cancer Prevention and Nutritional Therapies*, Keats, New Canaan, Ct., 1993.

64. American Cancer Society, Cancer Facts and Figures.

65. Ibid.

66. Ibid.

67. Bailor, John, et. al., "Cancer: Are We Losing the War?" *New England Journal of Medicine*, #314, May 8, 1986.

68. Op. cit. note #11.

69. "Cancer War Has Stalled," *New York Times*, Oct. 30, 1994.

70. Seely, Rod R., Ph.D., Stephens, Trent D., Ph.D., Tate, Philip, D.A., *Anatomy & Physiology*, Mosby, St. Louis, 1992.

71. "Breast Cancer—Speaking Out," PBS-TV, Oct. 13, 1993.

72. Walker, N.W., Dr., *Become Younger*, Norwalk Press, Phoenix, 1979.

73. Guyton, A.C., M.D., *Medical Physiology*, W.B. Saunders, New York, 1962.

74. Op. cit. note #20.

75. Ibid.

76. "Tonsils Bargain," *The London Observer*, Feb. 21, 1988.

77. Op. cit. note #4.

78. Op. cit. note #70.

79. Waldman, Hilary, "Breast Cancer: Lymph Node Removal Re-examined," *Sarasota Herald Tribune*, Sept. 11, 1996.

80. Janofsky, Michael, "Results of Biopsy Show Simpson to be Cancer-Free, Doctor Says," *New York Times*, Aug. 16, 1994.

81. "Workers Told of Risks In Handling Cancer Drugs," *Los Angeles Times*, Sept. 13, 1983.

82. Friend, Tim, "Lymphoma's Progression Was Swift," *USA Today*, May 20, 1994.

83. Altman, Lawrence K., "Doctors Told Mrs. Onassis There Was Nothing More They Could Do," *New York Times*, May 20, 1994.

84. Ibid.

85. Ibid.

86. Ibid.

87. Ibid.

88. Altman, Lawrence K., M.D., "Lymphomas Are On the Rise In U.S., and No One Knows Why," *New York Times*, May 24, 1994.

89. The Surgeon General's "Report On Nutrition and Health," U.S. Department of Health and Human Services, 1988.

90. Welch, C., "Cinocoronary Arteriography in Young Men," *Circulation*, #42, 1970; Page I., "Prediction of Coronary Heart Disease Based On Clinical Suspicion, Age, Total Cholesterol and Triglycerides," Circulation, #42, 1970; Zampogna, A., "Relationship Between Lipids and Occlusive Coronary Artery Disease," *Annals of Internal Medicine*, #84, 1976; Jenkins, P., "Severity of Coronary Atherosclerosis Related to Lipoprotein Concentration," *British Medical Journal*, #2, 1978; Pocock, S., "Concentrations of High-Density Lipoprotein Cholesterol, Triglycerides and Total Cholesterol In Ischemic Heart Disease," *British Medical Journal*, #298, 1989; Rosengren, A., "Impact of Cardiovascular Risk Factors On Coronary Heart Disease and Mortality Among Middle-Aged Diabetic Men, A General Population Study," *British Medical Journal*, #299, 1989; Pekkanen, J., "Risk Factors and 25-year Risk of Coronary Hearth Disease: The Finnish Cohorts of the Seven Country Study," *British Medical Journal*, 299, 1989; Benfante, R., "Is Elevated Serum Cholesterol Level A Risk Factor for Coronary

Heart Disease In the Elderly?" *Journal of the American Medical Association*, #269, 1990; Castelli, W., "Epidemiology of Coronary Heart Disease: The Framingham Study," *American Journal of Medicine*, #76, 1984; Kannel, W., "Cholesterol In the Prediction of Atherosclerotic Disease: New Perspectives Based On the Framingham Study," *Annals of Internal Medicine*, #90, 1979; Stamler, J., "Is the Relationship Between Serum Cholesterol and Risk of Premature Death From Coronary Heart Disease Continuous and Graded?" *Journal of the American Medical Association*, #256, 1986; Connor, W., "The Key Role of Nutritional Factors In the Prevention of Coronary Heart Disease," *Preventive Medicine*, #1, 1972; Pritikin, N., *The Pritikin Program For Diet and Exercise*, Grosset & Dunlap, New York, 1979; McDougall, J., *McDougall's Medicine: A Challenging Second Opinion*, New Century, New Jersey, 1985; Ornish, D., *Dr. Dean Ornish's Program For Reversing Hearth Disease*, Random House, New York, 1990; Whitiker, J., *Reversing Heart Disease*, Warner, New York, 1985; Connor, W., "Serum Lipids In Men Receiving High Cholesterol and Cholesterol-Free Diets," *Journal of Clinical Investigation*, #40, 1961; Imai, H., "Angiotoxicity of Oxygenated Sterols and Possible Precursors," *Science*, #207, 1980; Keys, A., "Lessons from Serum Cholesterol Studies In Japan, Hawaii and Los Angeles," *Annals of Internal Medicine*, #48, 1958; Levy, R.I., "Declining Mortality In Coronary Heart Disease," *Arteriosclerosis*, #1, Sept./Oct., 1981; Shekelle, R.B., "Diet, Serum Cholesterol and Death from Coronary Heart Disease," *New England Journal of Medicine*, #304, 1981; Wissler, R.W., "Studies of Progression of Advanced Atherosclerosis In Experimental Animals and Man," *Annals of New York Academy of Science*, #275, 1976; Samuel, P., "Further Validation of the Plasma Isotope Ratio Method for Measurement of Cholesterol Absorption In Man," *Journal of Lipid Research*, #23, 1982; Insull, W., "Cholesterol, Triglyceride and Phospholipid Content of Intima, Media and Atherosclerotic Fatty Streaks In Human Thoracic Aorta," *Journal of Clinical Investigation*, #45, 1966; Katz, S., "Physical Chemistry of the Lipids of Human Atherosclerotic Lesions: Demonstration of A Lesion Intermediate Between Fatty Streaks and Advanced Plaques," *Journal of Clinical Investigation*, #58, 1976; Proudfit, W., "Selective Cine Coronary Arteriography: Correlation With Clinical Findings In 1,000 Patients," *Circulation*, #33, 1966; Blankenhorn, D.H., et. al., "Dietary Fat Influences Human Coronary Lesion Formation," *Circulation*, #78 (SuppII). 1988; Brown, E.G., et. al., "Arteriographic Assessment of Coronary Atherosclerosis, Review of Current Methods, Their Limitations, and Clinical Applications," *Arteriosclerosis*, #2, 1982; Gould, K.L., et. al., "Improvement of Stenosis Geometry by Quantitative Coronary Arteriography After Adequate Cholesterol Lowering In Man," *Circulation*, #80, 1989; Leaf, A., "Management of Hypercholesterolemia," *New England Journal of Medicine*, #321, 1989; Shekelle, R.B., "Dietary Cholesterol and Ischemic Heart Disease," *Lancet*, #1(8648), 1989.

91.   Sorenson, Marc, *Mega-Health*, Sorenson, Utah, 1993.

92.   Whitiker, J., *Reversing Health Risks*, G.P. Putnam's & Sons, New York, 1988.

93.   Glick, D., "New Age Meets Hippocrates," *Newsweek*, July 13, 1992.

94.   "Second Opinions For Bypass Surgery," *Health & Healing*, Vol. 2, #1, Jan. 1992.

95.   Op. cit. note #91.

96. Cragg, Juli, "No Fault Of Their Own," *Sarasota Herald-Tribune*, Dec. 5, 1993.

97. "Smokers Have A Higher Breast Cancer Death Risk," *New York Times*, May 25, 1994.

98. Willit, W.C., et. al., "Relation of Meat, Fat and Fiber Intake to the Risk of Colon Cancer In A Prospective Study Among Women," *New England Journal of Medicine*, #323, 1990; Whittemore, A.S., et. al., "Diet, Physical Activity and Colorectal Cancer Among Chinese In North America and China," *Journal of the National Cancer Institute*, #82, 1990.

99. Kolata, G., "Animal Fat Is Tied To Colon Cancer," *New York Times*, Dec. 13, 1990.

100. Katsuoyanni, K., "Diet and Breast Cancer: A Case-Control Study In Greece," *International Journal of Cancer*, #38, 1986.

101. "Council Urges Major Changes For U.S. Diet," *Los Angeles Times*, March 2, 1989.

102. McMurray, M., "The Absorption of Cholesterol and the Sterol Balance In the Tarahumara Indians of Mexico Fed Cholesterol-Free and High Cholesterol Diets," *American Journal of Clinical Nutrition*, #41, 1985; Wells, V., "Egg Yolk and Serum Cholesterol Levels: The Importance of Dietary Cholesterol Intake," *British Medical Journal*, #1, 1963.

103. Connor, W., "The Interrelated Effects of Dietary Cholesterol and Fat Upon Human Serum Lipid Levels," *Journal of Clinical Investigation*, #43, 1964.

104. Op. cit. note #32.

105. Ibid.

106. Lea, A., "Dietary Factors Associated With Death Rates from Certain Neoplasms In Man," Lancet, #2, 1966; Caroll, K., "Experimental Evidence of Dietary Factors and Hormone-Dependent Cancers, *Cancer Research*, #35, 1975; Drasar, B., "Environmental Factors and Cancer of the Colon and Breast," *British Journal of Cancer*, #27, 1973; Armstrong, B., "Environmental Factors and Cancer Incidence and Mortality in Different Countries With Special Reference to Dietary Practices," *International Journal of Cancer*, #15, 1975; Knox, E., "Foods and Diseases," *British Journal Coc. Preventive Medicine*, #31, 1977; Hiryama, T., "Epidemiology of Breast Cancer With Special Reference to the Role of Diet," *Preventive Medicine*, #7, 1978; Gray, G., "Breast Cancer Incidence and Mortality Rates in Relation to Known Factors and Dietary Practices," *British Journal of Cancer*, #39, 1979; Hems, G., "The Contributions of Diet and Childbearing to Breast Cancer, *British Journal of Cancer*, #37, 1978; Howe, G., "A Cohort Study of Fat Intake and Risk of Breast Cancer," *Journal of the National Cancer Institute*, #83, 1991; Henderson, M., "Cancer Incidence in Seattle Women's Health Trial Participants by Group and Time Since Randomization," *Journal of the National Cancer Institute*, #83, 1991; Yu, S., "A Case-Controlled Study of Dietary and Non-Dietary Risk Factors for Breast Cancer in Shanghai," *Cancer Research*, #50, 1990; Van't Veer, P., "Dietary Fat and the Risk of Breast Cancer," *International Journal of Epidemiology*, #19, 1990; Willett, W., "The Search for the Causes of Breast and Colon Cancer," *Nature*, #338, 1989; Berrino, F., "Mediterranean Diet and Cancer," *European Journal of Clinical Nutrition*, #43 (Supp. 2), 1989;

Howe, G., "Dietary Factors and Risk of Breast Cancer: Combined Analysis of 12 Case-Controlled Studies," *Journal of the National Cancer Institute*, #82, 1990; Brisson, J., "Diet, Mammographic Features of Breast Tissue, and Breast Cancer Risk," *American Journal of Epidemiology*, #130, 1989; Foniolo, P., "Calorie-Providing Nutrients and Risk of Breast Cancer," *Journal of the National Cancer Institute*, #81, 1989.

107. Op. cit. note #3.

108. Goldin, B., "The Relationship Between Estrogen Levels and Diets of Caucasian-American and Oriental-Immigrant Women," *American Journal of Clinical Nutrition*, #44, 1986.

109. Schultz, T., "Nutrient Intake and Hormonal Status of Premenopausal Vegetarian Seventh-day Adventist and Premenopausal Non-Vegetarians," *Nutrition and Cancer*, #4, 1983.

110. Bennet, F., "Diet and Sex-Hormone Concentrations: An Intervention Study for the Type of Fat Consumed," *American Journal of Clinical Nutrition*, #52, 1990; Woods, M., "Low-Fat, High-Fiber Diet and Serum Estrone Sulfate in Premenopausal Women," *American Journal of Clinical Nutrition*, #49, 1989; Rose, D., "Effect of a Low-Fat Diet on Hormone Levels in Women With Cystic Breast Disease," *Journal of the National Cancer Institute*, #78, 1987; Rose, D., "Effect of a Low-Fat Diet on Hormone Levels in Women With Cystic Breast Disease,II. Serum Radioimmunoassayable Prolactin and Growth Hormone and Bioactive Lactogenic Hormones," *Journal of the National Cancer Institute*, #78, 1987; Gorbach, S., "Estrogens, Breast Cancer and Intestinal Flora," *Review of Infectious Diseases*, #6 (Supp. 1), 1984.

111. Op. cit. note #7; Frommer, D., "Changing Age of Menopause," *British Medical Journal*, #2, 1964; Trichopoulos, D., "Menopause and Breast Cancer Risk," *Journal of the National Cancer Institute*, #48, 1972; Armstrong, B., "Diet and Reproductive Hormones, A Study of Vegetarian and Non-Vegetarian Postmenopausal Women," *Journal of the National Cancer Institute*, #67, 1981; Hill, P., "Environmental Factors of Breast and Prostatic Cancer," *Cancer Research*, #41, 1981.

112. "Breast Cancer—Complacency Is the Enemy of Cure," *FDA Consumer*, July/Aug., 1991.

113. Kagawa, Y., "Impact of Westernization On the Nutrition of the Japanese: Changes in Physique, Cancer, Longevity and Centenarians," *Preventive Medicine*, #7, 1978; Op. cit. note #171; Haenzel, W., "Studies of Japanese Migrants, I. Mortality From Cancer and Other Diseases Among Japanese in the U.S.," *Journal of the National Cancer Institute*, #40, 1968; Kolonel, L., "Nutrient Intakes in Relation to Cancer Incidence in Hawaii," *British Journal of Cancer*, #44, 1981; Buell, P., "Changing Incidence of Breast Cancer in Japanese-American Women," *Journal of the National Cancer Institute*, #51, 1973; Wynder, E., "Strategies Toward the Primary Prevention of Cancer," *Archives of Surgery*, #125, 1990.

114. Powell, Bill, & Myers, Patrick S., "Death By Fried Chicken," *Newsweek*, Sept. 24, 1990.

115. "Fat Poses Dual Threat of Breast Cancer," *Science News*, Vol. 138, #19, Nov. 10, 1990.

116. Ibid.

117. Op. cit. note #33.

118. Ibid.

119. Recer, Paul, "Broccoli Extract Shown to Block Breast Cancer," The Associated Press, (*Sarasota Herald-Tribune*), April 12, 1994.

120. Lem, Sharon, "OJ Fights Breast Cancer," *Toronto Sun*, August 7, 1997.

121. Carper, Jean, *Food—Your Miracle Medicine*, HarperCollins, N.Y., 1993.

123. Ibid.

124. Kritchevsky, David, Ph.D., "Nutrition and Breast Cancer, *Cancer*, #66(6), Sept. 15, 1990.

125. Howe, Geoffrey, R., Ph.D., et. al., "Dietary Factors and the Risk of Breast Cancer: Combined Analysis of 12 Case-Controlled Studies," *Journal of the National Cancer Institute*, #82, 1990.

126. McKeown, L.A., "Diet High in Fruits and Vegetables Linked to Lower Breast Cancer Risk," *Medical Tribune*, July 9, 1992.

127. "Strong Views on Origins of Cancer," *New York Times*, July 5, 1994.

128. Ibid.

129. Ibid.

130. "Low-fat Diet Slows A Cancer in Mice, Study Says," *New York Times*, October 4, 1995.

131. Power, Lawrence, M.D., "Lowering the Risk of Breast Cancer," *Los Angeles Times*, Dec. 4, 1984.

132. "Personal Health," *New York Times*, Feb. 16, 1994.

133. Op. cit. note #12.

134. Op. cit. note #11.

135. Holland, Jimmie, M.D., "Cancer Do's—Cancer Dont's," *Health Confidential*, Vol. 7, #12, Dec. 1993.

136. "New Risks For Meat Eaters," *Science News*, Vol. 146, #3, July 16, 1994.

137. Op. cit. note #12.

138. Dowling, Claudia G., "Fighting Back," *LIFE*, May 1994.

139. Campbell, T. Colin, M.D., et. al., "Cornell-Oxford-China Project on Nutrition, Health and Environment, Diet Life-style and Mortality In China: A Study of the Characteristics of 65 Counties," Oxford University Press, The China People's Medical Publishing House, 1990.

140. "Huge Study of Diet Indicts Fat and Meat," *New York Times*, May 8, 1990.

141. Mead, Nathaniel, "The Champion Diet," *East-West Journal*, Vol. 20, #9, Sept., 1990.

142. Ibid.

143. Regan, Tom, "But For the Sake of Some Little Mouthful of Flesh," *The Animals Agenda*, Vol. 2, #1, Feb. 1989; U.S. Dept. of Agriculture, Agriculture Statistics, 1988.

144. *Eat For Life: The Food & Nutrition Board's Guide to Reducing Your Risk of Chronic Disease*, National Academy Press, Washington, D.C., 1992.

145. Hellmich, Nanci, "In Healthful Living, East Beats West," *USA Today*, June 6, 1990.

146. Sherman, H., "Calcium Requirements Of Maintenance In Man," *Journal of Biological Chemistry*, #44, 1920.

147. Bresala, N., "Relationships of Animal Protein-Rich Diet to Kidney Stone Formation and Calcium Metabolism," *Journal of Clinical Endocrinology and Metabolism*, #66, 1988; Zemel, M., "Calcium Utilization: Effect of Varying Level and Source of Dietary Protein," *American Journal of Clinical Nutrition*, #48, 1988.

148. Lewinnek, G.E., "The Significance and a Comparative Analysis of the Epidemiology of Hip Fractures," *Clinical Orthopedics and Related Research*, Vol. 152, Oct., 1980; Solomon, L., "Osteoporosis and Fracture of the Femoral Neck in the South African Bantu," *Journal of Bone and Joint Surgery*, Vol. 50B, Feb. 1968; Unite Nations Food and Agriculture Organization, *FAO Production Yearbook*, Vol. 37, 1984, and *Food Balance Sheets*, 1979-1981 Average; Walker, A., "The Human Requirement of Calcium: Should Low Intakes Be Supplemented?," *American Journal of Clinical Nutrition*, Vol. 25, May, 1972; Walker, A., "Osteoporosis and Calcium Deficiency," *American Journal of Clinical Nutrition*, Vol. 16, March 1965.

149. "Consensus Conference: Osteoporosis," *Journal of the American Medical Association*, #252, 1984.

150. Op. cit. note #139 & 140.

151. Op. cit. note #139 & 140.

152. Abdulla, M., "Nutrient Intake and Health Status of Vegans, Chemical Analysis of Diets Using the Duplicate Portion Sampling Technique," *American Journal of Clinical Nutrition*, #34, 1981; Ellis, F., "Veganism, Clinical Findings and Investigations," *American Journal of Clinical Nutrition*, #23, 1970; Sanders, T., "Hematological Studies On Vegans," *British Medical Journal*, #40, 1978; Anderson, B., "The Iron and Zinc Status of Long-Term Vegetarian Women," *American Journal of Clinical Nutrition*, #34, 1981.

153. Op. cit. note #91.

154. Op. cit. note #139 & 140.

155. Ibid.

156. Op. cit. note #139 & 140.

157. Chalmers, Irena, *The Great Food Almanac—A Feast of Facts From A to Z*, Collins, San Francisco, 1994.

158. Op. cit. note #145.

159. Ibid.

160. Op. cit. note #141

161. Op. cit. note #138.

162. "Position Paper of the American Dietetic Association: Vegetarian Diets—Technical Support Paper," *Journal of the American Dietetic Association*, Vol. 88, #3, March 1988.

163. As cited in *Vegetarian Times*, Feb. 1991.

164. Op. cit. note #70.

165. Blair, S.N., et. al., "Physical Fitness and All Cause Mortality: A Prospective Study of Healthy Men and Women," *Journal of the American Medical Association*, Vol. 262, #17, Nov. 3, 1989.

166. Op. cit. note #70.

167. Op. cit. note #165.

168. Koplan, J.P., et. al., "Physical Activity, Physical Fitness, and Health: Time to Act," *Journal of the American Medical Association*, Vol. 262, #17, Nov. 3, 1991.

170. Rippe, J.M., *Dr. James M. Rippe's Complete Book of Fitness Walking*, Prentice Hall Press, New York, 1989.

171. Ibid.

172. Ibid.

173. Ibid.

174. "Progress Toward Achieving the 1990 National Objectives for Physical Fitness and Exercise," Centers for Disease Control, MMWR #38, 1989.

175. "Leisure-Time Physical Activity Levels and Risk of Coronary Heart Disease and Death," *Journal of the American Medical Association*, #258, 1987.

176. Ibid.

177. Wiley, C., "Walk This Way," *Vegetarian Times*, Jan. 1992.

178. Ibid.

179. Op. cit. note #168.

180. Gavin, J., *The Exercise Habit*, Human Kinetics Pub., Illinois, 1992, as quoted in *Bottom Lines*, Vol. 13, #14, July 30, 1992.

181. "Study Links Exercise to Drop in Breast Cancer," *New York Times*, Sept. 21, 1994.

182. Bazell, Robert, NBC Network News, Sept. 20, 1994.

183. Kolata, Gina, "Study Bolsters Idea That Exercise Cuts Breast Cancer Risk," *New York Times*, May 1, 1997.

184. "A.M. Exercisers Stay With It," *Aviation Medical Bulletin*, Dec. 1990.

185. Op. cit. note #170.

186. Ibid.

187. Ibid.

188. Ibid.

189. Ibid.

190. Ibid.

191. Ibid.

192. Hottinger, B., "Walking Your Way To Fitness," *Vegetarian Voice*, Vol. 18, #4.

193. Study conducted at the Veterans' Affairs Medical Center, Salt Lake City, reported in *Bottom Line*, Vol. 12, #19, Oct. 15, 1991.

194. Study by David Nieman, Exercise Physiologist, reported in *Bottom Line*, Vol. 12, #21, Nov. 15, 1991.

195. *The Wellness Encyclopedia*, University of California Berkeley Wellness Letter, Houghton Miflin, Boston, 1991.

196. Op. cit. note #177.

197. Study headed by James R. White, Ph.D., Director of the Exercise Physiology and Human Performance Lab at the University of California, San Diego, reported in *Bottom Line*, Vol. 12, #12, June 30, 1991.

198. Data from Betty Kamen, Ph.D., writing in "Let's Live," reported in *Bottom Line*, Vol. 13, #1, Jan. 15, 1992.

199. Op. cit. note #170, 177, & 192.

200. Op. cit. note #177.

201. Ibid.

202. Carter, Albert E., "The Miracles of Rebound Exercises," Natl. Inst. of Reboundology & Health, Edmonds, Wa., 1979.

203. Leahy, M., "Can This Man Help You Live To 140?" *Los Angeles Magazine*, April 1983.

204. Trichopoulou, Antonia, "Consumption of Olive Oil and Specific Food Groups In Relation to Breast Cancer Risk In Greece," *Journal of the National Cancer Institute*, #87(2), Jan. 18, 1995.

205. Osborn, T., "Amino Acids in Nutrition and Growth," *Journal of Biological Chemistry*, #17, 1914.

206. Clinton, S., "The Vegetarian Perspective—An Examination of Nutrition Education and the American Diet," *Vegetarian Journal*, Vol. 9, #3, May/June, 1990.

207. Ibid.

208. Ibid.

209. Ibid.

210. "U.S.D.A. Cancels Nutrition Chart: Who's Being Served?" *New York Times*, May 8, 1991; U.S.D.A. Wilts Under Pressure, Kills New Food Group Pyramid," *Washington Post*, April 27, 1991.

211. Ibid.

212. Op. cit. note #210.

213. Nesmith, J., "Pyramid's Something to Chew On," Cox News Service (*Sarasota Herald-Tribune*), April 29, 1992.

214. Op. cit. note #204.

215. "Fear of Fat," CBS-TV, 48-Hours, Oct. 9, 1994.

216. Howell, Dr. Edward, *Enzyme Nutrition*, Avery Pub., New Jersey, 1985. Lopez, D.A., M.D., Williams, R.M., M.D., Miehlke, K., M.D., *ENZYMES The Fountain of Life*, Neville Press, S. Carolina, 1994.

217. Pottenger, Francis M., "The Effect of Heat Processed Foods and Metabolized Vitamin D Milk on the Dentofacial Structures of Experimental Animals," *Amer. J. Orthodontics & Oral Surgery*, #8, Aug. 1946.

218. Op. cit. note #216.

219. Cousins, N., *Anatomy of An Illness*, Norton, New York, 1979.

220. Talan, J., "Good Thoughts—Good Health," *Sarasota Herald-Tribune*, June 12, 1991.

221. Ibid.

222. Chopra, D., *Quantum Healing*, Bantam, New York, 1989.

223. Frank, J.O., *Persuasion and Healing: A Comparative Study of Psychotherapy*, Johns Hopkins University Press, Baltimore, 1973.

224. Op. cit. note #222.

225. Cushing, H., *The Life of Sir William Osler*, Oxford University Press, New York, 1940.

226. Shelton, Herbert M., *Natural Hygiene: Man's Pristine Way of Life*, Dr. Shelton's Health School, Texas, 1968.

227. Benson, H., "The Placebo Effect," *Journal of the American Medical Association*, #232(12), June 23, 1975; Booth, G., "Psychobiological Aspects of Spontaneous

Regressions of Cancer," *Journal of the American Academy of Psychoanalysis*, #1(3), 1973; Everson, T.C., et. al., *Spontaneous Regression of Cancer*, Philadelphia, 1966; Simonton, O.C., *Getting Well Again*, Tarcher, New York, 1978; Anderson, R.A., *Dr. Robert A. Anderson's Comprehensive Guide To Wellness Medicine*, Keats, Connecticut, 1987.

228. Vaux, K., "Religion and Health, *Preventive Medicine*, #5(4), Dec. 1976; Seventh-day Adventist Mortality Study, 1958-1965, School of Health, Loma Linda University, California.

229. Oberleder, M., *Avoid The Aging Trap*, Acropolis, Washington, D.C., 1982.

230. Beecher, H.K., "Surgery As Placebo," *Journal of the American Medical Association*, #176(13), July 1, 1961.

231. Klopfer, B., "Psychological Variables In Human Cancer," *Journal of Projective Techniques*, #21(4), Dec. 1957.

232. Beecher, H.K., "The Powerful Placebo," *Journal of the American Medical Association*, #159(17), Dec. 29, 1955; Wolf, S., "The Pharmacology of Placebos," *Pharmacology Review*, #11(4), Dec., 1959; Pogge, R., "The Toxic Placebo: Side and Toxic Effects Reported During Administration of Placebo Medicine," *Medical Times*, #91, August, 1963.

233. Brown, S., "Side Reactions to Pyribenzamine Medication," *Proc. Soc. Exp. Bio. Med.*, #67(3), March, 1948.

234. Goleman, Daniel, "Placebo Effect Is Shown To Be Twice As Powerful As Expected," *New York Times*, Aug. 17, 1993.

235. Ibid.

236. Chopra, D., *Unconditional Life*, Bantam, New York, 1991.

237. Op. cit. note #88.

238. Wright, K., "Going By the Numbers," *The New York Times Magazine*, Dec. 15, 1991.

239. Ibid.

240. Becnel, T., "Looking To The Future," *Sarasota Herald-Tribune*, Dec. 18, 1991.

Index